The Anatomy of Job Loss

Doreen Massey
and Richard Meegan

The Anatomy of Job Loss

The how, why and where
of employment decline

METHUEN *London & New York*

First published in 1982 by
Methuen & Co. Ltd
11 New Fetter Lane, London EC4P 4EE
Published in the USA by
Methuen & Co.
in association with Methuen, Inc.
733 Third Avenue, New York, NY 10017
© *1982 Doreen Massey and Richard Meegan*
Typeset by Keyset Composition, Colchester Essex
Printed in Great Britain by
Richard Clay (The Chaucer Press)

British Library Cataloguing in Publication Data

Massey, Doreen
The anatomy of job loss.
1. Unemployment
I. Title II. Meegan, Richard
331.13'7   HD5706

ISBN 0-416-32350-2
ISBN 0-416-32360-X Pbk
(University paperback 773)

Contents

Acknowledgements

The authors and publishers would like to thank the following for their kind permission to reproduce copyright material: *British Business* for figure 11.2; *The Economist* for figure 4.1; D. L. Farrant and the *Foundry Trade Journal* for table 5.4; the *Financial Times* for figure 11.9; *The Guardian* for figure 5.2b; Her Majesty's Stationery Office for figure 3.1; London Brick Company for figure 9.1; the National Economic Development Office (reproduced by permission of Her Majesty's Stationery Office) for figures 3.2, 3.3, 3.4, 3.5; Vaughan Associates for the advertisement on p. 82; Michael Ward and the *Sunday Times* for figure 11.3; Clive Woodcock and *The Guardian* for figure 11.8.

Preface

The arguments in this book emerged out of a wider research project looking at the geographical impact of different forms of production change within industry in the context of recession. As we worked in this general area it became clear that few studies had been done on the mechanics and the geography of job loss, and on the relation between the two. In particular, there has been little work relating employment decline to wider economic and political circumstances, on the one hand, and to what is actually going on in production, in the factory and the office, on the other. The general assumption that the decline of employment is, more or less, equivalent to the decline of an industry is inadequate. Job loss *may* go along with industrial decline, but it may also be the means of avoiding decline, or even be an outcome of the process of growth. Labour's loss is not the same as capital's loss. What is more, these different circumstances and causes of employment decline may have different geographical implications, and raise different issues about the nature of capitalist production.

All these issues were raised in the context of our main concern – that of explaining the geography of job loss. It was soon clear that such an explanation had to go beyond what are often considered to be the interests of 'geography' as such. We hope, therefore, that the book will be of interest and use not only to geographers and planners but also to those in related areas of work. Any adequate exploration of a topic such as this demands crossing established disciplinary boundaries.

The project began at the Centre for Environmental Studies (CES), a research institute established in the 1960s to carry out and to fund research work in urban and regional problems, both social and economic. The authors' interest in the subject matter of this book was greatly increased on the closure of CES during the writing up of this project!

As well as our colleagues from CES, we should like to thank the Social Science Research Council, whose grant enabled us to go beyond the initial work funded by the Department of the Environment and to complete the project as part of Doreen Massey's programme as SSRC Industrial Location Research Fellow. We should also like to thank the Department of Geography at the London School of Economics, where Doreen Massey is now based.

We derived our data and information from a wide variety of sources. In particular we received information from, and had helpful discussions with, people at the National Union of Tailors and Garment Workers, Sheffield City Library, the *Grimsby Evening Telegraph*, the Council of Ironfoundry Associations, the British Paper and Board Industry Federation, the National Economic Development Office, the Department of the Environment, and Dr Margaret Wray of the Hatfield Polytechnic. A large number of people were involved in one way or another in the work presented here. Among those who read and commented on the manuscript, or who helped with its final production, were Geoff Hyman, Ann Markusen, Andrew Sayer, Michael Storper, Marjorie Turton and John Whitelegg. We should like to thank them all.

Doreen Massey
Richard Meegan
January 1982

Part 1
Introduction

1
The issues

Job loss is high on the political agenda again. In the UK there has been talk of a return to the 1930s; May 1981 saw a People's March for Jobs. In the USA coalitions have been formed to fight plant closure. In France there have been mass demonstrations in a battle to preserve the industrial base of Lorraine. In 1980 the number of people looking for work in the European Economic Community (EEC) increased by 20 per cent. In August 1981 the EEC's jobless total stood at a record 9.1 million. In the same year in the countries of the Organization for European Co-operation and Development (OECD) the number of people officially registered as unemployed reached 25 million.

Closures of individual plants, even the decline of whole industries and regions, are not new to market economies. They occur even in periods of overall increasing prosperity. In the 1950s in Britain, when a government could be re-elected on the (in retrospect short-sighted) slogan 'You've never had it so good', the cotton-textile industry was in deep trouble, and jobs were being lost by the thousand in the cotton towns of Lancashire. What is different about the situation in the 1980s is that decline is now so general. The long post-war boom in advanced capitalist economies is well and truly over.

The British economy was one of the first to feel the effects of the ending of this period of more-or-less uninterrupted growth. Since the middle of the 1960s unemployment has never fallen back to the levels of the previous decade (figure 1.1). The number of jobs in manu-

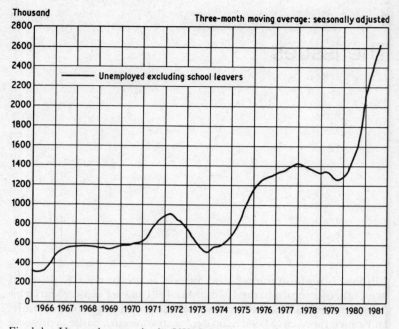

Fig. 1.1   Unemployment in the UK, 1966–81
Source   Department of Employment 1981b

facturing has slumped (see figure 1.2). By the mid-1970s manufacturing in the UK employed 1.3 million less people than it had ten years earlier, a decline of just over 15 per cent (Brown and Sheriff 1978). The decline has accelerated since then. In the second half of 1980, manufacturing employment in Britain was falling by an average of 77,000 jobs a month, over fifteen times the corresponding figure for the two years leading up to mid-1979 (Department of Employment 1981a). Layoffs in the manufacturing sector between 1980 and 1981 reached levels unprecedented since the Second World War. This cataclysmic fall in manufacturing employment has been exacerbated by a loss of jobs in the service sector. After a decade of almost continuous growth which provided over 1½ million new jobs, 1980 saw employment begin to fall in the service sector too. About ¼ million service-sector jobs disappeared in that year alone (Department of Employment 1981a). These years saw 'de-industrialization', 'British economic disaster' and 'alternative economic strategies' come to the fore in the debate over economic policy (see, for example,

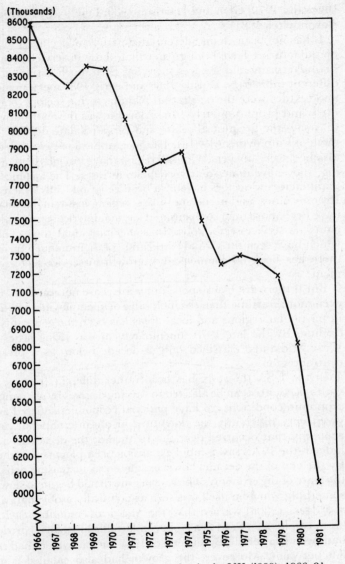

Fig. 1.2 Employment in manufacturing in the UK ('000), 1966–81

Source 1966–78 Department of Employment Gazettes
1979–81 Monthly Digest of Statistics (June figures/provisional)

Blackaby 1979; Glyn and Harrison 1980; London CSE Group 1980; Aaronovitch 1981).

It has not been an undifferentiated pattern of decline. Job losses in manufacturing have been greater than those in services, and within manufacturing and services there has been much variation between different industries. During 1980 and early 1981 metal manufacture and textiles were the hardest hit manufacturing sectors (both absolutely and proportionately). In services it was the distributive trades that saw the greatest absolute and proportionate decline (Department of Employment 1981a). The geographical pattern of decline has also been very uneven. While all regions have lost jobs in manufacturing, they have done so at very different rates. The fortunes of non-manufacturing sectors have also been geographically differentiated. In some cities, and in the South East region, losses in manufacturing have been more than compensated for, in numerical terms at least, by gains in service-sector jobs. In some individual towns, however, which have seen the virtual eradication of their manufacturing base, there has been no compensatory growth in service-sector employment.

But if there are black spots, other areas are not immune. Perhaps even more startling than the high rates of unemployment notched up in particular regions and local areas has been the generality of this decline. By the late 1970s unemployment was rising fastest in the West Midlands, classified only a decade before as a prosperous, central region.

In the USA the story has been rather different. Just as regions within a country can be affected to varying degrees by changing wider economic conditions, so have national economies suffered and survived very differently the downturn in the international capitalist economy that occurred over the 1970s. For the decade as a whole, indeed, the 1970s saw a rapid expansion of employment in the USA. By the end of the decade, however, there was increasing debate over the state of the economy. The rate of growth had begun to slow down, something which in itself was seen as politically problematical. *Business Week* (1980a) warned that 'the American credo that each generation can look forward to a more comfortable life than its predecessor had been shattered'. By the end of 1981 unemployment had reached 8.9 per cent. Moreover, the growth had also entailed a massive reorganization of the economy. Employment in manufacturing was giving way to employment in the burgeoning service sectors where the bulk of jobs offered low hourly pay, fewer hours and less possibility of advancement (Rothschild 1981). One result of this shift was the initiation of a major debate on how to 're-industrialize' the US economy (see *Business Week* 1980b, 1981; Rohatyn 1980, 1981; Etzioni 1980; Carnoy and Shearer 1980). Equally important has been the geographical reorganization of the US economy, with the shift from the 'Frostbelt' to the 'Sunbelt' (see Lonsdale and Seyler 1979; Bluestone and Harrison 1980; Varaiya and Wiseman 1978). Manufacturing job losses in the older industrial regions of the USA, in the industrial North and East, reached more than 1½ million in the decade between the mid-1960s and the mid-1970s. Even in the USA the generally more prosperous areas are not immune. Closures have occurred in the Sunbelt too (Bluestone, Harrison and Baker 1981), and even Los Angeles, one of the foci of net growth, is seeing major losses of jobs in its post-war manufacturing base.

This increasing concern with job loss brings to the fore a whole host of issues. It changes the terms of the relation between workforce and management, between labour and capital. It raises questions of how to defend jobs, of how, perhaps, to fight factory closure. In the UK, occupations of factories have taken place, and producer co-operatives and centres for the unemployed have been established. In the USA fights against layoffs, cutbacks and plant closure have assumed a new prominence (Metzgar 1980).

Employment decline also raises awkward issues of government policy. Questions of the location of new investment become more highly sensitive; it becomes more politically difficult to steer jobs to areas with the highest levels of unemployment when people in all regions are in need of work.

The increasing importance of employment decline has also raised analytical questions. The evidence and the numbers quoted above merely describe and map the fact of job loss. But what are the processes lying behind these aggregate numbers? The most general assumption is probably that jobs are lost in an industry because that industry is itself in decline, is in some way failing. As we shall show, however, things are not so simple; this is only one among a number of reasons for job loss. Still less is understood about the geography of employment decline. Most work on industrial location, both theoretical and empirical, has focused on questions of growth and movement: why new locations are chosen, why investment is shifted from one location to another. But little is known about why, for instance, job losses within an industry may hit some areas more than others. Thus, while it is frequently noted that the dynamics of industrial location and employment change have for long been dominated by questions of decline, it is also widely agreed (e.g. Townsend 1981;

Hall 1980) that little attention has yet been paid to the geography of job loss – why the spatial pattern of employment decline is as it is.

* * *

The purpose of this book is to examine these two questions: that is, first to look more closely at some of the different processes of employment decline, and second to present an approach to the analysis of its geography.

First, then, the processes: in part 2 of this book we explore some of the different roles that employment loss can play in a company's overall strategy and some of the different mechanisms by which it can occur. From what kinds of managerial strategies can job loss result? To what kinds of pressures is it a response? In what ways may it relate to what is happening in the wider economy, and to the structure of production for profit? An important thread of argument here is that 'employment decline' is not a simple category. A loss of jobs can result from all kinds of different pressures. Workers may lose their jobs because a firm is going bankrupt, or to stop a firm going bankrupt. They may lose their jobs because little investment has left the company uncompetitive, or as a result of new investment designed to make the company more competitive. Thus, for example, during the period on which we shall focus in this book job loss in the iron-castings industry occurred against a background of contracting markets and was accompanied by major disinvestment. In complete contrast, employment in the synthetic-resins sector declined by a similar proportion but was associated with rapid market growth and the introduction of major new investment. Employment decline was thus clearly, in terms of its causes and its purpose, a quite different phenomenon in each of these cases. A question which immediately arises, therefore, is: is 'employment decline' as it stands a sensible category of analysis? We argue here that for some purposes it is not. And especially we argue this is so when it comes to analysing the geography of job loss.

Perhaps the most common approach to the geography of employment decline is to start with the spatial pattern of job loss and to analyse that pattern in terms of 'factors' such as industrial structure and geographical characteristics. But this assumes (quite apart from other problems) that employment decline is all of a kind; and it says nothing about how and why jobs are being lost in the first place. Yet as we have seen, employment decline in an industry can result from a range of different processes. And in order to understand an effect (the geography of employment decline), it is necessary to analyse causes.

If these vary from industry to industry, or from company to company, it is incorrect to lump all that job loss together and to try to explain it as though it were all the same thing.

More formally, if a phenomenon is to be explained, it must be established as a category having a coherent relation to causality. To mix together the outcomes of very different processes as one and the same thing is mistaken if it is explanation that is needed. It is to combine the unrelated – a 'chaotic conception' (see Sayer 1980). Simply because objects are descriptively similar (they are all job loss) does not mean that together they form an adequate theoretical category (they are all part of the same causal structure). If the aim is to understand how and why employment decline occurs where it does, it is necessary to go beyond statistical descriptions to underlying causes; and this may in turn require more thought about the conceptualization of employment decline itself.

What we do in this book, therefore, is to examine more closely some of the different mechanisms and causes of employment decline and to use that in understanding the geography of job loss.

* * *

In order to pursue these themes we began by examining a number of sectors of the British economy that were losing employment over the years 1968 to 1973. This period of British economic history is a useful one to examine. The overall decline in jobs in manufacturing industry had set in two years earlier in 1966, and the parlous state of the economy was already an important issue. British-based industry was losing out in international trade, its manufactured exports were down as a proportion of all such trade between major industrial countries, while, conversely, levels of import penetration were rising. Profitability in manufacturing industry continued a fall that had begun in the late 1950s, and the rate of output growth in manufacturing began to fall (note that it was not yet in decline despite the net loss in employment).

Between 1968 and 1973 – the two end dates were chosen because they are at roughly the same point on the business cycle – well over half the industries in manufacturing were showing a net loss of jobs. Yet in spite of the fact that 'decline' in some senses was clearly setting in, a lot of things were going on. Manufacturing investment was relatively high. So was the rate of growth of productivity. There was an active attempt to reorganize and restructure industrial production. And there were important changes occurring in the geography of employment.

Table 1.1 Employment decline in the industries studied, 1968–73

mlh	Industry	Employment		Employment decline	
		1968	1973	No.	%
211	Grain milling	23,600	20,600	3,000	13
213	Biscuits	48,700	45,300	3,400	7
216	Sugar	15,000	12,800	2,200	15
231	Brewing and malting	80,400	71,600	8,800	11
261	Coke ovens and manufactured fuel	17,400	11,500	5,900	34
271	General chemicals	109,600	109,100	500	1
276	Synthetic resins and plastics materials and synthetic rubber	56,900	45,400	11,500	20
278	Fertilizers	19,300	19,100	200	1
311/312	Iron and steel (general)/steel tubes	313,500	296,100	17,400	6
313	Iron castings, etc.	101,000	81,800	19,200	19
321	Aluminium and aluminium alloys	58,300	52,100	6,200	11
323	Other base metals	24,700	19,000	5,700	23
332	Metal-working machine tools	72,100	58,800	13,300	18
335	Textile machinery and accessories	49,200	40,400	8,800	18
354	Scientific and industrial instruments and systems	121,500	96,300	25,200	21
361	Electrical machinery	167,700	138,600	29,100	17

MLH					
362	Insulated wires and cables	54,000	46,000	8,000	15
382	Motor-cycle, tricycle and pedal-cycle manufacturing	18,500	16,800	1,700	9
384/385	Locomotives and railway track equipment/railway carriages and wagons and trams	49,700	40,300	9,400	19
392	Cutlery, spoons, forks and plated tableware, etc.	16,100	14,500	1,600	10
413	Weaving of cotton, linen and man-made fibres	63,700	47,100	16,600	26
414	Woollen and worsted	141,600	109,000	32,600	23
415	Jute	14,200	10,100	4,100	29
419	Carpets	44,800	44,500	300	1
423	Textile finishing	53,400	46,100	7,300	14
431	Leather (tanning and dressing) and fellmongery	21,800	18,500	3,300	15
442	Men's and boys' tailored outerwear	100,900	94,900	6,000	6
450	Footwear	95,300	85,800	9,500	10
461	Bricks, fireclay and refractory goods	58,300	47,600	10,700	18
481	Paper and board	76,100	60,900	15,200	20
489	Other printing, publishing, bookbinding, engraving, etc.	212,700	194,800	17,900	8
	Total	2,300,000	1,995,400	304,600	13

Source Census of Production 1968 and 1973.
Note An 'mlh' is a 'minimum list heading', a subcategory of a major industry group, or Order, of the Standard Industrial Classification.

It was, in other words, a fairly 'active' period. Many different kinds of changes were under way in different industries. What we have done is to take a number of these industries and examine them further. The list of industries is given in table 1.1. It covers a wide spectrum. There are consumer-goods industries and industries producing basic capital equipment. There are labour-intensive industries and capital-intensive ones. They are industries based around very different technologies, and around very different forms of organization of work, or labour process. The structure and organization of capital in them also varies – it includes major corporations, nationalized industries and family firms. But what all of these have in common is that, between 1968 and 1973, the number of people employed in them in the UK declined.

*   *   *

What we do in the next two parts of this book is explore how, why and where these jobs were lost. Under the present economic system in the UK, it is the process of production for profit to which employment decline ultimately needs to be related. But this relationship is not simple and undifferentiated. The 'imperatives of capital accumulation' can produce, in different economic and political circumstances and in different industries, very different responses. The collapse of the iron-castings industry and the 'labour-saving' new investment in synthetic resins referred to above, are good examples of the very varied ways in which the pressures of production for profit in different parts of the same economy and during the same period led to job loss. They are different strategies. They have completely different implications for what is happening to accumulation and to the health of the companies concerned. Yet each resulted in employment decline. It was these different relationships that we were interested in exploring. We began by identifying the actual mechanisms through which the job loss had occurred, the kinds of changes that had been introduced in the scale and organization of the production and labour processes in the different industries. What we discovered was that employment decline had taken place in the context of a number of very different forms of production reorganization. Moreover, these varying kinds of change within production could each be directly related to the exigencies of production for profit – to the system's overall dynamic. This stage of the analysis is presented in part 2.

The implications of all this for the geography of employment decline are explored in part 3. The first step in this stage of the argument was to examine the relationship between the different forms of production reorganization and the spatial pattern of job loss. To do this, we started by examining the main features of the different forms of production reorganization as we defined them and by exploring their different spatial implications. It was the possibility of drawing out these implications that provided the other major reason for structuring our analysis around the forms of production reorganization: they provide a link not only backwards to the cause of employment decline but also forward, through the changes in production and labour processes which they involve, to the spatial pattern of that decline. They therefore allow an approach to the understanding of both how and why job loss took the geographical form that it did. It became clear that the different forms of production change that we had identified had different implications in terms of the geographical pattern of job loss in which they may result. By examining the causes and mechanisms of employment decline it is possible, in other words, to gain a greater understanding of its geography. Indeed we would argue that it is the only way in which its geography can really be explained.

Part 4 pulls together some of these arguments, and takes them further. Understanding the wider mechanisms of employment decline can have other implications too – we show how the different forms of production change that lie behind job loss can be related to very different kinds of conflict between labour and management, and raise different issues about the organization of production on the basis of profit. We take up a few methodological issues, and in particular argue that some of the techniques currently adopted in geographical studies, while useful in description, can not approach explanation. One of the reasons for this, and a point which underlies the whole of our argument here, is that production and location are far more closely linked to each other than most studies allow. Owing to the long-standing pattern of disciplinary job demarcation within academe – in particular between geographers and economists – these links are often missed.

Finally, we turn to consider the changes that have taken place in recent years, in the late 1970s and the early 1980s. The fact of continuing employment decline has had a number of wider effects, both social and political. In Britain, regional and other locational policies have fallen into abeyance, yet the geography of unemployment remains uneven, and the effectiveness of what regional policy there is declines. Job loss itself has accelerated and spread, and the kind of employment decline, we argue, has changed. By the early 1980s job loss, or the threat of it, had become an important weapon in the battle between labour and capital.

Part 2
Job loss and production change

2
Forms of production reorganization and job loss

This chapter examines more closely some of the things which can be involved in the apparently simple term 'employment decline'.

It has been pointed out elsewhere (Massey and Meegan 1979b) that any net change in employment is actually the numerical result of two other movements, in output and in productivity. Thus, for example, in some circumstances job loss may be linked with a straightforward loss of output. In others, however, substantial increases in output may occur with a much reduced labour force as a result of an even faster growth in labour productivity. The nature and implications of employment decline in these different situations are clearly different. In the latter case, and in contrast with the former, the loss of jobs is not equatable with a downturn in accumulation; in other words, it is a problem for labour but not for the owners of capital. We are concerned in this book with the problem of job loss experienced by labour.

But to disaggregate the loss of jobs in particular circumstances to output and productivity components is simply an arithmetical dissection. It neither explains, nor exposes the mechanisms behind, this decline in employment. We would argue that to understand why and where employment decline occurs it is necessary to investigate these mechanisms.

Such an investigation requires the identification of the different kinds of changes within production through which jobs are lost. In the case of the thirty-one industries introduced in the last chapter,

Table 2.1   Important forms of production reorganization in the industries studied, 1968–73

Rationalization	Intensification	Investment and technical change
Grain milling	Cycles	Biscuits
Iron castings	Textile finishing	Sugar
Metal-working machine tools	Leather	Brewing and malting
	Men's and boys' tailored outerwear	Coke ovens
Electrical machinery		General chemicals
Insulated wires and cables	Footwear	Synthetic resins, etc.
	Other printing and publishing	Fertilizers
Locomotives and railway track equipment/ railway carriages		Iron and steel/steel tubes
		Aluminium
		Miscellaneous base metals
Weaving of cotton, linen and man-made fibres		Textile machinery
		Scientific and industrial instruments and systems
Woollen and worsted		Cutlery
Paper and board		Jute
		Carpets
		Bricks and refractory goods

we were able to identify three specific examples of forms of production reorganization that had been particularly important in leading to the job losses that these sectors had experienced. We labelled these forms 'intensification', 'investment and technical change' and 'rationalization'. Table 2.1 shows in which sectors these different changes in production were important.

The three forms are defined in detail in the chapters which follow, but briefly: *intensification* is defined as being changes designed to increase the productivity of labour but without major new investment or substantial reorganization of production technique; *investment and technical change* is where job loss occurred in the context of significant investment often related to changes between techniques of production; and *rationalization* is defined as a simple reduction in total capacity. 'Employment decline' in the thirty-one industries we studied was thus quite clearly a differentiable category. Three very different mechanisms were at work.

* * *

A few points should be made here on methodology. First, the selection of the thirty-one industries. The work presented here derives from a broader exploratory project which examined the relationship between different forms of intra-sectoral production reorganization and spatial employment change in the context of recession. In this broader project, fifty-eight industries were studied. These were selected on a number of bases.

To begin with, on the assumption that rising labour productivity provided a good indication of the likelihood of some production reorganization, sectors were included that had experienced significant absolute and relative losses of employment in the context of productivity increases (see Massey and Meegan 1979b). This was a major criterion for selection, and thirty-three industries of the fifty-eight were chosen on this basis. The national importance of this group of industries is clear not only from its significant levels of productivity increase but also from the fact that it contained most of the industries that dominated aggregate employment change. Of the twenty industries in which employment either grew or fell by 10,000 or more jobs over the study period, fourteen were within this group (ten net losers and four net gainers). This in itself is a further indication of the importance in employment change of shifts in productivity. To give complete coverage of the industries that had dominated changing employment patterns, the remaining six industries were also included, even though four of these actually experienced declines in productivity. Further, given our specific interest in production reorganization in situations of economic retrenchment, it was also necessary to ensure that a reasonable number of industries experiencing output decline were examined. Output had fallen in only eight of the thirty-nine industries chosen on the basis of the productivity and aggregate employment change criteria (a notable point in itself). Thirteen industries that had substantial reductions in output levels were therefore also included. Finally, to ensure a basis for comparison over the whole range of output change, a small number of industries (six) was added which together covered the whole spectrum of output growth. These nineteen sectors included on the output growth/ decline criteria were chosen to reflect, as far as possible, potentially major differences in production reorganization within broad groups of industries (Orders of the 1968 Standard Industrial Classification). Thus within textiles, for example, carpets and man-made fibres, which increased output over the period, were included alongside the cotton-weaving, woollens, rope and narrow-fabric industries in which output fell. Similar sectoral contrasts were identified in other industrial groupings.

The fifty-eight industries finally selected for investigation comprised a cross-section of manufacturing activity over the study period. With the exclusion, for data reasons, of shipbuilding they included minimum list headings (mlhs) from all manufacturing Orders and employed 4,924,000 people in 1968, 63 per cent of 'all manufacturing industry'. As far as employment change was concerned, they contributed 67 per cent of the jobs created over the study period by industries growing in employment terms, and 80 per cent of the job loss caused by industries declining in employment. Forty-two industries lost employment over the period whilst only one of the sixteen employment gainers increased employment by more than 30 per cent. Retrenchment in employment terms, as in the manufacturing sector as a whole, was dominant.

The three forms of production reorganization that we identified were based on the behaviour of companies in thirty-nine of these fifty-eight industries. We did not, of course, expect all industries to be substantially reorganizing their production processes over the study period. We came across cases, for example, of 'extensive growth' – what Salter calls 'growth which merely reproduces a given situation' (1969, 3). In these industries production and labour processes remained essentially unaltered with the additional capacity being provided by a duplication of existing production techniques. Capacity expansion of this kind does not imply, of course, any reduction in jobs. We also did not expect employment change in every industry we examined to be dominated by a single form of production reorganization. Thus we were not surprised to find a number of cases in which employment loss appeared to result from a very heterogeneous mixture of production changes. In these cases it was impossible to pin down the bulk of employment loss to any single kind of production strategy. Finally, there were cases where we were reluctant to classify industries simply because of the inconclusive nature of the evidence we were able to piece together on production change. This was particularly true where the classification had to depend heavily on official statistics alone (see below for our reservations about these data). The thirty-one industries listed in tables 1.1 and 2.1 are the ones that, of the forty industries classified, actually reduced their workforce over the study period. In 1968 they employed 2,300,000 people, 29 per cent of employment in all manufacturing industry (Census of Production).

This leads us to the second methodological point: how did we actually decide which particular forms of production change had been important? For each industry an attempt was made to identify the main changes that were introduced in production and labour processes over the study period. Were existing production techniques being significantly altered? Were work practices being changed and if so how? What was the impact of these changes on productive capacity? A form of production reorganization was deemed to be particularly important when it seemed that the bulk of employment and productivity change within the sector in question could be attributed to it. Thus, to say that over the period 1968–73 intensification was important in the footwear industry does not mean that in those years there were no jobs lost due to other causes, but simply that intensification was the main systematically identifiable cause. It is, of course, extremely unlikely, both logically and empirically, that one form would account for all employment decline in a whole sector. There are almost bound to be mixtures, even of the three forms discussed here. It is highly unlikely, for instance, for there to be a significant fall in output without any consequent rationalization (closure of capacity). (It is possible: the newsprint section of the paper and board industry seems to have exhibited such behaviour in the period immediately prior to that studied here.) And, conversely, when a firm closes down some capacity it is unlikely that its remaining factories will be left unaffected. They may, for instance, be subject to cost-cutting measures. There will also be variations in behaviour between different firms in a given sector. Clearly intra-sectoral differences will exist between individual firms and this may lead to their experiencing different kinds of pressures and to their adoption of different kinds of production strategy. Such variations may distinguish large, multi-sectoral companies from small independents, for instance, or may occur because of sub-sectoral market differentiation. Studies that look simply at aggregate changes in sectoral employment levels might tend to overlook these important differences. An approach such as the one here, however, which seeks to understand the mechanisms behind employment change, pushes the research into an exploration of the intricacy of what is actually going on within individual industries. Accordingly, a number of instances of intra-sectoral disparities are analysed in the discussions that follow, and the implications for using 'sectors' as a basis of disaggregation are assessed in the final chapter. The aim of the initial classification exercise, however, was to characterize, at sectoral level, the dominant pattern adopted by any reorganization of productive capacity.

Thirdly and finally, we should report on the data and the methods we used in order to explore and identify the forms of production reorganization going on in these industries. As we have said, our main concern was with changes in employment. The question of classification was therefore decided by judgement of the impact of identified changes in production processes on levels of employment and productivity. The word 'judgement' is used advisedly, for analysis of the forms of production reorganization was based upon aggregate-level official statistics and immediately available secondary and more 'qualitative' sources. On the basis of this information, it was clearly not possible to allocate precisely every single employment change in individual industries to specific instances of production reorganization. A quantitative analysis of the employment impact of changing production processes would have required detailed and systematic information about production at company level. As part of the reason for the current preoccupation with quantitative analyses of aggregate sectoral employment numbers seems to reflect the difficulty of finding alternative data sources to company surveys or the aggregate employment data themselves, it might be worth going into in some detail the approach we adopted.

The first step was to see whether movements in the aggregate-level official statistics (chiefly output, employment, capital expenditure and numbers of establishments) conformed to any broad patterns which themselves suggested particular forms of production reorganization. A more detailed picture of these developments was then built up using such secondary sources as company reports, detailed industry and company surveys (by, for example, the National Economic Development Office (NEDO), trade unions and firms of stockbrokers), major financial and trade journals and reports of the Sector Working Parties set up under the Industrial Strategy. Heavy emphasis had to be placed on these qualitative sources because of the particular weaknesses, at least for our purpose, of using the aggregate-level official data on their own. Thus, for example, it was clearly important to get some idea of the extent of plant closure as part of the investigation of changes in productive capacity. The establishment data from the Census of Production, however, can only be used to show changes in net numbers over given periods.[1] A net reduction in numbers of establishments clearly implies some factory closure but this does not inevitably signify any loss of productive capacity, i.e. rationalization. A shift to fewer but bigger plants may have occurred. Alternatively the changed numbers may be concealing investment in fewer factories but with higher levels of labour productivity: this might be technical change.

Data on output and changing capital stock are clearly needed before any inferences on changes in productive capacity can be made.

Yet obtaining reliable data on these variables from official statistical sources is not at all straightforward.

As a major argument in this book is the need for a much closer integration of the study of changing production with that of changing geographical patterns of employment, we feel that it would be useful at this point to devote some space to a discussion of the main difficulties involved in finding and using these data on production. As far as the output data are concerned, the first difficulty arises over what is actually being measured in the official statistics. We are interested in 'value added', but because of the limitations presented by the basic data collected, the Census of Production figures for net output are only an approximation to it. Moreover, the basis of the calculation of net output in the Census has itself changed over time, making intertemporal comparisons problematical.[2] On top of these measurement difficulties, however, are the intractable problems involved in adjusting these data for inflation. Ideally changes in net output over time should be measured using a 'double deflation' method. This involves revaluing at constant prices both gross output and inputs (materials, fuels, services, etc.). The latter is then subtracted from the former. Lack of both detailed information on transactions and adequate price data make this method unreliable, however, and in practice it is only currently used in the UK to measure changes in agricultural production (see Central Statistical Office 1976). The Index of Industrial Production attempts to get around this problem by measuring changes in 'proxies' for net output. It is assumed in the compilation of the Index that net output in individual industries changes in line with either gross output or inputs. Gross output is measured either in terms of the physical quantities of goods produced or sold, or, where adequate price deflators are available, in terms of the value of sales or production at constant prices. Inputs are measured on the basis of either physical quantities of materials or employment numbers. The use of employment figures in this way clearly raises difficulties when productivity changes are being examined. Fortunately, however, only one industry is seriously affected by this measurement technique (shipbuilding).[3] Overall, input indicators are relatively unimportant in the construction of the Index. In the Index based on 1970, for example, materials used and labour together comprised less than 3 per cent of the Index. The bulk of the Index was accounted for by physical quantities sold or produced (33 per cent) and deflated values of sales and production (the remaining 64 per cent). Once the percentage movements in these different 'indicators' have been calculated, the changes are then combined in such a way as to reflect the relative significance of products and industries with weights given to each industry according to the value of its net output in the base year. The figures for net output used in this weighting exercise differ from those that appear in the Census of Production. Adjustments are made to allow for inter-industry payments of services and these estimates are then made consistent with the net output estimates in the national-level input-output tables, which are themselves based on national income statistics. The adjusted net-output figures used in the compilation of the Index thus correspond more closely to value added than do the Census of Production net output series. The use of base-year net-output weights in this way does mean, of course, that the Index operates on the assumption that the ratio between net output and gross output remains the same over the time period covered. Consequently, the Index measure of production movements understates the change when this ratio rises, and overstates the change when it falls. As the Central Statistical Office (1976) notes, however, the shorter the period of study the less restrictive this assumption becomes. Another problem involved in using the Index occurs when quantity indicators are used. In these cases changes in product mix are not reflected in the changed indices. NEDO (1978f), for example, refers to this problem in an interesting discussion of the implications of using the Index for measuring output change in food and drink manufacturing.

Two other methods of measuring output change present themselves. The first involves the deflation of Census gross-output figures using the wholesale price indices compiled by the Business Statistics Office (see, for example, Wragg and Robertson 1978). These indices, however, are not available for all mlhs and, because of the very real problems involved in compiling them, vary in reliability. Order-level indices could of course be applied to mlhs for which specific indices are not available, but to do this would run the risk of disguising significant intra-Order differences in rates of inflation. Thus, as deflating gross output using wholesale price indices does not not allow complete industry-wide coverage, some sectors have to be excluded. The second method of deflating Census output figures has little to recommend it. This method involves the use of an industry-wide deflator for all sectors. Thus Wood (1976), for example, applies the single deflator for gross domestic product at factor cost that appears in *National Income and Expenditure 1964–1974* (Central Statistical Office 1975) to net output figures in individual mlhs. Such a method, of course, makes no attempt whatsoever to allow for inter-sectoral differences in inflation rates.

On balance, and for our purposes, the Index of Industrial Production seemed to us to be the best measure. In the first place, deflated value indicators are only used where existing price deflators are sufficiently accurate. Secondly, the incorporation of quantity indicators for other sectors does allow inter-industry comparison across the bulk of manufacturing. Finally, the weights involved in compiling the Index are related to a net output figure which is adjusted in such a way as to allow the best available measurement of changes in value added. Table 2.2 shows the different indicators that are used to compile the Index of Production for the thirty-one industries in our study. It might be useful to bear these differences in mind when reference is made to output later in the argument.

Any investigation of production reorganization also requires an examination not only of changes in levels of capital expenditure, but also of the impact of such changes on the degree of capital intensity of the affected production processes. And again the official statistical sources pose problems for it is not possible to identify changes in capital intensity from statistics on capital expenditure. Ideally, capital-stock figures should be analysed, but reliable series of these data at the level of individual mlhs are not available. The Census of Production statistics only show annual expenditure on, and disposal of, plant and machinery, new building work, land and existing buildings and vehicles. These data are not cumulative and only indicate changes in levels of capital expenditure. And even these changes cannot measure the real extent of any scrapping of capital equipment because the data on disposals of plant and machinery do not include any amount for items that are written off. Nor is it possible using the official statistics alone to distinguish between simple replacement of plant and machinery of a given technique and major changes in the technical nature of the plant employed.

Some inferences can, of course, be made solely on the basis of the official data. Thus significantly increased expenditure on new building work occurring alongside increased investment in plant and machinery might indicate the possibility of brand new factories. Rapidly increasing capital expenditure on plant and machinery per employee and rapid increases in labour productivity might also be an indication of changing production processes.[4] The point to be stressed, however, is that no final decision on the nature of any production reorganization was made on the basis simply of inferences of this kind. Examination of the official data in a sense provided prima-facie cases for the further investigation of possible forms of

Table 2.2   Indicators of output change in the Index of Industrial Production

Rationalization		Intensification		Investment and technical change	
Industry	Indicator	Industry	Indicator	Industry	Indicator
Grain milling	Q	Cycles	Q	Biscuits	Q
Iron castings	Q	Textile finishing	Q/V	Sugar	Q
Metal-working machine tools	V	Leather	Q	Brewing and malting	Q
Electrical machinery	V	Men's and boys' tailored outerwear	V	Coke ovens	Q/I
Insulated wire and cables	V	Footwear	V	General chemicals	V
Locomotives and railway track equipment/railway carriages	V	General printing and publishing	V	Synthetic resins, etc.	V/Q
				Fertilizers	V
				Iron and steel/ steel tubes	Q
Weaving of cotton, linen and man-made fibres	Q			Aluminium	Q
				Miscellaneous base metals	Q
Woollen and worsted	Q			Textile machinery	V
Paper and board	Q			Scientific and industrial instruments and systems	V
				Cutlery	V
				Jute	V
				Carpets	V
				Paper and board	Q/V

Source   Central Statistical Office 1976
Notes
Q = quantities produced
V = deflated output/sales values
 I = material inputs
Q/V and Q/I etc. are mixtures
    Q/V = mainly Q
    V/Q = mainly V
    Q/I = mainly Q

production reorganization. Reference was then made to the secondary and qualitative sources already referred to for corroborative evidence.

It might be helpful to provide a couple of worked examples of what we did. The *bricks, fireclay and refractory goods* industry provides a good example of the problem of deciding upon the importance of specific forms of production reorganization. The official data for the first part of the period (1968–70) certainly suggested the possibility of rationalization. Employment fell by 12 per cent alongside a net reduction in levels of capital expenditure on plant and machinery of 20 per cent and a 10 per cent cut in output (see figure 2.1). At the same time the number of establishments was reduced from 824 to 584, a decline of 29 per cent. Over the period as a whole there was a loss of 329 factories, nearly 40 per cent of the original figure. This decline was reflected in the fact that disposals of land and existing buildings actually

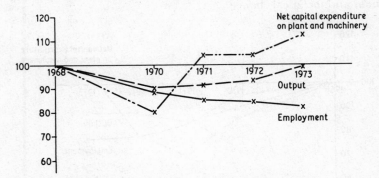

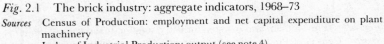

Fig. 2.1   The brick industry: aggregate indicators, 1968–73

Sources   Census of Production: employment and net capital expenditure on plant machinery

Index of Industrial Production: output (see note 4)

exceeded acquisitions in three of the five survey years (1968, 1971 and 1973) and matched them in one (1970). The index for capital expenditure on new building work moved from 100 (1968) to 64 (1970), 61 (1971), 76 (1972) and 112 (1973). Yet investment in plant and machinery had continued in the reduced number of establishments in the later part of the period to such an extent that from 1971 onwards the net total of plant and machinery expenditure actually exceeded that for 1968. The peaks in new building-work and plant and machinery expenditure in fact coincided at the end of the period. Taking an overall view of the period, therefore, it was difficult not to postulate that the plant closure had been an integral part of a process involving the introduction of new plant and machinery.

This new plant and machinery clearly could embody technical change, a proposition greatly reinforced by the significant increases in labour productivity that accompanied its introduction. Secondary sources were therefore consulted, Mooney and Wheatcroft (1977), for example, noted the drop in productive capacity in the industry up to 1970 and pointed to the impact on output and productivity levels of the introduction of continuous kilns in the period following 1970. And, as we shall see in chapters 4 and 9, other sources (including the annual reports of the leading company in this sector, the London Brick Company) provided fairly conclusive evidence of the crucial importance of investment of this type for the industry's overall performance. We concluded, therefore, that production reorganization in the industry over the study period had been dominated by investment and technical change.

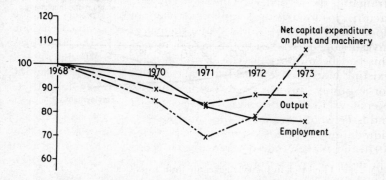

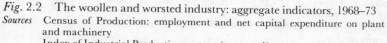

Fig. 2.2   The woollen and worsted industry: aggregate indicators, 1968–73
Sources   Census of Production: employment and net capital expenditure on plant and machinery
Index of Industrial Production: output (see note 4)

The period 1968 to 1971 appears to have been a crucial one for the *woollen and worsted* industry (see figure 2.2). Output and employment fell by 16 and 17 per cent respectively while 324 factories disappeared, over a fifth of the number in 1968 (1439). Disposals of land and existing buildings reached relatively high levels and spending on new building work, in constant price terms, slumped (from £2.5 million in 1968 to £1.7 million in 1971). Capital expenditure on plant and machinery also fell dramatically with levels of spending in constant price terms 15 or 30 per cent below the 1968 figure in 1970 and 1971 respectively. This decline was reversed in the two following years along with some recovery in output. The number of establishments continued to fall, however, with another seventy-six disappearing (making a loss, over the study period as a whole, of 400 factories, nearly 28 per cent). Employment also declined further. By 1973 the workforce was 23 per cent smaller than it had been five years earlier. The official statistics clearly suggested that rationalization could have played an important role in this contraction. And this initial impression was confirmed by a number of secondary sources.

The need for rationalization within the sector had been recognized by a study commissioned by NEDO (1969). This called for a major restructuring of the industry through mergers, company liquidations, factory closure and redundancies (see also the *Economist* 1968). The need for major re-equipment of plant and machinery was also stressed. In the early part of the period, when the loss of jobs was most dramatic, the secondary evidence suggested that company failure, factory closure and the scrapping of plant and machinery were the dominant factors at work. While there had certainly been some investment undertaken in this period, especially by the large firms, this had been rather piecemeal, and in many cases modification of existing machinery rather than replacement had been the rule (see, for example, British Wool Textile Industry Press Office 1971). Kershaw (1971b) also referred to the fact that larger companies in the industry were investing at this time but stressed the importance of liquidations and mill closures in the overall job loss (see also Kershaw 1970 and 1971a). Indeed he remained in general fairly sceptical about the industry's claims for its investment performance (Kershaw 1973). The Census of Production figures on capital expenditure (see figure 2.2) clearly support him in this view. Investment in the industry as a whole only began to be undertaken on a more substantial scale at the end of the study period. This increase in investment was assisted both by an upturn in markets and by the government's Scheme of Assistance which was introduced in July 1973 under the Industry Act 1972 (for a discussion of this, and a later scheme, see NEDO 1979a and 1980). But by this time the bulk of employment loss in the sector over the study period had already taken place (see figure 2.2). We therefore concluded that these jobs had been lost mainly through rationalization.

Moving between aggregate-level official statistics and secondary sources in this way we were able to distinguish between the three different kinds of production reorganization. These forms, in a sense, represent different kinds of response to recession, different ways of pushing forward, or attempting to push forward, the overall process of accumulation. But they remain only examples of mechanisms through which job loss occurs. To understand why these forms of production change are adopted, and why jobs are lost as a result, it is necessary to examine the different combinations of circumstances in which they occur. Not only does employment decline occur through a number of different mechanisms but also it may be the result of a range of quite different causal structures.

*   *   *

The organization of the chapters in part 2 of this book reflects this overall argument. Each of the chapters deals with one of the three forms of production reorganization that we have identified. In the first part of each chapter we examine in more detail two important aspects of the production change in question: first, how it affects 'what goes on on the ground' (or more precisely on the shop-floor) and second, how it relates to the structure of production for profit. This reflects the two sides of production in a capitalist society: the actual work process and capital accumulation. In a capitalist society it is the second that determines the first – profit is the driving force to which the organization of production must ultimately respond. The discussion attempts to demonstrate this relationship using general examples and, more especially, examples drawn from the industries we examined.

The second part of each chapter then takes a more detailed look at production change in one or two of these industries. We explore the precise circumstances in which production change took place. We examine such factors as the competitive position of the industry in question and the dominant pressures affecting it, the structure and organization of capital, industrial relations, and the main features of the production and labour processes. The aim of these industry studies is to explain why the specific form of production reorganization was so important and to examine in more detail the actual mechanics of the production changes. It should be stressed that they are not meant to typify the industries adopting that form of production strategy, to be in some way 'representative', from which generalizations can be made. They are meant more, as a group, to indicate various different types of situation in which employment decline can occur, and to provide the basis for part 3 of this book which tries to relate the geography of job loss to its wider determinants.

3
Intensification

The changes in production

One form of production reorganization that causes employment decline is intensification. By this we mean the reorganization of an existing production process, without abandoning capacity and without major investment in new forms of production, in order to increase labour productivity. Without any major changes in either the nature or scale of the labour process, therefore, the individual worker will, in a given amount of time, produce more output.

There are many actual methods by which an increase in output can be achieved on the shop-floor, ranging from the introduction of small work-aids to the increasing fragmentation of tasks, speed-up of the line in conveyor-belt production, minor mechanization, or simply exhortations and incentives to work harder. In the negotiations that accompany their introduction these methods go by such titles as 'increased flexibility' (the undermining of established rules of demarcation), 'changes in work practices', 'introduction of labour-saving devices', and 'reductions in overmanning' (getting one worker to do the work previously done by more than one).

In order to see what lies behind these changes in the process of production of a physical commodity it is necessary to look at what they mean in terms of the process of production of profit. As we have said, the effect of intensification is that the amount of output produced by the worker in a given time period is increased. There are two basic ways in which the time economy of a given production process can be altered to achieve this result. The first is to reduce those periods when the worker is not actually producing, when the worker is simply moving between different tasks, or preparing the tools or materials in readiness for production. Thus the amount of living labour going into the actual production of a particular commodity remains the same, but its cost is reduced; the wages paid to an individual worker are not reduced (they may even be increased), but the amount of useful labour got out of that worker increases. The second method of increasing output within a given time period is to increase the productivity of the actual work processes themselves. In terms of the kind of low-level investment strategy within a given production process that we are discussing here, there are two main methods of achieving this result: first by small-scale mechanization of previously manual processes, and second by increasing the fragmentation of tasks in the classic manner. Instead of reducing the amount of time spent not producing, this method thus increases the productivity of production time itself. In this case, therefore, the amount of living labour time going into the production of the commodity is reduced.[1]

Intensification may be used either to improve a company's profit rate within a given market or to increase its competitiveness, for instance within a market that is declining overall. It is essentially a cost-cutting measure.

The circumstances in which such measures may be adopted are many and varied. Intensification may simply be introduced to increase the rate of profit, it may be a response to labour shortage, or to rising wages (this combination seems to have been important in the clothing industry in the early 1970s, for instance; see NEDO 1974a and 1976), it may be introduced to retain a share of a declining market (through the ability to charge lower prices), or to compete against lower-wage producers. It may simply be used to get a product off the ground (or in this case on the road):

> Ford was convinced that his Model T was right. Right for him, right for Americans. It was black, cheap and functional. But it wasn't selling. Ford refused to change his ideas. He changed the price. An even cheaper Model T. At the cost of speed-up. (Beynon 1973, 25)

Intensification as such, then, is not a strategy that is inextricably associated with decline or recession. In particular, short-term increases in the speed of work may be negotiated to meet surges in demand. However, it is probably a strategy which is more likely to be adopted during set-backs than booms, and it is then, of course, that it is more likely to lead (as in the cases discussed here) to actual employment loss. On the one hand, intensification (squeezing more out of a given production process) may well be an alternative to major technical change as a means of cutting costs or increasing productivity. Given that there is some element of choice between the two, intensification may well be preferred during periods of restricted profits, liquidity or growth of output because it requires little or no investment. On the other hand, whilst various forms of intensification may be possible at all periods, they may only be attempted by management when times are bad, because of the potential industrial conflict. While this in turn may be worse during a period of recession – since intensification at such times is more likely to imply an actual loss of jobs for some of the workforce – the employees will also be at more of a disadvantage at such times because of the greater threat of unemployment (see chapter 11, and also, for instance, Elger 1979).

The reasons for such conflict become clear when the various methods for achieving intensification are elaborated. As has been pointed out, these methods may vary enormously; they will depend both on the nature of the labour process and on the state of labour relations. First, intensification may be achieved by simple speed-up, without changing any of the actual operations the workers carry out. The establishment and maintenance of such a change in tempo may itself be achieved by a variety of methods. At one extreme, there is the technique of simple exhortation and incentive. Clearly this is not the easiest or most reliable of methods. It may involve complex negotiations on changing work practices, it will probably involve increased supervision, and therefore some actual increase in labour costs, as well as other areas of potential conflict.[2] It may also involve incentive schemes of various sorts – profit-sharing, piece-work, group-working schemes, etc. (and here the difficulties of dealing with a human labour force become apparent: the Sector Working Party on the clothing industry bemoaned 'the ineffectiveness of work incentives' – primarily economic ones – as a major problem of the industry; see NEDO 1976, 3). One result of this facet of the strategy of intensification is, of course, that while labour costs per unit of output are cheapened overall, earnings of individual workers may well be increased. This in turn often performs a dual role in the production reorganization: by encouraging higher levels of labour productivity, and also by 'dividing and ruling' in order to break up workforce opposition to any proposed redundancies. Such methods of reducing 'porosity' in the working day tend to be of dominant importance only where the nature of the production process allows little else. This will be the case particularly in production processes where it is the individual worker, rather than a system of machinery who, in an immediate sense, controls the speed of production – in other words where explicit supervision, or mechanisms for gaining co-operation with the new work pace, are necessary to maintain the speed of production.

At the other end of the spectrum of the 'technology of speed-up' is the intensification that can be achieved by altering the pace of the whole system of machinery. This, of course, reflects a fundamental difference in labour processes. In these latter cases, and in terms of the actual job, the employees are subordinate to the machinery, their work and actions are geared to those of the machines, or the track. When these are speeded up, therefore, the employees have to speed up also. Indeed, speed-up is often seen as being almost an integral part of Fordism, or the mechanized mass-production, flow-line principle. One of the advantages, for management, of a switch between the two forms of labour process (which would be what we call here 'investment and technical change') is precisely the potential for this greater degree of control, through the technology itself, both over the work process as a whole and over the speed of work. But few changes are ever such absolute victories or defeats. The division of control between workers and management is not uniquely determined by technology. At minimum, the *change* in pace still has to be negotiated. Speed-up in assembly-line production has provoked conflict after conflict, and not only over the speed itself but also over who controls it. Employees as a group may win day-to-day control over the line speed.

Apart from these two extreme methods of simply getting employees to work faster, there are other methods of reducing the porosity of the working day. Small pieces of machinery may be introduced to reduce the dead time involved, for instance in handling, or in getting a job set up. The two industries studied in detail in the next section provide a number of examples, from automatic needle-threaders to pneumatic stackers and monorail trolleys. One obvious important example of porosity is that of the frequent re-tooling involved in small-batch production, and it is here, of course, that the introduction of numerically controlled machine tools has been so important; their use is fairly well advanced in the aerospace industry, for instance.

In other cases, productivity increases of the same sort may be achieved by the range of techniques based round time-and-motion studies. Once again, this can vary much in its complexity. It may be based on the sophisticated disaggregation and measurement of human activity in terms of units such as 'therbligs' or 'TMUs'.[3] Such was the approach used by the General Motors Assembly Division in its major reorganization, begun in 1968, of the jobs of both clerical and production workers (Braverman 1974, 178–9). At the other extreme, results of a similar nature may be achieved by simply reorganizing the layout of the workbench or the shop-floor. One of the industries to be looked at in detail in the next section (men's and boys' tailored outerwear) presents examples of this, for instance in the 'reorganization of the trouser room' (see figures 3.4 and 3.5).

Given, then, that both the circumstances under which intensification is introduced, and the concrete form that it takes, may vary from case to case, its precise effects on the labour force will also vary. We have argued that intensification may well be a strategy that is, on the whole, more likely to be undertaken in conditions of slow growth or recession. Under such conditions one result is likely to be a net loss of jobs. This, of course, was the case in all the sectors studied here (employment decline was the basis on which the sectors were selected). But such decline is not an intrinsically necessary result of intensification. Not only is employment decline the potential conse-quence of a whole range of different forms of production reorgan-ization, among them intensification, but the fact that intensification is being implemented does not necessarily imply that employment is being reduced. Descriptively similar phenomena will vary in their actual effects according to the circumstances in which they occur.

Similar points apply to the potential effects on the balance between different types of workers. By definition, if intensification is successful for management, the production workforce will be reduced relative to output. There may, however, be a bias within this reduction, with heavier losses among 'less direct' workers. It is also, as has been mentioned, common for intensification to involve an increase in the non-production workforce, and in particular the workforce of super-vision, as a result of the need to maintain the higher speeds of work now required of the production workers. Thus in the General Motors reorganization referred to earlier:

> the number of jobs was reduced and the number of operations assigned to each worker was increased, the number of repair or inspection workers reduced, and the number of supervisors to enforce the new standards was increased. It was this reorgan-ization which led to the 1972 strikes in the General Motors plants at Norwood, Ohio, lasting 174 days, and Lordstown, Ohio, lasting three weeks. . . . A vice-president of General Motors pointed out that in ten plant reorganizations conducted by the General Motors

Assembly Division after 1968, eight of them produced strikes. 'I'm not boasting', he added, 'I'm just relating relevant history'. (Braverman 1974, 178–9)

Out of the thirty-one industries for which we identified the main cause of job loss between the late 1960s and the early 1970s, there were six in which intensification was of particular importance. These are given in table 3.1.[4] All of these industries were characterized by similar forms

Table 3.1   The intensifying industries

Industry	Change, 1968–73, in:		
	Output	Employ- ment	Productivity
	%	%	%
Leather	−6	−15	+11
Footwear	−4	−10	+7
Cycles	+6	−9	+16
Textile finishing	+6	−14	+23
Tailored outerwear	+6	−6	+13
Other printing and publishing	+19	−8	+29
All manufacturing	+15	−6	+20

Sources   Census of Production: employment data
Index of Industrial Production: output data

of intensification. In none of them was simple speed-up of a conveyor belt a possible option. In all of them there was more reliance on changing work practices, small bits of mechanization, the introduction of subsidiary machinery into the interstices of the production process, time-and-motion study and incentives.

The connection between the importance of these kinds of intensification and the nature of the industries is clear. Two characteristics in particular stand out: the kind of capital involved in the industries, and the dominant forms of their labour processes. First, the sectors on the whole tended to be fairly fragmented, with a high percentage of small firms – table 3.2 gives the details. Such a predominance of small firms both reflects the nature of the production process and also restrains the amount of investment in new techniques which is likely to take place. Large firms were by no means absent from the industries, however, indeed in some sectors they played an important role (see later). The significance of this characteristic will be examined again, both in the detailed studies in the next section and in the final chapter. What the sectors shared most importantly, however, were relatively unautomated labour processes; none even approached full automation, none were structured around mechanized flow-lines. In all of them the individual employees retained a considerable degree of control over the detail and pacing of their own work. In footwear, outerwear and leather much of the work is based around individual, non-automatic sewing-machines. In many of the industries small-batch production is most common. In motor-cycle

Table 3.2   The importance of small firms in the intensifying sectors

Industry	Enterprises of less than 100 workers, as a percentage of total enterprises, 1968
	%
General printing and publishing	96
Leather	84
Tailored outerwear	83
Cycles	82
Textile finishing	79
Footwear	70

Source Census of Production 1968 Summary Tables, Enterprise Analyses. Calculations include figures for unsatisfactory returns. (The figure for all manufacturing is not available.)

production (part of mlh 382), perhaps the case where one would most expect a mechanized flow-line, the separate tasks were linked by the employees themselves moving the unfinished product on to the next station. Reports from the mid- and later 1970s – after the end of our study period – still refer to this. Thus the Boston Consulting Group's report for the Secretary of State for Industry, drawn up in response to the crisis in motor-cycle production in Britain, commented:

> The British motor-cycle industry has three rather antiquated factories in the Midlands. Investment has been low for many years and the equipment in the factories is old and mostly general purpose in nature. As a result, it is difficult to maintain product reliability and impossible to use modern, high volume, highly automated, low-cost methods. (HMSO 1975, 211)

In lighter vein, Leighton described 'the track' at one of these factories (Meriden in the West Midlands):

> to the casual visitor, it is difficult to follow the logic of the production line. Bikes are moved from one process to another by hand, engines are wheeled about in handcarts. It all has the stamp of the ingenious lash-up about it. (Leighton 1978, 18)

Two things should be noted. First, given this starting point, cost-cutting, short of major technical change, had to be of the interstitial and exhortatory form. Indeed, five out of six intensifiers (general printing and publishing was the exception) had a higher percentage of total pay in the industry on a payment-by-results system than was

Table 3.3   Employment change 1968–73 (1968 = 100) for different types of labour

	Operatives	Administrative, technical and clerical	Difference between operatives and administrative etc.
Cycles	89	95	6
Textile finishing	85	91	6
Leather	84	95	11
Outerwear	94	96	2
Footwear	89	96	7
Printing & publishing	91	94	3
All manufacturing	97	99	2

Source   Census of Production

typical of manufacturing as a whole (New Earning's Survey 1970).[5] This was also a higher proportion of industries than in either of the other two categories (the relevant percentages of sectors were: intensification 83 per cent, rationalization 56 per cent and technical change 44 per cent). Moreover, as table 3.3 indicates, job losses in all the industries were biased towards operatives. This was of course true of manufacturing as a whole during this period, but these industries typically had disparities in rates of loss that were greater than that for all manufacturing.

Second, the existence of labour processes such as these is not technically determined by the nature of the sector. Some American clothing and footwear firms now have production processes which include numerically-controlled sewing-machines, laser-cutting and injection-moulding. These techniques are used in Britain too, but to a far lesser extent (see later). Similar disparities exist within the motor-cycle industry, for instance between British and Japanese production. Rogers compared the techniques used for producing frames for small motor-cycles:

> BCG [the Boston Consulting Group] report that the Japanese industry uses pressed steel frames or sub-assemblies, using auto-mated, conveyor-based techniques wherever possible. Assembly times are about one minute per frame. An article in BSA [Bir-mingham Small Arms] Group News shows the equivalent stage at Small Heath. The brazing up of the frames was done as follows. Align all the tubes; 'paint' on a mixture of black lead and molasses to those areas not to be brazed; put the relevant joint into a vat of molten brass; remove, cool, and chip off the 'black lead toffee'. This was all done manually by about seven men, most of whom had over twenty-five years service with the company. The com-parison needs qualification, in that the situations compared are about ten years apart, but it demonstrates the attitude to pro-duction technology in either case. BSA, for instance, were not investing in more modern technology, as such investments would certainly have appeared in their Group News. (Rogers 1979, 27)

Major technical change clearly had been, and still was, possible. None of these processes and characteristics are in that sense com-pletely 'determined' by 'the nature of the industry'. The character of capital and the management involved in the industries, and the history of labour relations, were among the factors shaping the form of the production process, and that in turn was an important cause both of the need to cut costs, and of the kind of cost-cutting that took place.

We can see, then, that 'intensification' can both take a number of forms, and be a response to a variety of different economic circum-stances. It is, in other words, analysable as a strategy only in terms of the larger dynamic of which it is part. The next section takes up this point and pursues two detailed examples, exploring under what kinds of circumstance intensification was adopted by the industries during the period between the late 1960s and the early 1970s, and some of the forms that it took. This shows how production strategies, which as we shall see in part 3 have identifiable spatial effects, are related to a combination of circumstances structured around the need to respond to changing external conditions in a particular industrial-relations setting. This is, then, the first step in linking geographical change to the wider context of which it is part.

Case-studies: intensification in the footwear and men's and boys' tailored outer-wear industries

The two industries we are going to examine in detail are footwear and men's and boys' tailored outerwear (hereafter referred to as 'outer-wear'). The two cases are in fact so similar that they can be dealt with together.[6] Why did firms in these industries adopt a strategy of intensification within the UK during this period?

The first component of the explanation lies in the changing economic and political circumstances that these firms faced.[7] Not only did these changing circumstances imply increasing pressure on their ability to compete and to survive, but also the pressure was in the specific form of cost competition. First of all, world-wide demand was not buoyant; over the long term it had been either stable (outerwear) or only growing slowly (footwear). Second, within both industries the international pattern of production – the international division of labour – was undergoing a long-term shift, in particular towards production in certain Third World countries where wages are far lower than in metropolitan countries. In both sectors, within a context of sluggish aggregate demand, therefore, imports from the Third World to the UK had been gradually increasing. Moreover, the UK market was static, partly because of a slowdown in population growth, partly (in the case of outerwear) because of a shift in fashion away from tailored goods towards more casual clothing. Thus, the more immediate downturn occurred against a long-term situation which was already dismal. In the late 1960s/early 1970s, demand collapsed both world-wide and, specifically, in the UK domestic market. In the UK there was a slowdown, and reversal, in the rate of growth of personal incomes, both because of the recession itself and because of government incomes policies designed to dig industry out of recession, and this necessarily had severe effects on consumer goods industries[8] (Economists Advisory Group undated, para. 1:4; NEDO 1974a, para. 9). This decline in the rate of growth of income in the domestic market had a number of effects. First, overall demand slowed down even further as a result of both income and substitution effects – not only did incomes fall but there was some transfer of demand to other goods. Second, precisely because people were feeling the effects of recession and wage restraint, there was a shift within the overall footwear and clothing market towards cheaper products. This both immediately favoured imports from the Third World (Economists Advisory Group undated, para. 1.3; NEDO 1976) and further increased the pressure on domestic producers to cut costs of

Table 3.4   Trade balance in footwear, 1968–73

		% *Increase*	*Absolute increase*
1	Pairage imports	19	from 65.4m to 78.1m
	Pairage exports	3	from 16.2m to 16.7m
2	Import penetration 1968:	26%	1973: 31%

Source   *1* British Footwear Manufacturers' Federation 1969
          2 Department of Industry 1977

production. Other factors exacerbated the pressure of imports. In general the decline in growth world-wide encouraged national protectionism and therefore diverted even more commodities to those countries not operating import controls or quotas – the effect on the UK market of US bilateral agreements on clothing exports is a good example of this. UK import/export balances therefore deteriorated sharply at the end of the 1960s. The figures are given in tables 3.4 and 3.5.

In both industries, therefore, the combination of a shifting international division of labour with the effects of government policies both at home and abroad, led to a particular form of external economic pressure on the process of production in Britain. It was a pressure to increase productivity: it was directly competitive, it occurred in a context of slackening demand and the competition was largely in terms of cost.[9]

But if changing economic circumstances provided the stimulus to cut costs, it was the nature of the labour processes and of the organization of capital that influenced the form that cost-cutting took. The dominant form of labour process in both industries is a unitized, single-person craft operation based on the sewing-machine. This part of the process accounts for up to 75 per cent of total labour costs in outerwear and a similar proportion in footwear. Both industries are,

Table 3.5   Trade balance in men's and boys' tailored outerwear

	Imports	*Exports*	*Trade balance*	*Import penetration*
	£m	£m	£m	%
1968	13.9	8.7	−5.2	7.1
1973	63.5	18.2	−45.3	12.6 (1972)

Source   NEDO 1974a

overall, highly labour intensive. The fact that the dominant labour process is of this type has a number of effects, two of which are relevant here. First, it means that wages are the main cost item in production, and the pressure to reduce the wages bill was therefore strong. Moreover, both industries are predominantly employers of female workers, and were therefore coming increasingly into competition with other sectors, in both manufacturing and services, whose demand for female labour was expanding. The pressure on wages was therefore increasing from both sides. For clothing as a whole, NEDO commented that:

> The supply of labour is thus of the utmost importance to the clothing industry. The industry recruits largely female labour in competition with the light-engineering industry, distribution and the clerical trades. The industry requires as high or a higher degree of skill as any other employer of female labour without paying higher wages and the Department of Employment Gazette concluded in 1970 that, while the industry tended to gain recruits from the food, distribution and paper sectors, it incurred a net loss of workforce to the electrical and engineering industries and to 'professional and scientific services'. There is no reason to suppose that this competition for labour will decline in the future. (NEDO 1974a, 47)

The later Sector Working Party report demonstrated the industry's declining competitive position in the labour market: 'The average earnings of women over eighteen in the clothing industry had fallen back by 1976 to about 84 per cent from 98 per cent (in 1965) of the average for all manufacturing industries' (NEDO 1978a, 11).

Much the same picture was true of footwear. Here women's earnings had traditionally been above the all-manufacturing average, and they more or less kept up with that between 1963 and 1968, but fell back after that date (Economists Advisory Group undated; calculations from Wood 1976). Neither industry has an attractive image (NEDO 1974a) and in this period problems of labour availability and cost became acute. A nice example from footwear of management's perception of the relation between labour shortages and changes in production is given in the following quotation from the Footwear Industry Study Group:

> One of the most compelling reasons given for investing in more sophisticated semi-automatic equipment such as roughing machines and side-lasting machines was the shortage of skilled

labour for these operations. The first effect of such shortages is that the operatives in question become more demanding for higher rates of pay, knowing their strong bargaining position. This is obviously an added expense to the cost of producing the shoes but difficult to quantify. It is certainly an irritation to management. (1976, 35)

Second, the nature of the dominant labour process conditioned the *kind* of savings in the wages bill that could be made (given that abandonment of individual sewing-machine technology itself was not immediately on the agenda, see pp. 46–9). There was lots of room for intensification. The main stages in the production of shoes, and the associated labour processes, are shown in figure 3.1.

The dominance of relatively 'old-fashioned' labour processes is clear, as is the scope they provided for intensification of the labour process. Although there were differences in the precise kinds of changes made in the different stages of production, they were all of the small-scale intensification type (see pp. 49–53). Few major purchases of new kinds of machinery, embodying significantly new technology, were made. One indication of this is given by the age of machinery in the industry at the end of our period. In the mid-1970s, 80 per cent of the machinery in the closing rooms of the footwear industry in the UK was over ten years old. This is the stage of the process least amenable to change, but even in the cutting process (clicking) it was 31 per cent, and in the making-room 49 per cent of machinery was more than ten years old (Department of Industry 1977, 76).

A similar set of possibilities was open in the men's and boys' tailored outerwear industry. Here the main stages are cutting, sewing (assembly/machining), finishing and pressing. It is again the sewing stage which dominates the overall structure of production (see also p. 46), but it is only in cutting and pressing that advanced equipment has been introduced (NEDO 1974b). In machining, by contrast, where four-fifths of the operators' time is spent in handling (rather than actual machining), the scope for intensification of the labour process is considerable, through 'work-station engineering and lay-out, quality engineering and design specification and personal [*sic*] management' (NEDO 1974a, 49). Once again, the age and cost of machinery indicates the state of development. This is shown by, for instance, the NEDO (1974b) purchasing survey. This analysis of the penetration of more expensive and more advanced sewing machinery showed that it accounted for only a very small proportion of the total number of sewing-machines. The percentages were: 'advanced'

Clicking

When a design has been evolved and converted into working patterns (a process still largely dependent on handcraft) and when tooling has been obtained, footwear manufacture starts in the so-called clicking room with the cutting of the uppers and linings from leather skins or man-made sheet. Originally this was done manually by cutting around flat patterns. Now, except for uppers of the most expensive leather and for short production runs, the parts are cut out by operator-controlled hydraulic presses with swing arms using moveable shaped knives not unlike domestic pastry cutters. Cutting leather by this method is still highly skilled work; the 'clicker' has to reconcile the need to match the patterning of leather in pairs of boots or shoes and to use the natural stretch of the material to assist shape retention in wear with economy and with the avoidance of the blemishes in the skin.

The growing importance of plastic uppers has made it economic to introduce large overhead beam presses which can handle material up to six feet wide in several thicknesses on a continuous system, but even with these machines moveable shaped knives are used. The output from such presses is limited by the great variety of styles, sizes and fittings produced in each factory which necessitates constant pauses for knife adjustments.

Closing

The upper components are assembled in the so-called 'closing' room which is mainly equipped with sewing machines similar to those used for clothing but specially designed to deal with the diverse shapes, thick material and specialised types of stitching involved. Some 25 per cent of the equipment in closing rooms consists of machines other than sewing machines. Examples are machines marking numbers to indicate sizes and fittings, punching fancy patterns, skiving (i.e. edge tapering) leather components, folding over or taping edges and applying stiffeners in the toe area (toe puffs). The sewing machine is not easily displaced because of its flexibility and reliability, but the seams of some plastic uppers can now be heat welded, and various machines are being used to apply patterning which would formerly have been done by sewing. The most important recent advantage has been the embossing of certain types of PVC upper material by using low cost silicone rubber moulds or embossing dies in which the material is heated by energy from a high frequency capacitance generator. Close simulation of leather graining and of stitching is possible by this method.

Using traditional machine methods a single upper design can require as many as 20 operations and a typical range of, say, 12 styles produced by one factory can involve 34 different types of machine on which varying amounts of operative time would be required.

Lasting

The closed upper, the insole and the bottom components are brought together to construct the shoe in the lasting and making departments, the first major process in which is lasting. A last is a hinged wooden or plastic block shaped to take account both of critical dimensions of the foot and of the contours of the particular design of the shoe (e.g. pointed or square toes, low or high heels). Lasting consists of stretching the upper over the last and securing it to the insole (temporarily attached to the bottom of the last) so that the leather conforms to the contours of the last and retains that shape when the last is removed. The hitherto conventional process starts with the upper being 'mulled' (i.e. having water forced into its fibre structure) to improve elasticity and then treated on a pulling-over machine which pulls the lasting margin (i.e. the edges of the upper overlapping the insole) over the insole all round and tacks it to the insole temporarily. The waist (i.e. the sides), the toe and the seat (i.e. the heel) areas are then each lasted separately on different specialised machines which fold the lasting margin flat to the insole and secure it permanently by tacks or, in more modern machines, by adhesive. In recent years so-called two part lasting has been introduced to reduce the element of skill, speed up production and improve quality. With this method the first operation is to stick the heel area of the upper to the insole while at the same time forming the backpart of the shoe. The pulling over and lasting processes are then carried out on two machines of which one treats the toe area and the other treats the waist area. Combined pulling over and lasting machines in which the pincers and wiper plates have to carry out relatively complex movements adapted to a wide range of sizes and shapes of last are among the most sophisticated and expensive machines used in footwear factories. ☞

Making

Next the 'lasted uppers' (i.e. the combined upper/insole units on the last) are passed through a heat setting cabinet which successively forces steam into them and dries them out so as to relax the strains caused in lasting and to 'set' the upper permanently to the shape of the last. The whole process takes about four minutes whereas prior to 1960 the lasted uppers needed to be kept on the lasts for several days; it has thus brought about a substantial saving in the number of lasts required and the amount of work in progress. Some ancillary processes are carried out at this stage, notably, if the bottom is to be stuck on or moulded on by injection moulding, the insole and lasted margin must be roughed by hand or by machine to achieve good adhesion.

For the 'stuck-on' construction the pre-cemented sole or complete bottom unit is then attached to the lasted upper in a press which maintains for a pre-determined time the pressure required to shape the bottom and establish a permanent bond. If the heel is attached separately this is done by a heel nailing machine. If the bottom is to be 'injection moulded', the lasted upper is placed in a machine which clamps to its under surface a mould into which thermoplastic is forced under pressure and heat, thus forming and attaching the sole in one operation. The most common thermoplastic used is a plasticised PVC compound but more complex designs of machine using polyurethane (which has superior wear characteristics) are now being introduced. Some injection moulding machines deal with only one shoe or a pair at once but large rotary machines with up to 12 or more stations are in use for suitable applications such as football boots entailing long runs with limited size and fitting variations.

Finishing

With the modern processes described above the final finishing processes following the attachment of the bottom require only a limited amount of simple equipment such as polishers.

Fig. 3.1   The main stages of production in footwear manufacture
Source   Monopolies and Mergers Commission 1973, 78–80
Note   Some other techniques, such as laser-cutting, exist, and also the precise method of production varies with the style, performance required, and material used

machinery costing over £2000, 0.9 per cent; 'intermediate' machinery costing £1000 to £2000, 0.3 per cent; and 'special' machinery costing £500 to £1000, 4.9 per cent (NEDO 1974b, 47).

In both industries, therefore, the nature of the labour process restricted the possibilities of cost-cutting through major technical change, and this, together with other factors such as the nature of the raw materials, goes some way towards explaining the importance of intensification. But these factors do not altogether explain the kind of production reorganization adopted. Rather, they indicate that it was one of the possibilities. Much more dramatic forms of technical change could also have been adopted. The technological difference between the UK and American industries has already been noted. Indeed the figures just presented on the purchase of machinery indicate that there was a very low adoption of the advanced machines that were available. Much of the explanation for this lies in the structure of ownership in the industries, in the dominant kinds of capital involved. Precisely because of the predominance of sewing-machine technology, plant-level production economies of scale are extremely limited. Thus the NEDO survey of the clothing industry comments:

> *Technology and the Garment Industry* [NEDO 1971a] examines the special influence of the sewing-machine on the size to which establishments will tend. Its cheapness permits a proliferation of very small firms under twenty-five employees and its 'unitisation' limits advantages of scale both in machining and in peripheral production and management resources. The twofold fact that machining costs account for as much as 75 per cent of total labour costs, 20 per cent of the value of the industry's gross output and 41 per cent of its added value weakens production cost pressures towards attaining an optimum scale of factory. Processes such as cutting and pressing do lend themselves to economies of scale but only account for 25 per cent of total labour costs. (1974a, 16)

Exactly the same kinds of factors also operate to restrict the overall economies of scale in footwear (see, for instance, Department of Industry 1977). While *advantages* of scale certainly do exist (in terms of marketing, locational flexibility, etc.) the lack of *necessity* for scale in production has enabled the continued existence and importance of small companies. Table 3.2 has already shown that enterprises employing less than 100 workers form 70 per cent of all enterprises in the footwear industry and 83 per cent in outerwear. This structure has a number of effects.

First, in both sectors these small producers face markets controlled by single large firms (both upstream (leather) and downstream (retailing) in footwear, downstream in outerwear), and this has tended to increase the intensity of the external economic pressures upon them. The fate of large numbers of small manufacturing firms can become dependent on the decisions and ordering strategies of one or two retailing companies, for instance. Second, and most important from the point of view of the immediate argument, in both sectors organizational structure is part and parcel of the lack of significant technical change. Recommendations for methods of improving productivity in these industries frequently focus upon management, the need to make it more dynamic, more competitively capitalist. On footwear, the assessment of the Economists Advisory Group was unambiguous:

> One other important structural characteristic of the footwear industry should be referred to. This is the high average age of

companies. Very few new footwear companies have been formed since the Second World War and the majority of the medium and large companies date from the nineteenth century. In the mto [made-to-order] sector, in particular, this has resulted in a relatively high average age of managements in family business, much of which is in its second or third generation. This conclusion is based upon observation, there being no statistical evidence, but we understand that it is generally accepted in the industry as being correct. An ageing structure of enterprise and management is, it appears, a general characteristic of UK industry, but it may be exceptionally pronounced in the footwear industry where, in the nature of things, technological change has been relatively slow. (undated, 95)

It concluded:

The lack of new management blood has been particularly pronounced in smaller, family-owned firms. This is a direct cause of the introspection, lack of marketing energy, [and] poor financial controls shown by most firms and the failure of the industry to react to change.

The general quality of management in the industry is poor except in the few very large manufacturers where it is professional, trained and competent. Amongst the smaller family concerns, there is a preoccupation with the task of making the business simply provide a living for its owner which shuts out all thoughts of new investment and a new aggressive approach to marketing and reorganization. Many firms are living off their reserves and mto [made-to-order] companies have particularly been forced into this situation. Yet despite the fact that these firms will fail if the position is allowed to continue, nothing is done to attempt to correct matters. Management is very reluctant to attempt changes in the business which involve investment. (undated, 151)

We see here a very clear case of the point made in the last section that changes in production are not the 'deterministic' outcome of economic circumstances and technology. They are also dependent on the nature of management, industrial relations and the strength and organization of the workforce. A very similar situation pertained in the clothing industry. Thus the NEDO survey reported:

management in the garment industry is equipped to manage a craft industry of small technological content and small technical investment with short pay-off periods. Moves to raise technological levels and capital intensiveness in the garment industry will create large problems in management education. (1974c, 21; quoting NEDO 1971a)

Third, and reinforcing this lack of enthusiasm for technical change, the smallness of the companies may have restricted the amount of cash available to them for investment.[10] The important small-firm part of this industry therefore was both hit harder, because of its structural position, by the increased economic difficulties, and was less able to respond by going in for major technical change.

The fourth and final effect of the importance of such companies was that the smallness of the capital involved effectively ensured that these firms did not have the option of taking advantage of their competitors' more favourable conditions of production by investing abroad.[11]

Two other subsidiary factors remain to be mentioned, both primarily concerning the footwear industry. First, it has already been stated that the two industries came into increasing competition for female workers. Such competition seems to have been quite significantly spatially differentiated – both sectors seem to have suffered from the increased demand for female labour in the South East of England, for instance. But in other ways their experience was different as a result of their different initial geographical patterns; outerwear being concentrated in Yorkshire and Humberside, footwear in the East Midlands. It appears from both qualitative and statistical evidence (Economists Advisory Group undated, 35, 196; changes in female activity rates, etc.;[12] and references in chapter 8) that the pressure of competition increased over the period more in the East Midlands than in Yorkshire. This was probably due, in part, to the pattern of service-sector decentralization from the South East of England. It is certainly possible that the initial spatial pattern of the footwear industry increased the intensity of the difficulties with which it was faced. Second, this was reinforced by the effect of previous industrial relations agreements to retain the male/female division of labour in the footwear industry. Only women are employed in closing, men in clicking. It was therefore impossible to adjust to labour shortages in one sex by employing people of the other, and it is argued (Economists Advisory Group undated, 134) that this added to the pressure of finding enough female labour in the East Midlands over this period.

Thus in these two industries a whole variety of factors combined, first to produce the pressure for cost-cutting (the changing international division of labour, plus national geography and industrial relations) and second to influence the fact that the form taken by this cost-cutting would dominantly be that of intensification of the existing labour process (organization/ownership of capital, labour process).

This, then, is the broad structure of reasons why intensification was needed. It was, moreover, a very particular and 'classic' form of intensification: a combination of small modifications and machines, of work-study, and of attempts at devising payment schemes and forms of work organization that might encourage an increase in the pace of production. The overall character of the changes is indicated by the comment already referred to from NEDO on raising productivity in labour processes using the sewing-machine:

> the close association of operator with machine and the four-fifths of machining time spent on handling rather than machining suggest that the scope for intensification is great. Improvement of productivity by such means owes much to management input via training programmes, work-station engineering and layout, quality engineering and design specification and personal [*sic*] management. Investment in these and other management areas is a cost with tangible manufacturing returns although its worth cannot be measured by techniques such as the incremental capital–output ratios used to measure changes of productivity caused by modernisation of the manufacturing process. (1974a, 49)

There was a vast variety of small changes in individual parts of the labour process in both industries. Thus British United Shoe Machinery, in its evidence to the Monopolies and Mergers Commission (1973), claimed that, from 1969 to 1971, an annual average of about 540 modifications were included in new production of *existing* types of machines. Similarly in outerwear a later NEDO publication (1974c) entitled *Low-Cost Work-Aids for the Clothing and Garment Industries* presents details of sixty-two work-aids, most costing less than £50, all but one costing less than £150. The contents page is reproduced as figure 3.2 and clearly shows the emphasis on small time-saving devices, particularly on gadgets to reduce handling time and to reorganize workshop layout. The constraints of the labour process are clear. The classic nature of this attempt to achieve increases in worker output without major change to the production process is indicated by comparison of this list with what Braverman wrote in the same year on the US apparel industry. The Glossary of Terms from NEDO (1975b) is also indicative of the kind of increases in productivity being

In the manufacture of wearing apparel, every aspect of the production process is being energetically attacked. Since this is an industry which is characterized by the existence of many shops, most of them relatively small, a great many are still in the stage of traditional 'rationalization,' breaking down operations into a large number of smaller and simpler steps. At the same time these steps are being speeded up by the introduction of a variety of devices, chiefly attachments to sewing-machines such as needle positioners, automatic thread-cutters, pleaters, and hemmers. The use of two- or three-layer bonded materials, which eliminate separate linings, and synthetic fabrics, which may be processed by novel methods such as the electronic fusing of seams in place of sewing, opens up new vistas for cheapening and transforming mass-produced clothing. Advanced production methods are copied from sheetmetal and boiler-shop techniques: die-cutting to replace hand cutting, pattern-grading equipment which produces different size copies of a master pattern, etc. There is a photoline tracer which guides a sewing head along the path of a pattern placed in a control unit. Improving on this, a photoelectric control is used to guide a sewing head along the edge of the fabric. In these latter innovations we see the manner in which science and technology apply similar principles to dissimilar processes, since the same control principles may be applied to complex contours, whether on steel or cloth.

Source Braverman 1974, 211–12

Foreword
Preface
Introduction

Machine attachments (including guides, jigs and folders)
Sew on cuffs
Profile sewing jig
Special machine foot: join strip
Square ended bearer attachment
Folder strip to bra cups
Tab stitching jig
Ply separating foot
Guide: interlining to cuff
Join bust cups and lace
Special machine foot and folder: three stitch, strip and join
Pneumatically operated lap seam folder
Petersham banding skirts

Gauges or measuring devices
Braces button marker
Waist measuring gauge
Leg measuring device
Buttonholing gauge

Handling aids (and work handling systems)
Trouser hanger for rail conveyor
Batch clamp
Monorail trolley
Overhead conveyor
Work trolley
Carousel for hemming
Lable picker
Dual pick-up arm
Intermediate work clamp
Pneumatic stacker
Co-ordinated yoking clamp table
Automatic pneumatic lift (11 ft)
Packing in sewn paper sacks

Workplace layouts
Workplace: hip pocket make
Engineered workplace layout
Clamping table for yoking
Hem marking workplace
Buttonhole collars: tandem machines
Preparation of waistbands
Workplace and workholder for yoking

Machine conversions	Miscellaneous
Pneumatic conversion: eyeletting press	Button sewing aid
Pneumatic conversion of Juki buttonhole	Thread holder
machine L8H 76	Extension tester for narrow elastics
Pneumatic die-cutting press	Revolving inspection dummy stand
	Stretch fabric testing
Notch, weld, tack or baste	Polythene bag sealer
Halve and quarter collars	Precision elastic tensioning device
Staple baste fronts	Batch labelling
Staple rack sleeve vents	Stapling switch cards
Spotwelder: collar linings	Pneumatic buttoncovering machine
Halve and quarter collars	Lay manipulator for die-cutting
Bartack and staple tack waist adjuster	
	Pressing
Trim, cut or separate	Patch pocket pressing
Pneumatic tape cutter	Pocket flap press and mark
Tape cutter	Heated vacuum table for hand irons
Collar point trimming press	
	Appendix

Source Contents page of *Low-Cost Work-Aids for the Clothing and Garment Industries* (NEDO 1974c)

Fig. 3.2   In theory and in practice: changes in production in the clothing industry

sought (see figure 3.3). In particular, the definitions of 'excess costs' and 'standard costs' seem to reflect the notion of 'porosity' and the attempts to reduce dead time in which the workers are not actually producing output.[13]

In both industries some time-and-motion and work-study projects were carried out, although they were probably confined in actual application to a sub-set of companies. Thus the Economists Advisory Group (undated) study of footwear reported that in 1975 only about forty member-firms of the British Footwear Manufacturers Federation were operating time-study systems of payment, as distinct from traditional piece-work, though these included both small firms of between 100 and 200 employees, and very large ones. This, however, only refers to the use of time-study in payments; more firms were probably using the principles of such study in the organization of production. In the outerwear industry its use may have been quite widespread; certainly there was encouragement for its adoption during our period (see HMSO 1969; NEDO 1971b).[14] We reproduce here a case-study, mentioned earlier, from the second of these booklets (figures 3.4 and 3.5). One point that is significant to note is the importance of relations on the shop-floor being both a stimulus to

3 in 1 payroll system	An integrated system which enables individual performances, daily section performances and weekly gross pay information to be obtained daily from a single processing of the operators' work sheets.
60/80 incentive	A system of work measurement on which 80 is equivalent to 100 on the BSI system (*qv*) and where values are normally expressed at time work rate (80/60 × 'standard time' under the BSI system – *see also* Work content analysis).
BSI system	A system of work measurement which defines as 100 per cent the work output of an average operator who is working under incentive conditions.
Block scheduling system	A progressing system which identifies batches of work and which ensures that each unit in a batch is passed through an operation sequence before subsequent batches are allowed through.
Direct labour costs	The wages and costs of related benefits (e.g. national insurance, holiday) for those personnel employed on the factory floor who undertake operations that physically develop the product.
Excess costs	The difference between the actual wage costs incurred (not including related benefits) and standard costs (*qv*). These arise for example from operators waiting for work, working at less than standard performance or from the payment of overtime premium.
Handling time	Normally the time at a sewing operation when the garment parts are being picked up, manipulated or disposed and the sewing needle is at rest.
Indirect labour costs	The wages and related benefits (e.g. national insurance, holiday pay, etc.) for support personnel employed on the factory floor (i.e. excluding supervisors) whose operations do not physically develop the product.
Line balancing	The technique of ensuring adequate but not excessive levels of work in progress awaiting each operation in a sequence of operations.
Line bundle system	A production system in which garments usually of similar style and colour, pass together as a bundle through work stations laid out as a fixed production line.
Loose rates	Piecework rates based on an evaluation of standard time (*see* Work content analysis) which overstate the work content of the operations to which they apply.
Making through	A production system in which the whole (or a majority of the) garment is produced by one operator as one operation.
Operation bulletin	A chart which lists and describes each direct operation in the sequence which is required for the production of a finished garment. ☞

Operator	A member of the workforce who is trained to carry out a direct or indirect operation on the garment.
Overhead costs	All costs incurred in the business other than direct labour costs and material costs.
Production engineering	The shaping of a production system and production methods, and choosing machinery and equipment to manufacture a product at the lowest cost compatible with conditions imposed by outside factors such as delivery, flexibility or quality required.
Progressive bundle system	A production system in which garments, usually of similar style and colour pass together, as a bundle, through a sequence of separate operations (*contrast* Line bundle system).
Standard costs	In relation to direct labour, these are the wages costs (not including related benefits), that would be incurred if all direct operations were carried out in standard time (*see* Work content analysis). This is equal to the measured work content of the garments produced (i.e. number of minutes taken at the defined operator effort) multiplied by the yield rate per unit (i.e. agreed wage cost for standard time measured, for example, in pence per standard minute).
Throughput time	The time which a single unit would take in normal conditions to pass through a sequence of operations under a normal first in and first out basis at each operation.
Tote boxes	Boxes used to contain a bundle of work.
Transporter system	A production system which uses a 'transporter' (usually a belt conveyor or hanging garment system) to transport work from a central point to pre-selected operator positions for each operation.
Value analysis	The analysis of the real value of any feature of a product or its production and distribution in relation to the costs incurred in providing this.
Work content analysis	The evaluation of the standard time that an average operator working under incentive conditions would take to complete the direct labour tasks on part or all of the product analysed.
Work in progress	In a production department the total number of garments or the total work value which is in progress between either the previous department or store and either the next department to which the work goes or the finished goods store or dispatch.

Fig. 3.3 The language of intensification: the glossary of terms from the NEDO document *Unlocking Productivity Potential*
Source NEDO 1975b, 56–7

modifications in the labour process (in particular, in this case, the disruptive effects of absenteeism) and an important determinant of the success, from management's point of view, of their implementation. In this case, there was clearly resistance from the shopfloor, if not from the official union representatives. Similarly, in footwear, the Footwear Industry Study Group Report noted:

Operatives

There is always a resistance among operatives to the introduction of new machines particularly among the older ones who may have spent twenty years operating a particular machine and have great difficulty in reaching a reasonable performance with a new type. In addition, they will tend to suspect the management of wishing to obtain greater output at their expense, and there is also the obvious conclusion that some will lose their jobs unless the new machines are introduced at a time of increasing demand.

Unions

In some factories, the management have introduced labour-saving machinery without immediately re-costing the jobs involved. The result has been that the operatives' jobs have been made easier and they have received higher wages. In certain cases difficulties have arisen subsequently in re-negotiating the necessary adjustments to the rate for the job. (1976, 35–6)

This important element of change in labour processes is frequently underestimated (see, for instance, the comments of Elger 1979). Similarly, in geographical studies there has been a tendency to see management as the only 'actor', whereas these studies would suggest that more might be gained by focusing on the relation between management and workforce, capital and labour.

Finally, all assessments of the two industries during our period indicate a continuing discussion on the methods of payment most effective in increasing productivity. Simple payment-by-results, more complex forms of incentives, group schemes as against individual incentives – all are discussed, and experience of them is compared at length.

These two industries, then, provide good examples of intensification of a labour process not yet mechanized. The limits of such

Case study 4:
Re-organisation of trouser room to cope with increases in production

Problem
Diversification into trouser production resulted in a considerable actual and potential excess of demand over production facilities; the need was for a substantial increase in production.

Method and changes made
1 Consultants were commissioned (at this time there were no work study personnel in the company), and a broad analysis of the current production methods was made, together with an assessment of the costs, capital expenditure and consultancy fees that would be incurred if the trouser room was re-organised. The company decided to go ahead with the project and a resident consultant was appointed.

2 Production requirements were agreed between the company and the consultants in the light of forecast demand. The consultant then examined the operations of the trouser room over a reference period of four weeks chosen by the firm as being typical in order to establish average performance, wage costs, output and so on. This both served as a base period for comparison and also provided an opportunity to develop standard times, previously non-existent, for many of the more common operations. The total weekly output at this time was 2,400 trousers produced by almost 200 operatives.

3 The first changes proposed and accepted concerned the trousers themselves. The number of styles was reduced slightly, from 16 to 14, and previous minor variations in each style were eliminated. Further, 14 changes in garment construction were made, such as fitting only one size of pocket, and replacing the hand sewn, with a machine sewn, button stand tail. The major criterion of these changes was the possible effect on sales: where it was thought that any deterioration in quality and appearance would occur, the proposed change was rejected. This happened to three of the proposals.

4 Next, attention was turned to the layout of the room and the production flow. The previous layout and flow are shown in Chart 2, and the improved design in Chart 3. At the time of the study the cloth to be made up into suit and special trousers was received from a separate cutting section in the trouser room itself. The cloth from both these points was brought in boxes by hand to a temporary storage and preparation area in the centre of the room prior to being delivered, again by hand, to the start of two separate assembly lines. The smaller of the two lines started at the opposite end of the room and partly made up both the stock and special lightweight and golden grade trousers. This line had been causing some concern, mainly owing to absenteeism; and since there was only one girl per

☞

operation, bottlenecks and checks had been frequent. The trousers were pushed down the line along a conveyor belt; it had never been found practicable to switch it on.

5 The factory had no separate training centre: retraining required a great deal of effort on the part of the company. Representatives from the firms selling the machines and work aids gave instruction on the use of their machines where these were being installed; for the rest training was by the traditional method of example by an experienced operative.

6 The next stage was to balance production flow in a similar way to that used in the case study 3, by basing the calculating of the number of operatives required for each stage, or critical balance point to achieve the required production on the standard times. (See Table 4.1 for a more detailed example of the calculation of the number of machinists required for one operation – '3rd sew'.) There were six machinists of different performance rating, working different hours per week. The equivalent hours of work were calculated by multiplying the actual hours worked by the actual performance divided by the standard rating. Hence, for example, the equivalent hours for machinist 3 were:

$$\frac{31\frac{1}{4} \times 128}{100}, \text{ or } 40 \text{ hours.}$$

Two styles of trousers passed through this operation (styles A and B), with a production requirement of 1,000 style A trousers and 2,000 style B. With a target of 11.2 and 23 trousers respectively per standard hour the production times required were 89.1 and 87.0 hours, or a total of 176.1 hours.

The total 'equivalent hours' available in the section added up to 216.1 hours, or a surplus of 40 hours which could be allocated elsewhere. In addition to the operatives allocated to each section there were six highly skilled 'booster' or 'floater' operators who could be assigned to increase the production flow up to the necessary level through any critical balance point where a bottleneck was developing or to cover for absenteeism. For details of the problems encountered in the installation of the new scheme see the note on this page.

Benefits
The cost of all new machinery purchased was recovered in savings in labour costs within two years and once the scheme was fully operational, there were considerable financial benefits. At the start of the consultant's survey, nearly 200 operatives were producing 2,400 trousers per week. Nine months later with the equivalent of 125 operatives full time (39 hours per week) at 78 performance, output was just over 3,000 trousers per week. Production increased to a rate

☞

of just under 4,000 per 125 full time operatives, as performance rose to 100, a level reached first 18 months after the start of the consultants' survey. This large increase in labour productivity has been reflected in substantial improvements in unit production costs as well as in operative earnings. The financial benefits more than covered the cost of employing additional work study staff and others required.

Notes on problems encountered in the installation of the new scheme

A The installation of the new scheme was not easy. It was put to management, supervision and the union shortly after the consultants survey. Management came to accept it as capable, with few alterations, of achieving all that had been claimed for it. Supervisors and the union had more doubts. After further intensive explanation of the scheme, however, and in particular elaboration on precisely what the targets being set for each operation meant in terms of earnings to each operative, it was finally agreed that the scheme would be installed for a trial period of three months, at the end of which a vote should be taken in the trouser room on whether to continue it or not.

B A considerable weakness in the management of the project had been felt to be the lack of a permanent work study officer on the company's staff. This deficiency was finally made good at the end of the three month trial period. It was clear then that even though neither the consultant nor the management had lost faith in the possibilities of the scheme, it was not living up to its promises and both supervisors and operatives were expressing dissatisfaction with the scheme. Production was considerably below target; there was high absenteeism; and there was considerable work in progress. In fact it was so clear that the scheme was not being given a proper run that agreement with the union was sought, and reached, to delay the vote on acceptance for a month.

C The first grievance to be raised at a meeting with the trouser room committee concerned the targets; it was decided to check them. Ninety per cent of them were found to be correct; but the ten per cent found to be incorrect were altered. Nonetheless, the new targets were still not achieved, although detailed follow-up studies revealed clearly that many of the operatives who were not achieving target could do so. The many reasons for this were inter-related; even then there was lack of knowledge as to the significance of the targets and of the scheme in general. Hence, operatives were apathetic, so absenteeism was high. In respect of absenteeism, the guarantee of previous average earnings throughout the trial period was not helpful – although such a guarantee was of course absolutely necessary for the scheme to have a chance of acceptance. Absenteeism and poor performance disrupted the production flow and made it ☞

impossible for girls later in the line to achieve targets, increasing the dismay and frustration felt at the scheme. Work in progress was excessively high – and this problem was not helped in the early stages by an increase in output from the cutting room, where it was known that higher production was expected in the trouser room.

D Frequent meetings with the operatives in small groups were organised to iron out some of these difficulties. Further, the flow was rebalanced and the input from the cutting room was temporarily reduced in order to relieve pressure on the production line. Steady improvement was achieved. Nonetheless at the end of the extra month, even through 60–70 per cent of operatives were already achieving targets and were earning more than their previous average, the vote in the trouser room was split exactly 50–50. A second vote was subsequently taken and as a result of still more assurances concerning allowances for operatives learning new techniques and further explanations that the targets would not be cut even if they were exceeded, that further investigation would be made into the targets of those who were finding it difficult to achieve them, and finally that there were now permanent work study officers on the company's own staff to ensure continuity, the scheme was accepted by a small margin.

E Subsequently production increased steadily as experience increased, the guarantee of average earnings was removed and the target system fully installed. One group of four girls however, continued to fall considerably below target and it was quite clear from follow-up studies that they were deliberately holding back production. By use of these studies the union officials were convinced that this was the case; as a result, the girls were told that they did not have union support for their action and the problem disappeared.

F Installation of the project had certainly not been easy, particularly from the behavioural and human relations point of view. But once the scheme was operational, the benefits became very clear.

G The main production line was U-shaped and consisted of roller conveyers with the operators working at either side. After the final operation of bottom felling, the trousers were carried by hand across the brushing off section; from there they were taken to the pressing section and the final inspection and ticketing section. The new design (Chart 3) replaced both the previous types of conveyer thereby allowing both greater flexibility of production and the introduction of work aids in the form of chutes, clamps, trimmers, stackers etc. The two assembly lines were amalgamated; similarly, the two flows of cut cloth were coalesced into one by reallocating the cutting section in the trouser room to the cutting room. The boxes were replaced by trolleys. ☞

H An important part of the consultant's job was to recommend particular machines and work-aids required for the new method of production, based on his personal experience of them. The recommendation was of course, merely a selection for evaluation; it had first to be decided on the basis of an estimated rates of return on the investment whether to have such a machine at all; and secondly the rates of return to be achieved with different makes of machine were compared to choose the highest. Hence the sophisticated transporter systems were rejected as alternatives to the trolley system, and a semi-automatic machine for pocket welting was chosen instead of a fully automatic.

I Substantially different methods were introduced into the majority of the operations of the making-up and assembly. An example of simple modifications giving very high returns is given in case study 5. Standard times were developed empirically for most of the new methods. That is to say, a time study was made of an operative in the trouser room as she was carrying out the new method.

Charts 2 and 3 show the former layout of the trouser room and the improved layout. [see p. 60]

Table 4.1 Method of calculating the number of machinists required for one operation ('3rd sew')
Production required: 3000 trousers per week
Operation: 3rd sew

	Required	Target	Standard hours required
Style A	1000	11.2/hour	89.1
Style B	2000	23/hour	87.0
		Total	176.1

Machinist	Actual hours worked	Actual performance	Equivalent hours, or std produced hours
1	31¼	90	28.1
2	22½	104	23.4
3	31¼	128	40.0
4	39	127	49.5
5	30	118	35.4
6	31	128	39.7
	185		216.1
	Surplus: 216.1–176.1 or 40 hours		

Fig. 3.4   A case of intensification in the men's and boys' tailored outerwear industry
Source   NEDO 1971b

Chart 2 Trouser room, original design

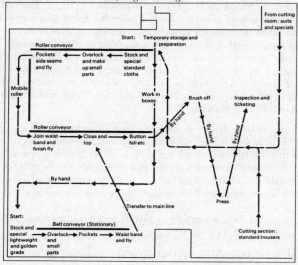

Chart 3 Trouser room, improved design

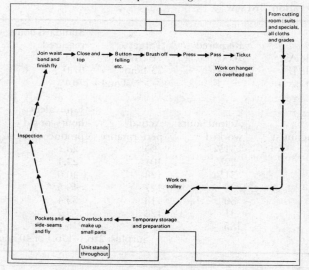

Fig. 3.5 Changes in work layout as part of intensification: the reorganization of the trouser-room
Source NEDO 1971b, 26–7

schemes are also clear. The real difference between this kind of labour process and the mechanized track of the car industry, in terms of the social relations involved, is well summed up by this suggestion from the Monopolies and Mergers Commission:

> Careful managerial control is thus necessary if high productivity in the closing room is to be achieved. One contribution to achieving this is to distribute work by a specially designed conveyor in which provision is made for an operative *to signal the supervisor when a batch of work is completed and a further batch is required.* Work is then delivered to the station by a belt which is set up to stop beside the operative and which also removes completed work. (our emphasis) (1973, 79)

In such a setting, rates of output have to be maintained by explicit supervision or by attempts to incorporate the production workforce behind the goal of increasing output. The debate on payment schemes is immediately indicative of the necessity of cajoling human workers to operate as management would like, and of the kind of frustration (and confusion) occasioned by management's relative lack of control of such labour processes through technology itself.[15] For footwear the Economists Advisory Group commented:

Relationship to management styles

Payment systems are an integral part of a firm's approach to management. Much has been discovered about motivation and management styles and experimentation has already begun in other industries. It would appear that when employees achieve a certain standard of living the relevance of incentive schemes declines. Factors such as atmosphere in the firm, identity with management and job satisfaction become more important to the employee.

Payment can thus only be seen in the context of the overall background of industrial relations in the industry and it seems probable that the footwear industry will have to pay more attention to behavioural factors, rather than expecting to be able to solve problems through payment systems. The [experiment at] Clarks . . . involves investigating the reorganization of a production unit into smaller autonomous work groups. (undated, 205)

Whilst NEDO reported on clothing:

Incentive systems

The incentive and payment systems in six of the seven firms had shortcomings in operation which hindered maximum operator performance. The most common defect was 'loose' or unrealistic rates, which caused inequities in payment and inefficiencies. Two firms were also operating money piece-rate systems. These were considered inappropriate because of operators' tendency to set arbitrary earning standards for themselves. One of these systems had a further shortcoming in that it applied to groups as well as individuals. Group-payment systems are not always conducive to the best level of productivity because the earnings and output of the groups will be limited by the length of the longest operation and/or the pace of the slowest girl.

In all cases the consultant's recommendations would remove these brakes on productivity by installing more relevant incentive systems and by attacking the causes of loose rates. (NEDO 1975b, 9)

4
Investment and technical change

The changes in production

So far we have looked at employment losses resulting from relatively minor modifications to the production process in a context primarily of output decline or slow growth. But employment loss can occur in other ways. In sixteen of the thirty-one industries we looked at employment decline in Britain was accompanied by heavy net capital investment. This investment was usually in the kind of major reorganization of the production process that resulted in a fairly substantial reduction in the amount of labour required for any given level of output.

The kind of physical change in production brought about by this investment varied considerably from industry to industry. In some cases, such as brewing and malting, there were significant increases in mechanization. In other cases there were major increases in scale that also incorporated some modification to the production process. Examples of this include the brick industry, and iron and steel. In yet other cases the labour-saving resulted from a change in the nature of the commodity being produced. This was true in the manufacture of cutlery, carpets and scientific and industrial instruments. In general, however, there was some kind of reconstruction of the production process as a whole. In most cases, too, this is the kind of reorganization of the labour process which leads, unlike intensification, to a noticeable shift upwards in the capital-labour ratio. It is through this means that the increase in labour productivity is achieved.[1] As in intensification, such labour-saving is, in most cases, achieved both by reducing the time not actually devoted to productive activity and by mechanization of the productive activity itself. In this case, however, it is likely to be the latter which dominates.

The first thing to note about this form of job loss is precisely the fact that it was accompanied by heavy capital investment. There is some tendency to assume that stagnation or decline in employment is associated with little activity on the investment front. The frequent assumption that a decline in manufacturing employment also necessarily implies a decline in investment and thus in the viability of policies to influence that investment, in particular its location, is a case in point. It is often argued, for instance, that regional policy cannot work during a period of employment decline because there will be no new investment whose location can be influenced. There is, clearly, often *less* investment under such circumstances, but even major investment projects are not absent. It becomes, therefore, particularly important to identify the conditions under which such projects may occur.

The point is reinforced by examination of table 4.1, which lists the industries in which employment decline occurred alongside significant levels of investment. It also gives their levels of output, employment and productivity. It is evident from this table that there is a wide range of different conditions under which major investment can both take place and lead to employment decline. At one extreme, six industries saw major investment even though output was actually declining over the same period,[2] and in three others output was growing only slowly (and way below the level for all manufacturing). Production reorganization in an overall context of retrenchment and a sectoral-level context of market decline, is thus not limited to relatively small-scale attempts to cut costs (intensification), or to closure and reallocation (rationalization). Even in such a context, fairly major reorganization of the production process, involving significant investment, may also take place.

The basic rationale for technical change in a capitalist system of production stems not from some neutral technological improvement, nor from 'need', but from competition and the requirements of profitability. Technical change in the process of production within a given product-market occurs as a result of the continuous attempt of firms to steal a march on each other. The commonest overall rationale is cutting production costs in some general sense. This may be either in the obvious immediate sense of reducing the combined costs of equipment and labour, or in the less direct way of enabling the use of a

Table 4.1 Industries where job loss occurred in a context of significant investment

| Industry | Output | Changes 1968–73 in: | |
		Employment	Productivity
	%	%	%
Misc. base metals	−9	−23	+18
Coke ovens	−6	−34	+42
Textile machinery	−5	−18	+16
Cutlery	−3	−10	+8
Fertilizers	−3	−1	−2
Bricks	−1	−18	+21
Biscuits	+2	−7	+10
Iron and steel	+3	−6	+9
Sugar	+4	−15	+22
Jute	+15	−4	+20
Instruments	+15	−21	+46
All manufacturing	*+15*	*−4*	*+20*
Brewing and malting	+18	−11	+33
Aluminium	+25	−11	+40
Carpets	+25	−1	+26
Chemicals	+30	−1	+32
Synthetic resins, etc.	+43	−20	+79

Source Census of Production: for employment data
Index of Industrial Production: for output data

potentially less organized workforce. It may also be that new technology is introduced in an attempt by management to gain a greater degree of control over an existing workforce through changing the labour process, or to eliminate a particularly unpliable part of the labour force. As we saw in the discussion of intensification, the development of a technology by no means guarantees its adoption. For example, even more 'advanced' than the new clothing-industry technologies referred to in the last chapter, is that reported by Harrison as now being advertised in the USA. This involves 'micro-computerized serving systems which remove control of the pace of piecework production from the stitchers and transform their work into a set of tasks that basically reduce to loading the pieces to be sewn into a feeder and removing the stitched section of garment a few seconds later' (1981, 71). The adoption of such technology may not occur while sufficient cheap labour is available to maintain the competitiveness of the sewing-machine system, or until, in a more general way, stimulated by the increasing power of labour. Thus, the very failure to push intensification any further, as a result of opposition from the shop-floor, may be what finally provides the occasion for more significant technical change. Burawoy, for instance, suggests that in some parts of American industry 'it has become more important and lucrative to change technology than to change rates' (Burawoy 1979, 182). All such technical change will enable the individual firm either to make above-average profits (because its costs are lower), or to capture a larger share of the market (because it can charge lower prices). In general these will, of course, be only temporary advantages as other firms, under pressure to stay in the race, also adopt the new production techniques. Those that don't may fail.[3] Such pressures apply in all kinds of economic conditions, whether growth or decline, but the nature and effects of such investment will vary a lot as a result of those conditions.

Major investment in the production process during a period of decline will often be 'defensive' investment (see, for example, Lamfallussy 1961); a major attempt by a company to increase a flagging rate of profit (through the increase in productivity) or to capture a larger share of a declining market (by cutting prices). It may also, of course, be the strategy pursued by the technically laggard firms in such a sector, in this case as a move forced upon them by worsening economic conditions, and a last attempt to stay alive. Failure to keep up technologically is much more likely to lead to actual failure in a period of decline than in a period of market growth. Many British firms managed to stay alive through the 1950s as they coasted along on the overall wave of expansion. Their failure to invest and modernize during that period came home to roost in the late 1960s and the 1970s. In such conditions, the actual technical change embodied in the new investment accords much more with what Fyfe calls 'technical application', namely 'the application of existing technical know-how in the production of existing goods and services for current markets' (1978, 87). In the period we are examining, such investment seems, at least, to have been not uncommon. Overall, the levels of manufacturing investment in Britain were high in the early 1970s; at the same time the rate of growth of output was slackening, and the ratio of the rate of growth of productivity to the rate of growth of output was relatively high until, precisely, 1973 (Singh 1977). The clear implication of this, of course, is that an unusually large proportion of the new investment was replacement investment. That is, instead of being embodied in new, additional capacity to produce additional output, to some extent at least the new investment replaced the existing capacity-operating at lower levels of productivity. The amount of any given investment level which functions as replacement investment will depend, in part, on what is happening to output. Assuming that in very general terms the amount of capacity is related to the requirement for output, then at zero rates of growth of output all new capacity necessarily has to replace existing factories. Building new plants, in other words, means the closure of others, either in the same firm or in others that have failed to keep up to date. Further, where output is declining, a greater amount of capacity has to be scrapped than the amount newly invested. Conversely, where output is growing part of the new investment is likely to be in additional capacity and part in replacement capacity. None of these market mechanisms work as perfectly as implied by this scenario, and indeed much of the next chapter will be devoted to examining how companies' rationalization strategies may vary. Nevertheless the general point is clear: the net effect on employment will vary according to the balance between output change and investment, and the lower the level of output growth the greater the likelihood that technical change will be accompanied by actual net job loss.

This point is significant in relation to some aspects of current debates. Both investment and technological change have, over the recent period, acquired increasingly bad names for their effect on employment levels. The announcement of major investment plans is often seen to be at least as likely to mean a loss of jobs as an expansion of them. And, at least in popular consciousness, the 'blame' for this is laid at the door of 'investment' and 'technological change' themselves. In fact, it is generally the combination of factors (more capital-intensive investment in a context of stagnating output) that is responsible for the employment decline. In most cases, had exactly the same investment taken place in a context of rapid output growth, it would have been embodied in new, extra capacity and would have been welcomed as a source of new, additional employment. Its degree of capital intensity in relation to existing techniques, its comparative levels of labour productivity, and consequently its comparative implications for employment, would probably have gone unnoticed. The same investment when undertaken in a period of stagnating or declining output can only too clearly be seen to be 'resulting in' job loss.[4]

It is, however, also possible for major 'labour-saving' capital investment to result in employment loss even where output is growing strongly. There are a number of such cases among the industries being examined here, general chemicals and synthetic resins and plastics being the two clearest examples. The fact that there was an actual decline in employment means, of course, that some of the new investment must, nonetheless, have replaced existing capacity. It is in such cases, where technological change in existing production processes is really the cause of employment loss, that it becomes most clearly incorrect to associate employment decline with any failure of accumulation. On the contrary, it is one of its necessary concomitants.

We have been talking so far about technical changes in the process of production. This, of course, is by no means the only form technical change can take. Major changes in industries, and in their employment structures, can result technical change in the nature of the product itself. The changes in telephone-switching equipment are probably the most notorious recent example. Over the economy as

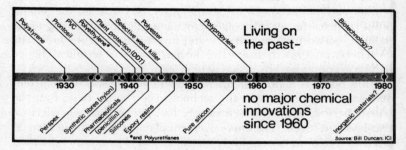

Fig. 4.1   Major chemical-product innovations
Source   *The Economist* 11 April 1981

a whole the two types of change are intimately interwined. A new product for one sector may be a new means of production for another, and automation of a production process may affect the nature of the product – mass-produced biscuits are different from hand-baked ones, in part because of the requirements of the production process. Moreover, the impetus behind product innovation also comes from competition. In some sectors, and at certain periods in the development of particular industries, competition through the technological advantages and sophistication of the product may replace cost as the main dynamic of inter-firm relations. At present this is perhaps particularly true in micro-electronics. It used to be true of chemicals in the 1940s and 1950s (see, for instance, Taylor 1979). Since that period, changes in process have become more important than changes in product, and the latter have consisted more of improvements to existing products than of major product innovations (see figure 4.1). The president of Imperial Chemical Industries (ICI) noted in an interview that between 1969 and 1980, while thirteen major process innovations were launched, there were only three major product innovations (the *Economist* 1980). Amongst the industries included in our research were some where product development was particularly important – it was true, for instance, of parts of the instrument-making industry. It was also true in a more defensive way of the cutlery industry (see pp. 75–8). On the whole, however, it has been investment and technical change in the process of production on which we have concentrated here, not because it is more important but because our intra-sectoral focus, and our concern with employment decline, threw up more examples of this type.

All this raises questions of spatial and sectoral definition. Technical change in both product and process are essential parts of capitalist competition and, as we have said, particularly in periods of slow or negative growth in output; those firms which do not innovate may die. When an industry is going through a period of technical change it may well be, as we have seen, that the new investment is in one area and the closure of now out-of-date factories occurs in another. There are many examples of this even within the UK. We have elsewhere (Massey and Meegan 1979a) pointed to a number of cases where inner-city closures went hand in hand with investment in new techniques outside the major conurbations. This raises two issues. First, it means that the definition of the main forms of production reorganization which is underway in an industry may depend on the spatial scale being examined. In principle, technical change in an industry within the UK may produce not only job loss in the UK but also closures of capacity and even greater losses of jobs in other countries. Conversely, rationalization in British industry may be a reflection of technical change elsewhere, and of the UK industry's inability to keep up with it. Similarly, as we saw, the intensification in the clothing industry in Britain in our period was a response to other kinds of changes (mainly growth in areas with cheaper labour) going on elsewhere. The different kinds of production change, in other words, are linked, and a whole range of changes may be occurring in a sector at the same time. It is important, therefore, to examine the changes going on in a particular area (such as the UK) within a wider context. In fact, as has already been intimated, much of the technical change in the UK in this period was of a defensive nature, and often rather late in the day. Second, it is important to emphasize the relation between production change and locational change. The two may be integral to each other, as when a change in production technology leads to new locational requirements, or when a move is a way of avoiding confrontation with the unions over proposed changes. They may also be alternatives to each other, as when movement to a new location, say with cheaper and less militant labour, obviates the 'need' for technical change. In this case changes in production and changes in location may be alternative ways of cheapening the labour force or of getting rid of well-organized workers.

The identification of dominant forms of production reorganization will also depend on the sectoral definitions adopted (the use of sectoral definitions is discussed again in chapter 10). Rationalization in one sector may be brought about by technical change involving a shift to another industry. This relates to the question of product development. In some cases – for instance the shift from woven to tufted carpets, or from electro-mechanical to electronic telephone switching systems – the shift takes place within one industry as defined by the data source we are using here (Census of Production). In other cases there will be a shift between the sectors for which the data are defined – an example would be the shift within textiles from natural to artificial fibres. Employment loss through rationalization in one sector may therefore be the losing end of a wider process of technical change and may be partially offset by gains in employment in the production of new products. In other words, just as it is important to set what is going on in a particular area in a wider geographical context, so also it is important to set changes in one sector in a wider industrial context. None of these changes in production are discrete, isolated happenings. They are all interrelated aspects of the pressure to increase profits within industries, and the search for higher profits between industries.

A good example of some of these sectoral considerations is provided by the jute industry in Britain. Employment in the jute industry (the manufacture of jute cloth) has been falling in the UK since about 1950, and has declined particularly quickly since the late 1960s. Output and capacity have been declining too. Between the mid-1960s and the mid-1970s, while employment dropped by 66 per cent, the output of yarn fell by 60 per cent and of cloth by 76 per cent. It was an area of production very clearly in trouble. The production of jute cloth is potentially subject to cost competition particularly from producers in India and Bangladesh; but, apart from losing some of the coarser end of production to capital in these countries, the decline was not primarily a result of such competition from cheaper producers. A long-standing protectionist policy prevented that.

> The explanation rather is that a synthetic substitute, polypropylene, has turned out to be cheaper than jute for a given technical performance in most end-uses and has therefore supplanted it. By 1976 polypropylene had replaced jute wholly or to a great and growing extent in most of its important traditional markets. There has also been some absolute reduction in a few of jute's traditional markets (e.g. linoleum backing). Over the past decade all the significant firms in the industry have diversified and are now much more concerned with the manufacturing of polypropylene. Polypropylene production is capital intensive, and jute production labour intensive. There has therefore been a net loss of jobs. (Odling-Smee 1977, xiv–xv).

There has, in other words, been a general decline in end-uses for jute cloth as a result of its substitution by other materials. Of these competing materials, cloth woven from polypropylene tape has been the most significant (McDowell and Draper 1978). Polypropylene's advantages derived both from its technical properties (weight, tenacity, etc.) and from its price, which was lower, more stable in the short run than that of jute, and declining over time.[5] There is also a great difference in technology between jute-cloth and polypropylene-cloth manufacture. Jute-cloth manufacture is based on a natural, and therefore variable, fibre using what is basically a traditional technology. 'Despite continuous improvements in productivity over the last five decades, its processes remain labour intensive and a jute mill in the 1970s looks much the same as a jute mill of the 1920s' (McDowell and Draper 1978, 8). In contrast, the manufacture of polypropylene cloth is capital intensive (it requires about one-sixth of the amount of labour to produce a given amount of cloth) and fast changing. Thus the halving of the labour force over our period may be explained largely in terms of the substitution of polypropylene for jute cloth in the product-mix of the industry (McDowell and Draper 1978, 9). This substitution, moreover, took place within an industry (mlh 415) as defined by the Census of Production, and is consequently included here as a case of technical change. In passing it is interesting to note how such changes reverberate through a whole string of industries. On the one hand polypropylene is shown in figure 4.1 as being one of the last product innovations in the chemical industry in the 1950s. On the other hand an important element in the changing market structure for jute has been the increasing importance within the carpet industry of tufted as opposed to woven carpets. At first the development of tufted carpets, and the increase in their production, provided a welcome new market for jute cloth, which was used as backing. It compensated for the decline of other traditional end-uses for jute, such as linoleum. However the tufted-carpet market turned out to be particularly vulnerable to competition from synthetic materials, and by the late 1970s polypropylene had ousted jute almost entirely from this end-use. By 1977 the total output of jute cloth for tufted-carpet backing was less than 10 per cent of what it had been ten years before. While in 1968 jute held 71 per cent of the primary-backing market for tufted carpets, by 1973, at the end of our period, it held only 5 per cent (McDowell and Draper 1978, 7, 15).

But why the change in carpet manufacture, an industry also included in our list of those undergoing technical change? Once again changes in product and changes in process are clearly linked. Between 1966 and 1972, while the total output of woven carpets remained more or less static, the output of tufted carpets more than doubled, and the latter's market share increased from 44 per cent to 60 per cent (McDowell and Draper 1978, 34; Central Office of Information 1978, 34). As a product, tufted carpets are cheaper than woven ones and their production opened up new markets for carpets by replacing hard floor coverings such as linoleum. And the reason that tufted carpets are cheaper than woven ones (such as Axminsters and Wiltons) is that the production process is completely different. The shift towards tufted carpets has been accompanied by a shift from natural fibre (wool) to synthetics (nylon and acrylic), and by the introduction of high-volume production based on a completely different way of making carpets. As the Central Office of Information pointed out, the main competitive advantages of the tufted process 'are that it enables carpets to be made at lower costs, with less labour and without many of the stages of production that woven-carpet manufacture requires' (1978, 35). Tufted carpets now account for about 75 per cent of carpet sales in Britain.

These examples thus form a whole chain of technical change of various sorts, each revolving in this case around changes in basic materials and, most significantly from our point of view, each involving reductions in the labour required for the production process. In each of these cases (chemicals, jute and carpets) it happened that the technical change took place within an 'industry', as defined for statistical purposes. In two cases (jute and carpets) the shift took place during our period. We have therefore, in these cases, caught both the declining and the growing ends of the process. In both industries, nonetheless, the net effect of this shift was a loss of jobs, and this in spite of the fact that, in our period, output continued to grow in both of these industries.

*   *   *

There is, then, a whole range of different circumstances under which major investment can take place and result in employment loss, and this range is reflected in the industries represented here. Moreover, the industries also display a fairly wide range of other characteristics. This is true, for instance, of the nature of the labour process. A glance down the list of industries in this category furnishes examples from many different manufacturing processes: from continuous or flow-line production (steel and chemicals) to large-scale partially-mechanized production (bricks), to small-scale, often craft-based, production (scientific and industrial instruments). Although there was a wide variety of manufacturing processes, indicating that such large-scale investments can take place in lots of different kinds of industries, there was also, however, a noticeable difference between the characteristics of these industries and those that, in this period, we found to be pursuing the other forms of production reorganization.[6] In particular, the group of industries which invested heavily included a much higher proportion of capital-intensive sectors than either of the groups of intensifying and rationalizing sectors. Moreover, the actual degree of capital-intensity in these sectors was also much higher than in the other groups.

A similar combination of both variety and distinctiveness characterized the ownership structure of capital in these sectors. The industries present a fairly diverse pattern in terms of company structure. As in the intensifying and rationalizing sectors, industries are included in which companies employing small numbers of workers are important (e.g. in cutlery, and fertilizer production), as well as those in which such firms were relatively less important (e.g. in the brewing and the coke-oven sectors – the latter predominantly owned by nationalized industries). Although small companies were most important in the intensifying industries, they had, on average, a relatively higher presence in the group of technical-change industries than they had in the rationalizing industries. Average plant size showed a similar range. However, examination of Census of Production figures on sales-concentration ratios indicates an important distinction between 'fragmentation' in these industries and that in the intensifying sectors. Table 4.2 lists, for each form of production organization, those sectors in which small companies, in employment terms, were particularly important, and shows for each main product the percentage of total sales accounted for by the five largest companies (in terms of sales).[7] In only two cases in the intensifying sectors did sales concentration exceed 50 per cent (although one was very high). In contrast, twenty-eight of the thirty-one technical-change products had sales concentrations above, and in many cases quite significantly above 50 per cent. This is sales. Perhaps more importantly concentration within production also seems to be more marked within these sectors than in those characterized by intensification, though data are hard to come by. What this means, of course, is that the role of 'leading companies', and large ones, was probably greater

Table 4.2   Sales concentration in industries with high proportions of small employers, 1968

*Form of production reorganization: industries with high presence of small employers**	*Percentage of total sales of principal products accounted for by the five companies with largest sales*
Intensification	
Printing and publishing	32
Outerwear	38
Leather	56, 21, 42
Cycles	95
(Average unweighted	47)
Rationalization	
Metal-working machine tools	41, 27, 50
Iron castings	42
Grain milling	81, 67, 94
(Average unweighted	57)
Technical change	
Instruments	57, 49, 30, 66, 37
Aluminium	51
Textile machinery	59
Bricks	57
Cutlery	71
Other base metals	71, 97, 92, 98, 71, 81
General chemicals	78, 97, 95, 65, 98, 95, 100, 74, 83, 97, 99, 85, 90, 79
Fertilizers	88
Sugar	99
(Average unweighted	78)

*for definition see note 7
Source   1968 Census of Production Summary Tables, Enterprise Analyses

in the heavily-investing sectors. But this does not mean to say that investment only took place in large firms. Cutlery provides a good example. Brutton (1975) talks of a company of only five workers where over £25,000 was invested in new machinery and where output was increased by breaking down manufacturing operations into a large number of very small, de-skilled processes. Clearly, the nature of the production reorganization was limited by the factor of size, but the fact of small size did not preclude significant production change and investment. Nonetheless, the greater ability of dominant firms to invest in new production techniques can further increase their power within an industry.

Partly for that reason, the process of major investment, and of possible technical change, is itself frequently accompanied by changes in the organizational structure of capital, and in particular by mergers and increases in concentration and centralization. This may, perhaps, be particularly true of industries in which the investment and technical change is taking place in the context of slowdown or decline. It is easy to understand a number of reasons why this might happen. On the one hand, mergers might be a necessary prerequisite for certain forms of investment and technical change in order to gain the necessary size in either financial or production terms. On the other hand, the very process of new investment and/or technical change by the strongest firms in a market might contribute to the subsequent failure and closure of the weakest (in other words a process of inter-firm compensatory scrapping – see note 4). This second situation can be seen in the cutlery industry over the period. Technical change had been going on in a number of ways in this industry and had occurred along with a substantial change in the organizational structure of the industry, through both mergers and liquidations (*Retail Business* 1974). A number of closures took place as a result of a failure to compete adequately with imports through such mechanisms as new investment and technical change – though in spite of this overall context, and as the report from British Silverware indicates (figure 4.2), closure was sometimes attributed to more immediate factors!

The jute industry provides a further interesting example of this relationship between technical change and organizational change. For most of its history the jute industry in Britain has been in the hands of small, often family-owned, businesses, which were confined to jute production and which sold an unbranded, almost homogeneous product through merchants (McDowell and Draper 1978, 20). These companies were not much concerned with market research

British Silverware close factories

The two Sheffield factories of British Silverware Limited, in Queen's Road and Heeley, are to close following a six-week strike. The announcement was made on November 9 by Mr. P. J. Daglish, chairman of the company, who said that insufficient number of the members of the National Union of Gold, Silver and Allied Trades had returned to work to enable the company to execute its commitments. The management had previously warned that closure was unavoidable unless adequate numbers returned to work. Less than 50 men out of 300 strikers in a work force of 550 responded to the call.

The strike had started over the suspension of six men for bad timekeeping. Mr. Daglish said this had developed into the union's refusal to accept the right of management to take disciplinary action over breaches of existing works rules. He said: 'We have therefore decided most reluctantly on closure of the two plants'. The union gave its official backing to the strike.

British Silverware was formed by the amalgamation of Mappin and Webb Limited with Walker and Hall Limited and Elkington and Company Limited of Birmingham in 1963. The statement on November 9 revealed cumulative losses of £1¼ million over the past seven years. The company is owned jointly by the Delta Group and Mr. Charles Clore's Sears Holdings. The retail shops of Mappin and Webb were not incorporated into British Silverware Limited.

Fig. 4.2   A rationale for a closure
Source   Watchmaker, Jeweller and Silversmith December 1970

or marketing. The industry was, however, fairly highly concentrated with one or two companies of substantial size. This structure of capital ownership both enabled technical change to occur within the industry, and was in turn affected by it. First, the presence of a few larger companies facilitated adoption of the new technology. McDowell and Draper write:

> it is interesting to speculate on the role of concentration in the jute industry in allowing it to respond favourably to the new technology. The presence of a few reasonably large companies in the industry who had the resources to respond . . . seems an important factor in enabling the Dundee jute industry to switch so readily to the new substitute. (1978, 21)

It was these larger companies that were able in the 1960s to diversify into synthetics, and by the end of that decade all the major jute companies had some polypropylene-weaving capacity, either themselves or through subsidiary companies, and some were integrating backwards into the extrusion of the fibre itself (polypropylene tape).

But the adoption of the new technology also had a reciprocal effect on the structure of the jute industry. First, the fact that some of the original jute companies were able to diversify into the new form of production has enabled both their survival and possibly the continuation of jute-cloth production at a higher level than might otherwise have been possible (there is evidence of cross-subsidization from polypropylene to jute – McDowell and Draper 1978, 8).[8] Second, however, it was the larger firms that were most able to diversify and survive in this way. The number of companies in the jute industry fell between 1963 and 1973 from forty four to twenty four. The process of change clearly increased the dominance of the already dominant. But it was not just the degree of concentration of capital which changed; it was also the nature of the capital. For one thing outside firms, with no previous connection to textiles but with a base in chemicals, entered the industry. Moreover, the nature of the new product and production process demanded a more dynamic approach. As McDowell and Draper put it: 'the jute companies, in diversifying, entered a very different industrial world from that to which they had long been accustomed' (1978, 8). Two changes in particular have been important. First it has been necessary for these firms to change their attitude to marketing – production for stock is no longer adequate. Second, in complete contrast to jute, polypropylene-based production is both a high-technology and a fast-changing affair. The firms, therefore, have both had to set up research and development and had to embark on a continuous process of product development, which in turn again means greater marketing ability. Technological change has therefore produced and required both a quantitative and a qualitative shift in the nature of the capital involved in mlh 415.

The combination of the wide range of different circumstances under which major investment can take place and result in employment decline, with the wide range of characteristics of the industries themselves, means, unsurprisingly, that this form of production reorganization included a considerable variety of actual behaviour. Thus, among the industries facing either static or declining markets, compare cutlery, brick making and biscuit making. In cutlery, the main pressure for modernization came from imports. One example of a response to this – technical change in a small firm – has already been given (see p. 75). Figure 4.3 illustrates two others: automation of the production process and a shift in its content (from making whole cutlery to simply plating it); all forms of change used less labour, and

One relatively recent arrival (1971) to Saltley is the firm of Arthur Price of England, which manufactures cutlery. It took over the old Parkfield Rolling Mills, expanded the facilities, and built some offices. The company employs less than 200 workers, and its position seems very insecure, although this may be exaggerated by the company in its concern to win protection against imports. The British cutlery industry has had to change dramatically since the 1960s in an attempt to adjust to the imports of cheaper goods from the Far East, which are produced on a larger scale in long runs and on more modern machines.

It has had to move up-market, to emphasise the craft skills involved, but at the same time introduce new techniques. The Saltley plant is Arthur Price's attempt to do this. Its offices are a central point in the company's marketing campaign of emphasising craft. Its works are integrated; sheet steel is unloaded automatically in one street, passes through the factory and is prepared for despatch as spoons and forks into a parallel street. New presses form the forks and spoons, which are glazed and polished automatically. In other words, while the old crafts are emphasised in the advertising, newer skills, closer to other engineering work, are actually being used.

The position as described by the company is a difficult one. John Price, the Managing Director, has said: 'It is literally a fight for survival. Eighty per cent of the cutlery in Britain is now imported. I can remember when there were 50,000 employees in this industry. Now there are just 3,000'. That estimate of present employment (made in 1975) has now been shifted downwards by Mr Price to 2,500, although other estimates put it at 10,000.

One response of many British manufacturers has been to import cutlery in blank form and then plate it – essentially giving up competing in the mass market. According to some spokesmen, the profit made on this has helped British manufacturers to invest in more modern production techniques, using less labour.

Fig. 4.3   Some changes in the cutlery industry in Saltley, Birmingham
Source   Birmingham Community Development Project 1977, 30

less-skilled labour (e.g. see David 1978; Ward 1978). In brick making, as we shall see in the next section, the investment was very much a 'leading-firm' phenomenon, and carried out in response to pressure on costs in the face of stagnant demand in a geographically predefined market. The nature of the change in production was also rather different. In this case, cost-cutting was achieved primarily through taking advantage of economies of scale and through aggregating together, in the new works, a range of small changes in the production process, each of which was already in operation individually in one of the existing plants. In this case, therefore, although there were

United Biscuits market leadership stems from pioneering production techniques

1950	First Biscuit Factory devoted to mass production of one product – (Penguin – Sales worth £5 Million per year).
1954	First Bulk Ingredient System for biscuits.
1955	First direct line of chocolate coating and baking led to Chocolate Homewheat, world's largest selling biscuit at £15 Million per year.
1956	First continuous plant incorporating three separate processes led to Jaffa Cake – and to sales worth £7 Million per year.
1958	First completely automatic Dough Mixing System.
1958	First continuous and completely automatic Cream Making System.
1959	First plant scale investigation into Radio Frequency baking.
1959	First automatic cake production line led to Jamaica Ginger – and sales worth £2½ Million a year.
1963	First Direct Linked Assortment System – oven to packet.
1964	First Biscuit Counter Blender Feeder to wrapping machines.
1966	First with rotary cutting of biscuits in UK.
1967	First (of three) automatic Chocolate Refinery.
1971	On-Line Computer Control of recipe process, stock records and bulk-handling ingredient system extended.
1972	Greater weighing accuracy resulting from new automatic biscuit cutting and packet loading equipment.
1973	First with a computerised plant info' system, leading to greater speed and accuracy of production control.

Fig. 4.4   The road to computerized biscuit making
Source   United Biscuits 1976

considerable increases in productivity, and consequent reductions in the number of workers per unit of output, there were almost no changes in the composition of the workforce.

The biscuit industry, too, is a concentrated one, with production being primarily in the hands of two companies. In this sector, the investment and technical change in the period 1968–73 was part of a much longer process in which automation was being introduced. Thus, the Commission of the European Communities reported:

> The biscuit industry is now highly concentrated, largely as the result of amalgamations and acquisitions among companies which had previously grown by internal expansion to some significant size. Two firms – United Biscuits Ltd and Associated Biscuit Manufacturers Ltd – accounted together for as much as two-thirds of the sales of all biscuits by UK manufacturers in 1972. In contrast to Continental Europe, biscuits have been mass produced and nationally marketed in the UK for many decades, and while imports of biscuits are limited, there has been a long-standing export trade as well as the development of overseas production by UK companies. (1975a, 205)

The 1973 annual report of the United Biscuits company talked of the installation of automatic refineries, of automatic cutting machines and of being 'well advanced on the road towards computerized biscuit making and plant monitoring and control' (United Biscuits 1973, 9), while figure 4.4 puts this in the longer-term context of automation within that company. In this case there was again a relationship between the changes in the production process and the structure of ownership in the industry (see Commission of the European Communities 1975a, 222, and Adam 1974). In 1972, for instance, the company took over Carr's Carlisle, Kemp Biscuits Ltd and Wright's Biscuits (all from Cavenham Ltd). Finally, although we do not have detailed information on the changes in labour-type brought about by this reorganization of production, in at least one aspect it was different from the other two cases. While the changes in the cutlery industry resulted primarily in a reduction of the skills required of the labour force, and while in brick making there was little change at all, in biscuit making the nature of the production change (towards relatively sophisticated automation) has led, over the long term, to a dichotomization of the labour force. Over the longer period of mechanization since the Second World War most of the jobs in the industry have become 'repetitive and boring', in the words of the industry's Sector Working Party (NEDO 1978e, 13). Indeed there have been efforts to offset some of the problems inherent in that process. The same document reports on efforts in the fields of job enrichment and consultation and worker participation (pp. 13–14). However, the same processes of technical change have also produced an increased demand for workers with technical skills. Clearly, given this variety of experience among the different industries, it would be wrong to assume that investment in technical change always and inevitably results in a simple process of de-skilling.

In all of these three industries (cutlery, bricks and biscuits), then, significant increases in productivity and losses of employment occurred in the context of declining or static output. The kinds of change in production process were quite varied, but the pressure for change frequently came in the form of cost competition. In complete contrast was the synthetic resins, plastics and synthetic-rubber industry. Here employment fell by a fifth even while output grew by nearly a half. The industry was, of course, already highly capital-intensive before the production reorganization took place so that further investment, even in conditions of fairly rapid growth, was not likely to increase employment substantially. In fact, however, employment fell dramatically. Therefore, in this industry, the new investment and the technical change was more than simply additional capacity; it must also have been embodied in replacement investment (i.e. in order for employment actually to fall). Nor was the technological change simply a response to the need to cut costs – technology in industries such as these is fundamental to competitiveness. Labour-saving capital equipment was often developed in association with advances in production and/or materials technology; capital investment was predominantly science based and, with the backing of substantial research and development expenditure, often at the forefront of technological development. And that technology was often as important to the nature of the product as to the process of producing it.

There is, then, a variety of means through which employment decline may be brought about alongside substantial investment. The next section presents a detailed study of one such set of circumstances and changes. The industry selected for study is that of brick making (part of mlh 461), a sector experiencing slow growth and retrenchment rather than great expansion. This choice derives from the overall concern of the wider project with the employment implications of the conditions of recession. It should not, however, be allowed to obscure the points of the last example: that job loss cannot, in any way, be taken as a simple surrogate for a slowdown in the rate of accumulation; and there are many causal mechanisms, and thus implications, hidden behind the chaotic conception that goes by the name of employment decline.

Case-study: investment and technical change in the fletton-brick industry

The position facing the brick industry at the end of the 1960s had many elements in common with the other industries examined in this book.[9] In this case, however, the factors were combined in such a way as to produce pressure for a different form of production reorganization: that of major capital investment embodying labour-saving technical change.

First, the market for bricks is entirely intra-national and indeed transport costs constrain the average size of market to a level below national. In this case-study, therefore, we are dealing with a whole production and market system.[10] Second, because of this total dependence of UK production on the UK market, the rate of growth of demand for bricks has been slackening over the medium term, having risen to a post-war peak in 1964, but declining thereafter (Monopolies and Mergers Commission 1976, 5). This national economic slowdown was the prime element in the situation facing the brick industry over these years. The situation was exacerbated by inter-sectoral shifts, in particular by increasing competition for housing bricks from concrete blocks (mlh 469.2), the nature of this competition being primarily that of cost – concrete blocks are less labour intensive both to make and to use. There was some shift between sectors, therefore, but this was a relatively minor pressure compared with the impact of the more general economic decline. The market for housing bricks is also highly cyclical, a factor adding to the industry's problems in a period when demand was relatively stagnant. Reports on the industry also mention the additional problems posed by the long-term increase in labour costs (Monopolies and Mergers Commission 1976, 61) and by the difficulty of attracting workers. The National Board for Prices and Incomes (1970) reporting on London Brick, the dominant company in the industry, wrote:

> Voluntary labour turnover averaged 40 per cent in 1969. Many workers are old and, despite improvements, working conditions are often hard. Despite recent redundancies the industry continues to find it difficult to attract an adequate and suitable labour force. A third of the workers entered the industry under foreign labour permits issued because British labour was not available. (p. 7)

It is not clear what 'suitability' and 'availability' mean, but the use of foreign labour presumably helped to keep down the level of wage increases. Clearly, the pressure on costs was considerable. Moreover, with the downturn of the mid-1960s the situation worsened and the brick industry found itself particularly badly hit as a result of its place in the national economic situation. The general downturn was reflected in the later 1960s in a decline in building overall (the first actual decline in many years) and in particular in house building.

Changing external economic conditions, therefore, produced a situation in which, in order to maintain profits, it was necessary to constrain costs in the face of stagnant demand. It was the conjunction of this with the current nature of the labour process in the industry and the industry's organizational structure, that primarily determined the form which this cost-cutting would take. The industry was capital intensive, with a well-established division of labour, operating in plants whose average age was high (all fletton production was in pre-war plant). Between 1964 and 1969, when the cost pressures were beginning to make themselves felt, savings were made in existing plants through improvements and extensions (Monopolies and Mergers Commission 1976, 62), the variety of bricks produced was cut down, there were attempts at intensification (National Board for Prices and Incomes 1970, 7), considerable extra mechanization took place, and the London Brick Company engaged in a classic rationalization programme concentrating a slightly reduced output on the largest, newest and most mechanized units within each major geographical area of production (e.g. the Bedford Group of brickworks, the Peterborough Group, etc.) (see, for example, London Brick Company 1970, 19). Such measures did reduce costs, but they had practical limits imposed by the existing buildings.[11] Thus, the 1972 annual report of the London Brick Company explained:

ever since the end of the war, we have been mechanizing and modernizing existing works and have now reached a stage where their very lay-out precludes scope for further improvement in efficiency. Only through the construction of new plants can we completely automate our production process and further increase our productivity. (pp. 13–14; see also Monopolies and Mergers Commission 1976, 61 and 72)

From 1968 a policy of building a completely new generation of brickworks was therefore embarked upon. These new works reduced labour content to one-third of its previous level in the case of the larger of the two new huge works (see London Brick Company 1970). Thus the annual report of 1972, quoted above, continues:

> Let me give you an example. At the old Kings Dyke Works, now demolished, eighty six men produced 600,000 bricks a week. When the expansion of the new Kings Dyke [works] is complete, 260 men will produce 3 million bricks a week – three times the labour force, producing nine [*sic!*] times the number of bricks. (p. 14)

These savings in labour costs were achieved by a mixture of economies of scale and technological advance. On the latter, the Monopolies and Mergers Commission wrote:

> The 'new generation' works at New Saxon and Kings Dyke . . . incorporate all the technical improvements, achieved over the years in the pursuit of lower labour intensities and better plant utilization including flexibility of production as between commons and facings. Some such improvements are in use at all works – some are in use at some works only; some works which were operating at the beginning of 1974 were comparatively old fashioned and, at the date of our Report, were closed. (1976, 38)

It is important to understand the context of this massive new investment. Demand was stagnant. This was a case, therefore, of technical change in replacement capacity, in order to cut costs and improve profitability, not in additional capacity to satisfy growing demand. The Monopolies and Mergers Commission assessed the role of the new investment as follows:

> In general, new works may be constructed either for the purpose of increasing capacity or reducing costs or both . . . brickmaking is not a growth industry and . . . for the last ten years fletton bricks have done little more than maintain their share of the total brick market. We have referred to LBC's [London Brick Company]

confidence that it can increase its market share in the longer term, but the main justification for new works has been to reduce costs rather than to expand overall brickmaking capacity. (1976, 72–3)[12]

Such investment can only be warranted if fairly substantial increases in competitiveness and/or profitability can be achieved. Thus, the report by the Prices and Incomes Board pointed out that 'brick kilns . . . have an almost indefinite life, given proper maintenance. Replacement can therefore be justified only by a substantial improvement in productivity' (National Board for Prices and Incomes 1970, 2). By the end of the 1960s it was calculated that the increase in labour costs, and the potential savings on such costs in new works, were such as to warrant the building of two huge new plants (New Saxon and Kings Dyke), and the complementary closure of some existing capacity. The Monopolies and Mergers Commission summed up the situation:

> LBC's capital consists partly of investment in manufacturing and partly of investment in distribution. Most of the investment in manufacturing is regarded by the company as a form of modernization or replacement investment as (a) it does not expect much growth in future brick production and sales, although it thinks that flettons will increase their market share; (b) a brickworks has an economic life much longer than the period for which the demand for its output can be forecast. LBC has, therefore, used its technological knowledge to build new works with unit costs that are lower, due partly to scale economies, than are those of existing works and has justified new works economically on the basis of their replacement of less efficient production units. LBC has also improved the production processes of some of its older works to the extent, in its view, that this is possible without rebuilding. An important consideration in new construction and modernization has been the high and increasing cost of labour, which has made investment in labour saving plant increasingly profitable. A further advantage has been the opportunity to improve working conditions thus making labour recruitment and retention easier. New works are environmentally more acceptable and have a more flexible product mix, with a nominal capability to produce 100 per cent facing bricks if required. (1976, 61)

The brick industry thus provides an excellent example of how major new investment may continue to take place even in the absence of significant output growth. The company predicted that 'Even if there is a downturn . . . these works can still operate profitably at a time when higher cost units are being phased out' (London Brick Company 1972, 14).

The new works were for the production of fletton bricks, and if the macro-economic pressures had provided the impetus for production reorganization, and their combination with existing technology had influenced its form, the organizational structure of that part of the industry was certainly important in *enabling* technological change and new construction on this scale. In effect, this was a classic case of a single major company taking a leading role, and the increases in investment and productivity went hand in hand with changes in ownership structure. The industry is capital intensive and the new investment required large amounts of capital. At the beginning of the period the London Brick Company already dominated the sector, and over the period it purchased Marston Valley (1968), the second largest producer, all the fletton interests of Redland (1971) and a works from the National Coal Board (1973). The company was therefore large enough both to provide adequate finance, and to be able to take advantage of production economies of scale.[13] This enabling structure of capital ownership, itself related to the nature of the dominant technology and capital intensity of the industry, was in marked contrast to the small-scale and old-fashioned management and capital structure that held back major technical change and investment in the footwear and outerwear industries.

5
Rationalization

The changes in production

We labelled the third and final form of production reorganization 'rationalization'. Unlike intensification and technical change, this strategy produces job loss as a direct result of disinvestment. The term 'rationalization' has become one of the theme-tunes of recession; its connotations of more sensible organization and of order are frequently appealed to in explanation of cutbacks in production and closures of plant. In this study the term is used to refer to disinvestment. Rationalization thus involves complete or partial plant closure, the scrapping of capital equipment and cutbacks in the labour force. No major reinvestment in plant and machinery, or new factory premises is undertaken. The only alteration to existing production and labour processes is thus one of scale, the end result being a reduction in the productive base of the industries in which it is undertaken.

The general reason for rationalization is a lack of profitability. As a result of this lack of profitability in a particular industry, capital is withdrawn from investment in that part of the economy, perhaps to be invested elsewhere. Rationalization in individual sectors is therefore a necessary by-product of changing relative levels of profitability, as investment flows to those areas of the economy where the return is highest. At the aggregate level, therefore, rationalization is not so much the result of a failure of profitability as a means for increasing or keeping up profits for capital over the economy as a whole; the same applies in conditions of more generalized recession. The scrapping of perfectly usable, but unprofitable, factories and machines is a means by which the capital which remains in production can increase its return. In such circumstances, rationalization is a mechanism for getting out of a crisis.

'Profitability', moreover, in this context is a relative term. The fact that a plant is closed down does not necessarily mean that no profit is made there. What is important is the relationship between current rates of return on capital in that part of the economy (national or international) and that offered by investment in other areas. Thus, as a result, for example, of the loss of major markets, the average rate of profit within an individual sector, though still positive, may fall below that prevailing elsewhere. Alternatively, profit rates may be rising faster, or offer the promise of greater stability, in other sectors. This could occur, for example, where new production techniques are developed and/or new markets opened. In both sets of circumstances, however, it would be more profitable for capital in the sectors with the relatively low rates of profit to shift to those where the returns are greater. Sectoral profitability thus needs to be viewed in relation to profitability throughout the economy as a whole. Therefore, it is clearly possible for plant closure and job loss, resulting from rationalization, to occur in sectors with positive rates of profit as well as in those where losses are being made.

One of the factors often put forward both as the reason for low or negative levels of profitability in individual industries and as the justification for the subsequent rationalization of production, is that there is 'excess capacity'. But as with 'profitability', it is again necessary to be clear about what this term actually means. In the first place, in a capitalist economy the criterion of 'excess' is profitability; capacity is only in excess in relation to the requirements of profitable production. The firms affected are either unable to make sufficient profits, or have the opportunity of gaining much higher profits from investing in other sectors of production. Excess capacity is thus itself *defined* by the demands of accumulation for profit.

The second and important point to note about excess capacity is the way in which it is continually *produced* by the very nature of accumulation. Within given markets firms are competing with each other to maximize profits, for only by so doing can production be expanded and further profits made. The pressure is on individual firms, therefore, continually to build up production in order to gain an advantage over competitors. All firms must follow this course if they are to accumulate: not to do so would mean a declining market share, falling profitability and eventual bankruptcy. We have already seen something of this in the discussion of technical change. In this way production is expanded, with investment in new capacity embodied in fixed capital equipment. This uncoordinated build-up of plant and equipment, of course, makes it increasingly difficult, over time, for all firms to achieve adequate profit rates. There comes a point where too much capital is chasing too little profit. The comments of industrialist Andrew Carnegie on the iron and steel industry in the USA in the latter part of the last century thus appear to have more general relevance:

> A demand exists for a certain article beyond the capacity of existing works to supply it. Prices are high and profits tempting. Every manufacturer of that article immediately proceeds to enlarge his works and increase their producing power. . . . In a short time the supply becomes greater than the demand and there are a few tons or yards more in the market for sale than are required, and prices begin to fall. They continue falling until the article is sold at cost. (quoted in Edwards 1979, 40–1)

Clearly, where profit is the motor of production, this situation cannot continue indefinitely and the only remedy is a withdrawal of capital from the industry, and the closure of some productive capacity. If accumulation is to continue then the capital structure must be reorganized. Burawoy puts it like this:

> the continual expansion of production, with either falling or constant wages, leads to crises of overproduction, which force capitalists to cut back production and render their capital idle. In short, the market forces individual capitalists to innovate and gain competitive advantages over one another, but, when they do so, they threaten their own existence as a class by intensifying class struggle, bringing down the rate of profit, and creating crises of overproduction. (1980, 195)

The same uncoordinated build-up of new production capacity can occur even in cases where current profitability is low or where there is already over-capacity, for, as we saw in chapter 4, it is often only by new investment that greater competitiveness can be achieved and, for the most competitive firm(s), larger market shares gained. It also holds true in declining and relatively stable markets as well as in conditions of market growth. In both instances, individual firms may invest in an attempt to outdo their competitors: in the former case to get a larger share of a shrinking whole, in the latter to gain a proportionately greater share of the forecasted market increase. Figures 5.1 and 5.2 illustrate these phenomena: how new investment can continue even in situations of existing over-capacity; how this results from the uncoordinated, private nature of investment decisions; how it is exacerbated in certain industries by the sheer scale of fixed capital investment and by the long lead-times necessary to build such facilities; and how, when the inevitable rationalization comes, it involves losses of employment and the concentration of capacity into still-profitable lines of production. The figures also, incidentally, show how dramatically the kinds of production change in an industry can change over time. The chemical industry has gone from product innovation in the period before 1960 to process innovation in the late 1960s (see figure 4.1) to rationalization, and continuing new investment, in the late 1970s and 1980s.

In very general terms, therefore, 'rationalization' is integral to the process of accumulation and to the search for profit. First, the need for rationalization is defined in terms of the potential rate of profit. Second, the relative lack of profits and the excess capacity, which are the rationale for rationalization, can themselves be a product of a system of production that is motivated only by individual-firm profits. Third, the process of rationalization is a means of increasing the rate of profit.

However, the way the process of rationalization actually operates in particular cases varies widely, as with the other kinds of production reorganization. Its character in particular instances depends on the combination of the economic circumstances in which it is adopted, and the particular characteristics of the industries affected.

Perhaps most obviously, the whole question of what is 'an adequate rate of profit' depends, not just on the alternative investment opportunities available, but also on the nature of the capital; the kind of firm involved. Sheer size may be an important factor; small companies with limited financial resources may, for example, be less capable of sustaining losses for any period of time than the larger, more diversified, companies which can operate some degree of cross-subsidization of their activities. The larger firms can either continue producing at a loss or lay off workers and leave capital equipment standing idle whilst waiting for their weaker competitors to collapse. When the market turns up again, or when sufficient capital has disappeared from the sector to allow profitability to rise once again, production can be resumed. In this case, because they have the financial strength to take the long-term view, larger firms may be less likely to cut capacity at any given rate of profit than the small ones. And of course this may in turn increase their power for with the next upturn some of the competition will have been removed, and their control of the market, and the concentration of ownership of capital in the industry, will have increased.

But the differential responsiveness to the rate of profit may also operate in the opposite direction. The greater inter-sectoral flexibility of some large firms may enable them to respond to fairly minor differences in potential rates of profit. In their major study of plant closures in Massachusetts, Bluestone and Harrison found that:

> Large modern corportations – and conglomerates in particular – *will* and frequently *do* close profitable branch plants or previously acquired businesses, for a variety of reasons directly related to the nature of centralized management and control. In other cases, the 'remote control' of operations by a home office far removed from the production site, or unfamiliar with the industry in which a subsidiary is competing, actually *creates* the unprofitability of the plant or subsidiary which then leads to an eventual shut-down. In no aspect of the problem is the textbook theory of perfect competition – with its mythical image of atomistic warfare among single-plant entrepreneurially-owned and managed businesses – more misleading. (1980, 199)

Obviously the conglomerate (inter-sectoral) structure is the basis for this greater flexibility of some larger firms. Rather than being committed to the production of a particular commodity, such a company is essentially a financial centre switching investment between sectors of production in response to relative rates of return. Smaller and medium-sized firms, and single-industry corporations, particularly in older-established industries, will often not be able to react in this way. They may find it difficult to shift their capital away from the rationalizing sector. They may lack the financial strength necessary for reinvestment in completely new sectors of production, especially when entry into these sectors can only be achieved by take-over or merger, and particularly when their existing production is confined to sectors with low rates of profit. Being a conglomerate already bestows great advantages, becoming one (i.e. the initial diversification) may be more difficult. Moreover, it is not just a question of size and structure. The social nature of capital is also important. The whole ethos of accumulation may vary substantially between different kinds of firms (different parts of capital). First, instead of the essentially financial orientation described above, many smaller and medium-

(a)

The European petrochemicals industry

Looking forward to ten years of overcapacity

The petrochemicals industry in the European community. It faces the prospect of living through the whole of the next 10 years with pronounced overcapacity.

...

It considers that some form of regulation of chemical markets is inevitable. Where steel and synthetic fibres have led the way, petrochemicals will follow. 'There is no solution but concerted action by manufacturers and governments together, to develop speedily the checks and balances which the market needs,' says the Eurofinance study. 'These checks and balances have to come. The question is not whether they will, but when? How much suffering can petrochemicals is growing for their products.

...

Why so much capacity installed in the first place? The answer stems from the extraordinary demand the industry faced before the oil crisis and in the months immediately after. As Eurofinance points out: 'Construction time of plant takes several years and manufacturers thought that, as always happened in the past, the market would gradually catch up with capacity. In fact, 1975 was the first year in the history of the petrochemical industry that an actual decline in demand occurred in the EEC for its products.'

So why, in view of all this, are companies still investing in more capacity? The report suggests a variety of reasons. Countries, such as the UK, which have their own oil and gas resources, consider they should upgrade and add value to these valuable feedstocks. Countries around the EEC wish to be self-sufficient in petrochemicals, even though some do not have a big enough market to absorb the production of one giant ethylene plant.

Eastern bloc countries with balance of payments problems view petrochemicals as a way of gaining more hard currency, and are less concerned about fully covering their costs. 'This leads sometimes to absurdities,' says Eurofinance, 'such as the recent export of Hungarian propylene to the Netherlands. The real freight cost was estimated at more than 50 per cent of the value of the material.' And some EEC manufacturers are busy building a strategic position for the moment when the market ultimately takes off.

EEC is facing the greatest crisis in manufacturers take before they its history, according to a study that apply to governments for concerted is being prepared for the European banking community.

...

It is unlikely that its dire prognosis would yet be accepted by all petrochemical manufacturers around Europe. If they are wanting to clutch at straws they can point to the small series of successful price increases implemented recently in the market sectors such as plastics and alcohols, which seem to have a good mark the beginning of what would be a long haul back to reasonable levels of profitability, and price increases will do little to halt the damaging growth of surplus plant capacity.

The fact is that Europe's petrochemical producers are still building plants faster than demand

(b)

How a new £25m. plastics plant took a Shelling

Despite the chronic surplus of plant in many sectors of the petrochemicals industry – units are often operating at only 60 to 70 per cent of capacity – companies are still investing in expansion. The decisions are only taken after many months, and sometimes years, of uneasy deliberation, but once made they quickly become irreversible. A typical example is the decision

taken by Shell Chemicals U.K. to build a second plastics plant at its Carrington site, near Manchester. Construction began in late 1976, and the plant is due on stream in 1980, but the company's subsequent heart-searching about the wisdom of the move illustrates clearly the troubles and uncertainties that are overtaking the industry.

'What we decided was: all right, it plainly is, no. ... looks marginal but the expansion is needed some time. Let's do it now with the advantage of the grant, which makes the investment immediately attractive; let's do it quickly, to beat a competitor to the punch, and let's build anti-cyclically.'

Two years later is Shell happy with the decision? The answer

'Petrochemicals in Europe is in a very sorry state – and certainly in plastics the industry is losing money, heavily. Brussels is worried, they are searching around for remedies for this new industrial crisis. Such is the environment into which our plant will be born.'

Fig. 5.1 The European chemical industry in 1978: overcapacity and new building
Source Extracts from the *Financial Times* 25 April 1978

(a) ICI sparks off a European shake-out

In rather the way Britain's chemical giant, ICI, had been hoping, its decision to close down the bulk of its loss-making polyester filament operations appears to have succeeded in unlocking a previously tight logjam in Europe's fibre industry.

Within months of the announcement, one of ICI's European rivals, the Dutch group, Akzo, has unveiled plans to shed a similar total of 4,000 jobs at fibre plants in the Netherlands, Germany and Northern Ireland and to withdraw from parts of the nylon and polyester filament market.

In France, Rhone-Poulenc, which like ICI and Akzo has made earlier attempts to bring fibre capacity into line with demand, is also cutting 4,000 jobs – roughly half the total in its textile division.

Most recently of all, Britain's other big fibre group, Courtaulds, has announced its withdrawal from nylon filament, with the loss of 1,900 jobs. Courtaulds, like other European groups, has also scaled down its involvement in polyester filament.

. . .

The pattern that has begun to emerge under the pressure of chronic overcapacity (estimated recently by Akzo as likely to reach 600,000 tonnes by 1985 if no action is taken) is a narrowing by Europe's fibre groups of the range of fibres they make.

'Even the biggest groups are now finding it difficult to fund the costly research, technical and marketing effort necessary to operate across a broad front in the fibres business. As a result producers in Europe are concentrating on those fibres and on the end-uses where they already have a sizeable share of the market,' Mr John Stuart, chairman of the British Man-Made Fibres Federation points out.

(b) Why add to existing over-capacity?

At Wilhelmshaven in Germany, with a cold wind whipping in from the grey and dismal North Sea, ICI earlier this month proudly inaugurated a complex described by one of its competitors as 'the greatest white elephant in Europe.'

. . . We haven't built these plants for today or even tomorrow – they are here to produce the products we believe Europe will need through the 1990s and into the next century.'

To quote Mandy Rice-Davies: 'long-sighted before the planners' judgements were confronted by the 1979 oil price explosion and the 1980 recession – ICI must now more than double its PVC sales in Europe if its new plant, due to start operation in October, is to run at commercial before the planners' judgements was at least partly caused by the drop in domestic demand during the recession.

The truth is that the European chemical industry faces a short-term pincer movement of high feed-stock prices and depressed demand.

At a cost of £250 million ICI now has one plant on the Wilhelmshaven site capable of producing 300,000 tonnes of vinyl chloride monomer a year and another plant capable of turning out 115,000 tonnes a year of polyvinyl chloride.

The only problem is that Europe already has all the bulk petrochemicals and plastics it needs, and especially PVC (the raw material for seemingly everything from the plastic buckets to sou'-wester oilskins). So why on earth add to existing over-capacity?

Denys Henderson, ICI's Scottish commercial director, tackled the question head on: 'The faint-hearted will point to the short-term problems of the European chemical industry and say that Wilhelmshaven is an investment made at the wrong time. We reject this argument because chemicals is a business for the determined and the 'Well he would say that, wouldn't he?' The underlying question remains: is the chemicals industry making the same kind of misjudgements perpetrated by the steel industry before the 1974 oil shock, and – if so – will chemicals in Britain become a Government-nourished lame duck like steel, cars and shipbuilding?

It is almost impossible to over-estimate the importance of the chemical industry in the overall economy. Last year the UK chemical sector achieved a balance of payments surplus of £2.1 billion, nearly two thirds of the entire surplus achieved by manufacturing industry. At the same time, the European chemical industry spent a record £1.3 billion on UK investment.

But the figures can mislead. Output was 8.5 per cent down on a 1979, meaning a £450 million drop in earnings, and the export surplus For the British industry the situation is made still worse by the imposition of energy costs substantially higher than in France and West Germany.

. . .

The question is what can the industry do to avert potential disaster. One answer is 'rationalisation' – a euphemism for ICI's 6,000 redundancies last year and 6,000 more this year. Another is informal price-fixing: one company will raise a product price and others will follow suit.

There is also a third – and dangerous – answer: for individual companies to fight it out to the death. Dangerous because the stakes are high and no company can be confident of winning.

But this appears to be the only rationale for the Wilhelmshaven complex. Trapped by an investment decision taken four years ago – capacity.

Part of this can be achieved by scrapping old capacity. ICI now plans to take about 50,000 tons out of its existing European PVC capacity of 450,000 tonnes a year.

But the fact remains that ICI is now leaping from sixth to fourth or possibly third in the league of 27 Western European PVC producers, and the jump is bound to hurt someone.

Closest to home will be ICI's joint operation with Solvay of Belgium in the four Salvic PVC plants located in Italy, Spain, France and Belgium. ICI makes the only reply possible: that Solvay has its own PVC operation outside the joint venture and cannot complain if ICI does likewise.

. . .

With hindsight, ICI must wish it had never heard of Wilhelmshaven.

Fig. 5.2 1981: Rationalization in fibres, new building in chemicals

Source Extracts from (a) the *Financial Times* 25 March 1981 and (b) *The Guardian* 30 June 1981

sized firms are committed to the production of particular commodities. This might well have been true, for instance, in the case of
the jute industry explored in the last chapter. Thus Odling-Smee
wrote:

> The original jute firms have therefore been able to secure a future
> for themselves. Whether they would have done so had there been
> no synthetic substitute for jute and the alternative would have
> been to move into a different industry altogether is more doubtful.
> (1977, xvii)

We have already referred in chapter 3 to the conservative and inward-
looking managements typical of small clothing firms. Where such
attitudes prevail, the option of shifting capital to more profitable
areas of production may not even be considered. Furthermore, and
especially in the case of old-established family firms, even a very low
or temporarily negative rate of profit may not deter continued production. For such firms are not simply in the business of maximizing
profit; they are the family identity, something to pass on to the next
generation. And what, anyway, would the possibly ageing owner-
managers do instead?[1]

An important distinction needs to be raised here between small
independent firms and small subsidiaries of larger enterprises. Not
only are they difficult to distinguish in many statistical series, but they
have often been confused in the recent debate over 'small firms' and
their potential for employment generation (Brimson, Massey,
Meegan, Minns and Whitfield 1980). Thus, as we have seen, small
independent firms may survive the rationalization process with at
least some capital intact, simply because they are willing to accept
much lower rates of return on their capital than are larger companies.
For small subsidiaries, however, the position may be different.
Decisions on the acceptability or otherwise of particular rates of
return will ultimately be decided by the parent company which will
have broader investment horizons than its smaller subsidiaries.
Talking about the job loss between 1966 and 1972 in Canning Town
following the closure of subsidiaries of major companies, the Canning
Town Community Development Project argued that:

> Companies which are closing down subsidiaries in Canning Town
> are not unprofitable. They are planning ahead on a long-term
> perspective with a view to finding better rates of profit elsewhere.
> The closure of firms which are providing too low a return in-
> evitably improves the company's overall performance. Unilever's

returns improved with rationalization of animal feeds which were not doing well at the end of the sixties. Shipping companies such as P & O [Peninsular and Oriental Steamship Company] and Furness Withy which shed their ailing subsidiaries and reinvested in a diversified way, are now thriving – the only thing to decline is the jobs. In some cases firms which are profitable but not providing a sufficient return have been axed. The larger companies are more inclined to operate on a higher ratio of profit to capital employed. For example this ratio was 15.6 per cent for Unilever, 11 per cent for Courtaulds, whilst for a small private firm the acceptable margin would be half of this. (1977, 18–19)[2]

It would be wrong, then, to try to establish empirical 'rules' of behaviour, of ways of responding to different comparative rates of profit, for different kinds of companies. What is clear, however, is that that behaviour may vary substantially; it is not a question of some immediate and automatic response, as might be predicted by theorists of perfect-market situations.

In part, what these differences reflect is variation in the degree of control which different kinds of firms have over their fates. Large firms are able to undertake rationalization in a much more planned way than are smaller, independent or subsidiary companies. They may be able to control the inter-sectoral shift of investment. Such planning will involve profit comparisons, often on an international scale, not only between sectors and companies but also between individual factories. Where a large multi-plant company decides to retain some interest in an industry, which as a whole is being rationalized, it is often able to undertake co-ordinated capacity-cutting with selective plant closure and possibly some degree of concentration of capacity. Firms of this type can plan within their own organization the inter-sectoral shifts of investment within the economy as a whole. Smaller and single-sector firms do not have this ability; instead of being able to plan, to some degree, the overall flows of capital within the economy, they have to respond to the external mechanisms of the market.

Not only, therefore, may different kinds of firms pursue different strategies of rationalization, but also rationalization may have different implications for firms themselves. In some cases, where sectoral rates of profit collapse, plant closure may go along with company liquidation. Not only are jobs lost but individual firms go out of business. But, as we have argued above, rationalization does not necessarily imply company failure. In the first place, companies may attempt to stay in business in the sectors affected precisely by cutting their production levels. Workers will be laid off and short-time working may be introduced. Capital equipment will be scrapped and renewal of plant and machinery may be cut back or put off indefinitely. In some instances, recently completed production lines or whole factories may not be brought into production. Figure 5.3 is a recent example which illustrates a number of these points, the plant that was closed was relatively new, and very modern; in physical terms, in other words, it was perfectly capable of producing cars. There is reference to 'over-capacity' in the car industry, yet there are clearly many people who still need a car, and many socially important products which the labour, skills and equipment in the car industry could be producing (Institute of Workers' Control Motors Group 1978). Finally, in other words, the purpose of the cutbacks was to enable, not the production of cars, but the production of profits.

In other situations, firms may close down capacity and switch capital into other areas of production with higher profit rates. There was an element of this, too, in the Solihull closure (figure 5.3). Another example from among the largest UK firms is that of the General Electric Company (GEC). In the late 1960s and early 1970s the company as a whole was disinvesting fast. There were major closures in the heavy engineering side of its business with many jobs lost, plant closures and scrappings of capital equipment (see Massey and Meegan 1979a). As Lorenz (1975) pointed out, its fixed-asset base only began to expand again in 1973–4 with heavy investment particularly in electronics, gas turbines, electric motors, telecommunications and radio and television. The transformation of the company's activities had thus been achieved by a planned withdrawal from a sector in which profit rates were rapidly declining, to new and more profitable areas of activity. Similarly, the Birmingham Community Development Project (1977) documented another recent case, that of Metro-Cammell, where the job losses in Birmingham were associated with the company's shift of production from the manufacture of general railway equipment to buses. In this case the shift did not involve anything like the level of investment that GEC had undertaken; nevertheless, the result of its long-term rationalization and change of direction was to raise its share of the Laird Group's pre-tax profits from £1.8 million in 1975 to £2.7 million in 1976 (Birmingham Community Development Project 1977, 24). It should be stressed that in all these cases the shifts of investment were the logical outcomes of the situations in which the companies found themselves. They were operating in sectors with declining profit-

BL to close Rover plant and end TR7 production

By Kenneth Gooding and Nick Garnett

BL is to close the £27m Solihull Rover plant and also production of the TR7 sports car as part of a new package of cuts. The Solihull plant in Birmingham was heralded as one of the most modern in Europe when it was opened only five years ago.

It is unofficially estimated that the combined impact will cost at least another 4,000 jobs and possibly as many as 6,000 throughout the BL Cars industrial complex.

Mr. Ray Horrocks, chairman of BL Cars, said yesterday that the recovery plan for the company was threatened by a fall in demand for cars, made worse by some Budget measures. These have encouraged a switch from larger, highly-profitable vehicles to smaller economical cars such as the Metro.

'The car companies must face up to reality and that means we must accelerate cost reductions to cope with the continuing recession and maintain progress with the recovery plans. Government money for new products will be spent on new products. We must absorb extra costs ourselves.'

Reaction from union leaders, obviously shocked by the scale of the latest rationalisation proposals was muted, even though they expected few and far between, given the current over-capacity in the motor industry.

Car assembly at Solihull will end by next April, with production of the Rover transferred to Cowley. Nearly 3,000 people are employed in the Rover plant which has been producing only 800 cars a week compared with its capacity for producing 3,300. Land-Rover operations at Solihull will not be affected.

BL said the Rover plant would be maintained so that it could be used either for future vehicle assembly or offered for sale to another company.

. . .

'The changes in demand have hit us hard in 1981. The worst thing would be if we failed to face up to them and wasted the progress we have achieved in the past three years,' Mr. Horrocks said.

If the latest round of cuts is implemented, BL cars should still be able to move out of losses by 1983, he said.

Fig. 5.3   The 'rationalization' of a modern factory
Source   Extracts from the *Financial Times* 13 May 1981

ability and world-wide 'excess capacity'. Rather than taking the risk of losing out in the competitive rationalization of these sectors, they chose to get out. For the companies, the move was successful: profitability was increased. For the workers and areas affected by this withdrawal of capital, the move was disastrous: jobs were lost and factories closed.

To recapitulate: in all cases rationalization is part of a process of increasing the rate of profit on capital as a whole; but the effect on individual capitals as 'institutions' can vary widely. For some, the shift to areas of higher profit will be encompassed within the firm; other companies will simply be on the receiving end of market forces. And as we have seen, this different relationship to the overall process (to capital as a whole, one might say) in turn influences the behaviour of companies when faced with declining rates of profit. In all cases, however, whether or not jobs are gained elsewhere, employment is lost at an existing point of production. This variation in the different fortunes of capital and labour can clearly affect the potential for resistance.

Rationalization may, therefore, occur in different ways and be a response to different conditions, in different sectors. At sectoral level the consequences for employment of a low rate of profit may vary. However, although for some firms profits may be too low in relation to other investment opportunities, even where markets are growing overall, removal of capital in these market conditions is less likely to result in massive aggregate losses of employment. For closures are more likely to be at least partially compensated for by the opening of new capacity by other firms. It is when profits and markets are declining, or relatively static, that employment decline as a result of rationalization is likely to be dominant within a sector. Indeed, as we said earlier, rationalization is an integral feature of periods of recession.

For the same reason it is rare, however, that rationalization will be the only form of change occurring in the production of a particular commodity. For where profits are falling, attempts will be made to make parallel cuts in cost; where markets are declining competition will hot up. Thus the factories that remain open are also likely to be affected by the overall sectoral reorganization of production. Although having avoided complete (or perhaps even partial) closure of capacity in the rationalization process, the factories that remain in production are still faced with a battle for competitive survival amongst themselves. This may involve, for example, cost-cutting strategies of the intensification type. Thus, while overall employment decline in the sector is dominated by rationalization, more job losses may ensue as the firms operating the remaining capacity undertake further production reorganization. Indeed the very fact of rationalization will often make such further reorganization easier for management to introduce (see chapter 11). As Bluestone and Harrison noted, when discussing plant closure:

> Among the more difficult qualitative impacts to measure . . . but no less important for that subtlety . . . is the chilling effect on industrial relations in the plants that remain, where workers can be made aware (if they were not already) that militant action or even just assertive collective bargaining may lead to *their* shop being shut down. (1980, 102–3)

One other effect of rationalization may be a change in the pattern of ownership within the sector. For not only may the organizational structure of capital influence the nature and pattern of rationalization, but also the process of rationalization may be part and parcel of the changing ownership structure of capital. This may be simply because of differential rates of closure by large and small firms, but, perhaps more importantly, mergers and takeovers may be a condition of capacity-cutting, through enabling either quicker elimination of competition or co-ordination of cutbacks. Thus, following a merger, competing capacity can be closed down and excess capacity reduced. This need not be instigated by firms within the affected sectors. In the early 1960s the two large textile producers, Courtaulds and Imperial Chemical Industries (ICI), embarked on a policy of take-over and rationalization of their customer industries in the textile trades because the prevailing excess capacity and uncoordinated rationalization of these sectors threatened their own survival (see, for example, Commission of the European Communities 1975b). Financial reorganization of this sort may be promoted by the State for this very purpose, as the activities of, for example, the Industrial Reorganization Corporation testify (Massey and Meegan 1979a). Inter-sectoral mergers may also be used by individual firms as a device for shifting their interests away from the rationalizing industries to other more profitable areas of production. Thus, for example, immediately prior to our study period, English Electric (now part of GEC) acquired Elliott-Automation in an attempt to lessen its dependence on the contracting heavy electrical engineering sector and to move towards the expanding, and more profitable, electronics business. Mergers are not, of course, essential for this redeployment of

capital assets but they do provide, for firms with sufficient resources, a
relatively quick way into new areas of production.

* * *

In nine of the industries we looked at, rationalization was an important phenomenon, and responsible for the bulk of the jobs lost in the
late 1960s and early 1970s. As explained in chapter 2, in some cases
particular sub-sectors dominated the performance of the industry as a
whole. Thus in grain milling it was the production of wheat products
in general and flour milling in particular that were rationalized. In
the electrical machinery and insulated wires and cables industries,
rationalization of the production of, respectively, heavy electrical
equipment and supertension cables accounted for a substantial
amount of the job loss. As we shall see later, rationalization of newsprint production was particularly important in shaping the overall
employment performance of the paper and board industry. In the
other cases rationalization was fairly widespread throughout the
sectors.

Some indication of the pressures that these industries were under
is given by their different output performances. These are shown in
table 5.1. In six sectors output fell, while in only one of the sectors in
which output grew was the growth rate above that for all manufacturing. Ideally, as we have said, these figures should be set against

Table 5.1   The rationalizing industries

	1968–73 percentage change in:		
Industry	*Output*	*Employment*	*Productivity*
Electrical machinery	−23	−17	−7
Locomotive and railway track equipment/railway carriages	−20	−19	−1
Cotton weaving, etc.	−15	−26	+15
Woollen and worsted	−12	−23	+14
Metal-working machine tools	−7	−18	+13
Iron castings	−4	−18	+19
Paper and board	+2	−20	+28
Grain milling	+11	−13	+28
Insulated wires and cables	+17	−15	+38
All manufacturing	+15	−4	+20

Sources   Census of Production: employment data
Index of Production: output data

those for the changing rate of profit, since it is that which, above all, governs the process of rationalization, but comprehensive and comparable figures are not available at mlh level. Nonetheless, the rationalization was clearly not associated with growth. But neither was it simply associated with a decline in output. As was suggested above, the immediate circumstances in which excess capacity manifested itself varied quite considerably between sectors. On one side were the capital goods and intermediate goods industries affected by the general slowdown in national economic growth (machine tools, iron castings and paper and board). On the other were the sectors experiencing problems associated with international competition. Thus, for example, electrical machinery, insulated wires and cables and locomotives and railway equipment industries were hit by the loss of overseas markets, whilst the cotton-weaving, paper and board (again) and machine-tool (again) sectors were all facing growing competition from foreign producers in the domestic market. The industries are all producers of non-final goods but they display, like the technical change group of industries, a quite varied set of production characteristics. On the one hand, for example, there are industries with oligopolistic structures operating relatively capital-intensive labour processes (grain milling, insulated wires and cables and paper and board). On the other hand, there are sectors characterized by a much more fragmented ownership structure and employing relatively more labour-intensive labour processes (iron castings, machine tools, cotton weaving and woollen and worsted). Therefore, even at this fairly superficial level of distinction, quite different industries were pursuing the same strategy.

The impact of rationalization in these industries was dramatic. The official data present a depressing picture of employment cuts alongside declining levels of net capital expenditure and disposals of plant and machinery. In complete contrast to the industries looked at in the last chapter, no significant amounts of new building work were undertaken. Some of the closures, however, were extremely significant. We have documented elsewhere (Massey and Meegan 1979a) some of the major plant closures in the electrical machinery and insulated wires and cables industries, and there are further examples in the other sectors. In metal-working machine tools, for example, there was the collapse of the joint Anglo-American venture, Herbert-Ingersoll, and the closure of its Daventry factory in 1972. In grain milling, two years earlier, the Co-operative Wholesale Society had closed one of its flour mills while the Scottish Co-operative Wholesale Society had closed all three of its mills. Table 5.2 gives a graphic example of the impact of

Table 5.2   Capacity in spinning and weaving (in thousands)

	1968	1973
Spindles in place	3860	2660
Spindles running (average)	3470	2470
% operating on 3-shift days or 7-day working week	26	45
Looms in place	90.1	54.9
Looms running	77.3	48.7
% operating on 3-shift days or 7-day working week	23	35

Source Commission of European Communities (1975b)
Note It should be noted that the table relates to both mlh 412 (spinning and doubling on the cotton and flax systems) which is not included in this study, and mlh 413 (weaving of cotton, linen and man-made fibres) which is.

rationalization on productive capacity in the spinning and weaving textile industries over the study period. The number of spindles and looms in place was reduced by 31 and 39 per cent respectively over the five years. Employment fell by over 32 per cent (from 164,200 to 111,400 jobs; Commission of European Communities 1975b, 21). Table 5.2 also helps to demonstrate the point made earlier that rationalization may be accompanied, or followed, by changes in the operation of the capacity that remains. The percentage of spindles actually running to those in place was increased from 89.9 per cent to 92.9 per cent over the period. For looms the corresponding increase was from 85.8 per cent to 88.7 per cent. The elimination of production capacity, in other words, just kept ahead of the decline in the need for it. Moreover, the problem was exacerbated because of cost-cutting measures in the capacity which was left. As table 5.2 shows, the proportion of capacity being operated on a three-shift day or seven-day-week basis was increased substantially. This would help to reduce the fixed costs of production per unit of output. But for those working in the industries it meant, not only that there were fewer jobs around as a result of the rationalization, but also that those remaining offered worse conditions of employment: more shift-work, more night-work, more weekend work.

As in the technical-change industries, a number of mergers appear to have been undertaken in the sectors we studied in order to facilitate a co-ordinated rationalization of capacity. Indeed, State aid was given in a number of instances expressly to promote such strategies as, for example, in the restructuring of the heavy electrical machinery and supertension cables industries in the late 1960s. In grain milling a

Table 5.3   Employment change 1968–73 (1968 = 100) for different types of labour

Industry	Operatives	Administrative technical and clerical workers	Difference between operatives and admin., etc.
Grain milling	92	77	−15
Iron castings	78	96	18
Metal-working machine tools	79	86	7
Electrical machinery	85	78	−7
Insulated wires and cables	86	96	10
Locomotives and railway track equipment/ railway carriages	79	96	17
Weaving of cotton, linen and man-made fibres	73	81	8
Woollen and worsted	75	88	13
Paper and board	77	92	15
All manufacturing	97	99	2

Source   Census of Production 1968 and 1973

major merger in 1972 (Spillers' acquisition of the milling and bread-baking interests of the Co-operative Wholesale Society (CWS)-Lyons, forming Spillers-French Holding Ltd) was followed by the closure of three mills (see Commission of the European Communities 1975a).

The impact of rationalization on the workforce was severe. 146,400 jobs disappeared from the nine rationalizing sectors over the study period, an overall reduction of 20 per cent. The impact varied for different types of worker. Direct or production workers are usually most threatened by rationalization for it is, after all, productive capacity that is being cut. Table 5.3 shows how the number of operatives in all manufacturing industries declined by 3 per cent over the study period, 2 per cent more than administrative, technical and clerical workers. This difference in the rates of decline between operatives and administrative, technical and clerical workers was in the same direction, and more pronounced, for seven of the nine rationalizing sectors.

In individual cases, the cuts led to some bitter struggles between managements and unions over closure and redundancy plans.[3] GEC, for example, announced its plans to reduce the workforce in its power engineering and electrical components companies in the North West by 4300 workers with the following statement:

> There is an urgent need for design, manufacturing and marketing resources to be rationalized in order to reduce unnecessary duplication of activities and thereby to increase the company's efficiency and competitive ability. This requirement coincides with an unprecedented decline in home-market demand for power-engineering products which causes or aggravates severe problems of over-capacity. (*The Times* 1969)

In the weeks that followed there was a series of strikes throughout GEC's plants. At one stage, plans were mooted by the workforce for the occupation of three of the company's factories. In the end, however, this opposition broke down; the threatened plants were closed and jobs were lost.

Case-studies: rationalization in the iron-castings and paper and board industries

Both the iron-castings and the paper and board industries underwent major rationalization in the period between the late 1960s and the early 1970s. In some ways the two industries are similar. Both, for example, are in the capital goods/intermediate goods parts of the economy and this influences their relationship to the performance of the economy as a whole. In other ways, however, the two are very different: in terms of the kinds of firms most common in the industry and, concomitantly, in terms of the organization of capital in the sector. The two together, therefore, provide a good basis for examining some aspects of the process of rationalization.

* * *

To understand why rationalization was so important in the iron-castings industry over the study period we need, as in the case-studies in the previous chapters, to look first at the wider economic pressures the industry was facing. As we have said, the industry is mainly a producer of intermediate goods; the national input-output tables (Central Statistical Office 1973) classified 97 per cent of its output as intermediate in 1968. Its main final products are ingot moulds (castings for the steel industry – the actual moulds in which the metal is formed) and pressure pipes and fittings; other outputs include engine blocks for the car industry, and a host of other products for a wide variety of other industries, particularly engineering. Because its main markets are other industries, the sector is highly sensitive to the

Table 5.4   The UK ironfoundry industry 1952–73

Year	Production ('000 tonnes)	Number of foundries (end year)	Total employment ('000)	Tonnes per person per year
1952*	3892	1919	154	25
1953	3696	1863	143	26
1954	3805	1796	140	27
1955	3988	1775	145	28
1956	3962	1706	144	28
1957*	3775	1673	138	27
1958	3542	1585	132	27
1959	3554	1518	125	28
1960	4032	1475	130	31
1961	3867	1439	130	30
1962	3582	1387	124	29
1963	3718	1306	120	31
1964*	4214	1243	123	34
1965	4149	1176	123	34
1966	3928	1111	115	34
1967	3603	1037	106	34
1968	3614	965	100	36
1969	3816	920	101	38
1970*	3833	887	101	38
1971	3346	843	94	36
1972	3281	806	85	39
1973	3445	768	86	40

*53-week year
Source   Farrant 1977

overall growth of the wider economy and the performance of its main customers. The general slowdown in the rate of growth of the economy since the mid-1960s has thus had particularly serious implications for the industry's performance. As table 5.4 and figures 5.4 and 5.5 show, while there has been a long-term decline in employment in the industry, it was not until 1964 that output began to fall seriously.[4] After following a classic cyclical pattern through the 1950s to the mid-1960s, when there was a downturn, production failed to recover to levels of previous cyclical peaks. Table 5.4 also shows, however, that employment in the industry had been declining since well before this date. There had, in fact, been a substantial build-up of productive capacity in the industry in the later 1950s/early 1960s. Despite a decline of nearly a third in the number of ironfoundries and of nearly

Employment ('000)

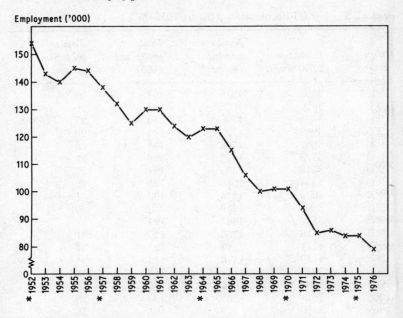

Fig. 5.4   Employment in the UK ironfoundry industry, 1952–76
Source   Farrant 1977
Note   *53-week year

a seventh in employment over the decade from the mid-1950s to the mid-1960s, output was still increased (see figure 5.5). The available evidence suggests that this can largely be explained by the increasing relative importance of large ironfoundries. Table 5.5 shows that the two largest size categories of ironfoundry were the only ones to increase in number and output over that period. Table 5.5 needs to be interpreted with care as it is affected not only by closures and openings but also by movements between size classes. The table suggests nevertheless, that the reason why output could be increased alongside such a marked reduction in the number of foundries and employment during the period, lies in the fact that it was the small foundries, providing a relatively minor portion of total capacity but with much more labour-intensive production processes, that were closed, whilst production was increasingly concentrated in the larger more up-to-date and relatively more mechanized foundries (see also NEDO 1974d). The first point, then, is that the employment decline

('000 tonnes)

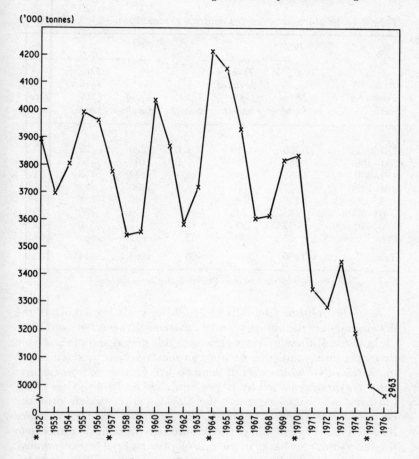

Fig. 5.5   UK ironfoundry production 1952–76 ('000 tonnes)
Source   Farrant 1977
Note   *53-week year

in the industry up to the early 1960s had not been associated with any significant cutbacks in production capacity. While some individual companies certainly went out of business, the loss of jobs was associated more with changes in the internal structure of the sector than with any failure of accumulation over the industry as a whole. This picture was to change, however, with the onset of recession in the overall economy in the mid-1960s: domestic demand collapsed.

Table 5.5   Production by size of foundry, 1955 and 1964

Tonnes per year	1955			1964		
	No. of foundries	Tonnage produced ('000 tonnes)	Total tonnage	No. of foundries	Tonnage produced ('000 tonnes)	Total tonnage
			%			%
Under 200	493	46	1.1	290	22	0.5
201–400	285	85	2.1	188	56	1.3
401–800	336	194	4.9	232	138	3.3
801–1200	177	176	4.4	120	122	2.9
1201–2000	189	299	7.5	140	223	5.3
2001–5000	184	593	14.9	146	460	10.9
5001–10,000	72	506	12.7	76	528	12.5
Over 10,000	63	2089	52.5	73	2665	63.3
Total	1799	3988	100.0	1265	4214	100.0

Source   Data provided by the Council of Ironfoundry Associations

A study published by NEDO (1974d) gives a breakdown of the development of the industry's major markets between 1963 and 1972. Only three of these markets grew over this period and of these only two were important (iron castings for motor-vehicle production and ingot moulds), whilst overall demand fell. Output of iron castings between these years fell by 12 per cent (NEDO 1974d). Clearly the industry was suffering from the slowdown in growth over the economy as a whole. Moreover, that slowdown was soon to make itself felt in other ways, in particular through the political response to the recession. Cut-backs in the rate of growth of public expenditure, and eventual absolute cuts, served to exacerbate the industry's problems in certain sub-markets (notably pressure pipes, used in construction, and castings used in railway work). There was, further-more, little hope of extending markets by expanding sales overseas through exports or by import substitution (NEDO 1974d). There was, and is, very little trade in iron castings across UK frontiers, the high bulk/value ratio of the product being an obvious deterrent. The industry's average import penetration over the years 1968–76 was the sixth lowest in all UK manufacturing (calculated from Wells and Imber 1977 – note that the figure in this case is for the whole of mlh 313). The UK also had a positive trade balance on the small amount of international trade that did occur. Finally, whilst there was some increase in competition from other processes and other materials, such as plastics and aluminium (NEDO 1974d; Farrant 1977), taken overall 'most of the blame for the lower output of the past few years can be placed on the generally depressed economic climate of the country' (Farrant 1977, 464). The reduction in output, therefore, resulted from a decline in demand overall rather than from competitive pressures reducing British producers' share of that demand. And there was little hope of market expansion simply by becoming 'more competitive'. Competition was not the problem. If profitability was to be maintained there was clearly a need to cut capacity – in other words to rationalize.

Companies in the sector therefore had to compete for a declining total market. Macro-economic conditions were thus clearly exerting pressures for some capacity reduction. But this was at sectoral level. Within the overall context of demand decline, the individual firms were competing to stay alive, or not to have to close capacity. So although changes were likely in the scale of production, there was also pressure on individual firms to change the organization of production in order to cut costs and retain a viable share in the shrinking market. Such a cost-cutting element might have been the dominant force shaping the changing level and pattern of employment.

In fact, however, this was not the case. While there was certainly some intensification and a limited degree of technical change in the industry over the study period, these did not rival rationalization in their employment effects. This was primarily because of the nature of the dominant labour processes. The industry already had a high level of division of labour and it was difficult, without massive changes, to introduce any further division of labour into the production sequence (Gooding 1977). Moreover, although some cost-savings were possible within each of the stages of production, few were dramatic, or involved changes in employment, of either numbers or type. This is indicated in table 5.6. One other possibility for labour-saving was standardization of the product, but although standardization was possible in some parts of the sector (in, for example, the production of iron castings for the motor-vehicle industry), in many areas it was not a real option. Many of the sector's customers, such as the machine-tool industry, demand, in general, small-batch production of iron castings. Small craft foundries working on a 'jobbing' basis closely geared to customer specification thus find themselves, when faced with difficult market conditions, unable to switch production rapidly, if at all, to more standardized operations. This relationship between market and production in turn further reduces the possibilities for mechanization. Given the present state of technological development and the amount of capital available to these small firms, a reduction in labour content in small-batch production is difficult to achieve.[5] The employment loss that did take place through technological shift within the industry occurred, not because of technical change as such, but because of different rates of decline in different parts of the sector. The various product markets moved, as we have said, at different rates,

Table 5.6   The stages of production in iron castings

Major stages of process	Possible cost-cutting changes	Major implications for labour requirements
Melting and pouring	Some changes in type of cupula	None
Mould and coremaking	Long-term trend towards mechanization Some degree of automation	Some loss of labour, and deskilling
Fettling and cleaning	Hand process Very difficult to mechanize	—
Heat treatment	Some speed-up of processes	Possibly some loss of labour

some even continuing to expand. The growth in the market for iron castings in motor-vehicle production, for example, enabled some mass production and continued the longer-term shift towards larger, more mechanized plant (see Farrant 1977; and chapter 7). All in all, therefore, employment loss through changes in the technology of production was limited, and was far outshadowed by that which resulted from closure of capacity.

In the ensuing rationalization it was the small foundries which were hit particularly hard, as a comparison of table 5.5 with table 5.7 shows. All size categories showed a decline in output from the 1964 level suggesting fairly widespread cuts in capacity but, as in the late 1950s/early 1960s, the large foundries still managed to perform relatively better. In fact, over the study period itself, the number of foundries and level of production in the largest size category actually increased. This might indicate, as well as shifts between sub-sectors, some degree of capacity concentration by the largest firms, a tactic not available to the smaller ones. There was an overall decline of 23 per cent in the number of ironfoundries in production (a fall from 999 to 791, see table 5.7) and a 14 per cent cut in the number of jobs (from 100,000 to 86,000, see table 5.4). Within the workforce, the employ-

Table 5.7   Production by size of foundry, 1968 and 1973

Tonnes per year	1968			1973		
	No. of foundries	Tonnage produced ('000 tonnes)	Total tonnage	No. of foundries	Tonnage produced ('000 tonnes)	Total tonnage
			%			%
Under 200	193	19	0.5	133	13	0.4
201–400	159	48	1.3	111	35	1.0
401–800	179	104	2.9	130	77	2.2
801–1200	91	92	2.5	76	73	2.1
1201–2000	107	167	4.6	89	137	4.0
2001–5000	128	415	11.5	117	358	10.4
5001–10,000	72	501	13.9	62	433	12.6
Over 10,000	70	2268	62.8	73	2319	67.3
Total	999	3614	100.0	791	3445	100.0

Source   Data provided by the Council of Ironfoundry Associations

ment cuts were heavily biased against operatives (see table 5.3) and continued the long-term decline of craftsmen in the industry (see, for example, Foundry Industry Training Committee 1978). Just between 1970 and 1972 membership of the engineering union (Amalgamated Union of Engineering Workers (AUEW)) fell by 13 per cent in foundries (though these figures include both ferrous and non-ferrous foundries) and the number of skilled moulders and coremakers declined by 23 per cent (NEDO 1974d). The bias in the cuts towards skilled manual workers might explain why wages in the industry, although above the all-manufacturing average in 1968, rose less quickly over the period (data from Wood 1976).

The impact of all this on the industry is indicated by the fact that a year later NEDO was arguing that there was still 'ample physical capacity available' (NEDO 1974d, 27). Yet output in 1974 was only 3,190,000 tonnes, 24 per cent below the 1964 figure. The industry had clearly moved on to a much smaller productive base. Further rationalization was still on the cards.

* * *

As in the iron-castings industry the pressure towards rationalization in the paper and board industry clearly came from developments in the national economy. Paper and board, like iron castings, experienced a fall-off in the rate of growth of demand for its products over the study period. This took a different form, however, in paper and board.

In paper and board there was again a great deal of intra-sectoral differentiation in performance. The problems centred above all on newsprint, with declines also in kraft (very strong paper and board made from sulphate pulp) and food wrappings, bulk printings and writings, packaging and paper-making based on imported esparto grass. The production of corrugated case materials and soft tissues continued to expand at a reasonable rate. But for the sector as a whole:

> As in other countries, growth in consumption of paper and board has been closely linked with growth of the national economy, and growth of the UK economy and hence paper consumption has for many years been less than that of other developed nations. (NEDO 1978b, 7)

In this respect then, the paper and board industry was very much like the iron-castings sector. Unlike the latter, however, paper and board was particularly vulnerable to developments in international competition and this added to the problems that it was facing as a result of the slow growth of the UK economy. Thus the economy was already turning down when the UK's accession to the European Free Trade Association in 1967 greatly increased competition from Scandinavia and Austria. Between 1967 and 1973, the UK was the only major importing country in Europe to admit duty-free imports of paper and board from the Nordic countries (NEDO 1978c). Producers in these countries and in Austria could, unlike those in the UK, manufacture from slush pulp in integrated mills and using relatively cheap hydro-electric power. Their industries were also major sectors within their economies and used the countries' main natural resource. With such a prominent position in their overall national economies, these industries received considerable support from their respective States. In the Sector Working Party's own words: 'The advantage enjoyed by these producers, combined with tariff-free entry to the UK, enabled them to sell many grades, particularly newsprint, magazine papers and sack kraft, at prices UK mills could not match' (NEDO 1978b, 7). The devaluation of the pound sterling in 1967 did not help. Pulp prices went up (thus increasing input prices to the UK industry) but not paper prices (because of the convention that pulp prices are denominated in dollars or krone, but paper in pounds sterling).

Between 1966 and 1976 the percentage margin of paper prices over pulp prices dropped by two thirds for newsprint and over a half for bleached kraft paper and woodfree printing (NEDO 1978b, 8).

Imports into the already stagnant British market increased between 1970 and 1972 from 50 per cent to 69 per cent for newsprint, and from 30 per cent to 36 per cent for other grades of paper (NEDO 1973, 81). At a wider geographical level, the OECD reported over-capacity, not only because of falling demand but also because new capacity was just coming on stream. The industry thus provides a further example of the way in which competitive investment strategies can carry the seeds of over-production. Once again, as in the chemical industry, this problem of supply and demand co-ordination through competitive, private decision making is exacerbated by the long lead-times involved in building new plants. In such a context, it was extremely difficult to increase exports. Indeed it was difficult even to fight import penetration, because UK companies in pulp-based production were dependent on a raw material (pulp) which was supply-controlled by producer-competitors (NEDO 1978b, 7). In newsprint these problems were made worse by the fact that producers had to face a domestic market dominated by news-paper monopsonists and were unable to raise prices (British Paper and Board Industry Federation undated).

As in iron castings, output in the paper and board industry had increased over the early 1960s, albeit at a slower rate than for manu-facturing as a whole. The deflated figures from the Business Statistics Office (1978) show that the industry's gross output increased by 25 per cent between 1958 and 1968, compared with 42 per cent for all manufacturing. But unlike in iron castings, this increase in output had not been accompanied by any loss of jobs. Employment in the industry stayed relatively stable throughout the 1960s (NEDO 1978b, 22–3). Production capacity had thus not seen many major changes in the years immediately preceding the downturn in the economic situation. With the downturn, however, previously usable capacity became 'excess'. The absolute decline in demand meant that capital throughout the sector was faced with the prospect of drastic-ally reduced returns. As in iron castings, the pressure on the sector as a whole was for reduction in capacity.

This pressure was reinforced by the nature of the industry's labour processes. The division of labour in paper-making, like that in iron-castings manufacture, was already highly developed and would have required quite dramatic changes in production technology for it to be altered. It was also somewhat different from that in iron castings, being based around relatively more capital-intensive operations. To quote Wilkinson:

> modern paper mills are built the size of cathedrals at costs which can be at least £100 million for a new plant. A single new newsprint mill producing 200,000 tonnes a year could supply the whole of Belgium or getting on for a third of the requirements of France. (1980, 19)

This meant that low-capacity working had a serious effect on profits. Newsprint machines need to be run at about 90 per cent capacity per annum (British Paper and Board Industry Federation undated). NEDO (1978b) notes that, between 1969 and 1974, pre-tax profits for the industry as a whole averaged about 8 per cent compared to the all-manufacturing figure of 14 per cent. In newsprint 'little or no profit' was made in the early 1970s (British Paper and Board Industry Federation undated). Moreover, the continuous nature of the production processes and the already high level of shift working made further intensification difficult. NEDO concluded: 'the paper-making process does not lend itself to individual incentive schemes' (1978b, 23). The main stages of production are given in table 5.8. With-

Table 5.8   The stages of production in paper and board

Major stages of production	Possible cost-cutting changes	Major implications for workers
Preparation	Within newsprint, some investment in de-inking of waste paper	Some increase in numbers
Machine stage	—	—
Finishing	Some mechanization Some reduction in process	Reduction in numbers

in newsprint manufacture there was some investment in the preparation stage involving the de-inking of waste paper as a substitute for imported pulp,[6] but this had little impact on overall labour processes and in fact was relatively ineffective in relieving the pressure for capacity reductions in this sector. Indeed, one of the two companies which were involved in these investments was eventually forced to close its newsprint operations (Peter Dixon & Sons). The finishing stage was the only one amenable to any labour-cost savings through production change. This stage was still very much an individual and hand-done process and it employed mainly women.

During the study period, some degree of mechanization was introduced in this stage, resulting in reductions in the number of jobs for women. There was also some reduction in the level of finishing operations with increasing amounts of paper being sent out on reels, unfinished. This caused further losses of jobs for women in this industry. Where customer industries took on the finishing process themselves, these latter jobs would have been re-created there.

In contrast to these comparatively minor employment losses resulting from changes within production, the rationalization was drastic. In the words of NEDO:

> much of the productive capacity (particularly of newsprint, magazine papers and sack kraft) . . . had to close or switch to other products, jobs were lost, profits fell, investment capital was difficult to generate, and it became harder to provide financial justification for new investment. (1978b, 7)

In the three worst years, 1970–2 (inclusive), the OECD (1975) recorded a decline in productive capacity of nearly 7 per cent (from 5,336,000 to 4,985,000 tonnes) for the industry as a whole. The cuts were much greater in newsprint and kraft paper and paper-board sectors, however, with capacity declining by 28 per cent (from 890,000 to 640,000 tonnes) and 35 per cent (from 275,000 to 178,000 tonnes) respectively. In fact 1970 marked a turning point in the industry's recent history. Between then and the mid-1970s twenty-one mills and fifty-one machines were closed (NEDO 1978b, 23), most during our study period. Fifteen thousand, two hundred jobs disappeared from the industry between 1968 and 1973, a decline of 20 per cent. As in iron castings, this employment loss was heavily biased against manual workers, whose jobs were cut by 23 per cent, whilst the number of administrative, technical and clerical jobs fell by 8 per cent (table 5.3). Unlike in iron castings, however, the operatives affected were predominantly unskilled and, due to the developments in the finishing stage of production, referred to earlier, contained a higher proportion of female workers. Like iron castings the industry moved on to a much reduced productive base. But this did not mean major liquidations of firms within this sector. This was different from the case in iron castings; in that industry closure of a foundry often occurred together with the liquidation of a company. But the different structure of capital-ownership in paper and board meant that here closure was more often a means of saving a company, or of increasing its profits. Whilst there was a number of bankruptcies among the smaller independent mills during the rationalization, the larger companies continued to pursue their long-standing policy of diversification. Thus while the proposed merger of the pulp and paper-making activities of Reed International and the Bowater Paper Corporation was abandoned in 1971, the two companies continued to expand their interests outside the sector: Bowater acquired Liquid Packaging Ltd in 1969 and, in 1972, the Beautility Ltd furniture company and the Ralli International trading company; Reed International acquired the International Printing Corporation (IPC) printing and publishing company in 1970 and Twyfords Holdings Ltd a year later. Capital within the sector was thus shifted to other parts of the economy whilst the capacity cuts were taking place. While jobs were lost, most companies remained intact. No new jobs were created by the companies' diversification since this mostly took place by takeover, that is by a transfer of ownership between companies rather than by new investment in production. Within the industry, too, capital assets were saved. Thus the collapse of Peter Dixon's newsprint activities left the company, at the end of the study period, offering to sell the assets of its packaging subsidiary for £5½ million cash (Stock Exchange Official Year Book 1973–4). In the event, however, the whole company was taken over by Bowater in 1974. This not only saved the packaging subsidiary but also transferred Dixon's 34.2 per cent share of the capital of British Tissues[7] to Bowater, thus increasing its interests in the major expanding sector in paper and board. Rationalization was therefore also part and parcel of a further reorganization of ownership within the sector.

The performance of the industry at the end of the study period provides a fitting end to this chapter. The brief upturn in the UK economy in 1973 saw some improvement in the sector's fortunes. Yet the rationalization had itself set constraints on expansion; in the words of one commentator: 'The only limits on demand were production capacity and the availability of pulp' (Financial Analysis Group 1975, 3). There was now a *shortage* of capacity. The new question was which firm(s) could expand production fast enough to benefit from the expected market increase. The cycle began again, and with the same result.

> By the end of 1974 however, the picture was quite different: mills were closing, demand had collapsed; and the British Paper and Board Industry Federation estimated that 20 of its 160 member mills were on short-time working. Orders in January 1975 were down to only 5 to 6 weeks against 10 to 12 in the previous Autumn. (Financial Analysis Group 1975, 3)

The uncoordinated search for profit had thus resulted in excess capacity appearing yet again in the industry: 'paper makers who had been eagerly expanding their production capacity in late 1973 and early 1974, or diversifying into waste paper at the height of the pulp famine, now ruefully found themselves busy building new machines whilst demand evaporated' (Financial Analysis Group 1975, 3).

Part 3
Production change and the geography of job loss

6
Forms of production reorganization and the geography of job loss

It has been argued that employment decline can result from a range of different forms of production reorganization, and that these can themselves be adopted in order to cope with a range of different circumstances. This is interesting because it indicates that job loss may have a number of different implications for what is going on in production and for the state of economic health of the industries and areas affected. Now, in part 3, we aim to demonstrate that the identification and explanation of the different mechanisms can also make a significant contribution to the understanding of the geography of employment decline. All too often, attempts to explain the geography of employment decline – why some parts of the country lose more jobs than others – have concentrated on trying to find an association between the map of employment decline and the characteristics of different areas. We argue that this is not enough. First, it is analytically inadequate; the form of production change through which jobs are lost may be at least as important for an understanding of the geographical pattern as the locational characteristics, and even locational characteristics may vary in the way they operate, depending on the kind of production change. Second, the difference between the two approaches is politically important. The approach which looks immediately for a correlation with the characteristics of declining regions tends more easily to slip into an argument which essentially 'blames the victim'. What we argue here is, not that such geographical characteristics are unimportant, but that their degree of importance, and the way in which they operate, depend on the kinds of production change that are causing the job loss. It is not enough to go straight from the geography of decline to seek its explanation in geographical characteristics ('Merseysiders go on strike more often' for example). It is also necessary to understand the reasons why, and the processes by which, the jobs are being lost in the first place.

* * *

To begin with, when considered in their pure forms each of the different kinds of production reorganization has different geographical implications. Not only do they differ in terms of the changes they represent within production, but these different changes are also likely to give rise to different geographical patterns of job loss.

Consider first *intensification*, which is probably the simplest of the three forms of production reorganization we have studied. The basic aim of intensification is to reduce aggregate labour costs per unit of output by cuts in the number of workers employed, and this is achieved through the reorganization of existing production and labour processes. It therefore involves reductions in the level of employment at existing plants; it does not involve either plant closure or significant levels of new investment. Its impact is confined to the existing geographical distribution of plants in the sector(s) concerned. There are no location choices to be made; indeed, no region will experience any expansion in employment. Unequal effects between regions will not be produced by job transfer or by the creation of new jobs at existing locations, but only by the differential distribution of job loss. This is important; what it means is that in situations where employment decline takes place entirely through intensification, there will be no potentially mobile employment. The concept of 'potentially mobile employment' is an important one in any discussion of the geography of employment decline. It relates to the possibility that different forms of production reorganization offer for individual regions/locations to secure employment gains even though the aggregate sectoral context in which these occur is one of decline. Such gains could occur as a result of investment in new production capacity, or the re-location of existing capacity. Where production reorganization potentially involves either, or both, of these kinds of change individual locations may experience some employment growth; the jobs involved are 'potentially mobile'. Intensification, as defined here, clearly cannot generate such potentially mobile employment as it is, by definition, concerned solely with the reorganization of production and labour processes within existing factories.

Rationalization is different. Like intensification it does not involve any investment in new productive capacity. It involves no new locations and all changes in employment levels take place within the existing geographical distribution of employment. Unlike intensification, however, it may generate some potentially mobile employment. This is the case if the rationalization involves redistribution of production between sites as part of the process of cutback. In particular, it may involve the closure of smaller, outlying plants and the concentration of capacity at one or two larger sites. The reorganization of the heavy electrical engineering industry in the late 1960s/early 1970s provides good examples of this phenomenon. The concentration of capacity involved both inter- and intra-regional shifts of production, but the amount of employment actually gained by the location on the receiving end of the transfers was very small and paled into insignificance in relation to the job loss with which it was linked. The employment gained by individual locations as a result of the geographical concentration of capacity is invariably tied to substantial employment losses elsewhere, where such reorganization occurs as part of an overall strategy of rationalization. There is, nonetheless, a geographical shift of jobs: there is mobile employment.

The fact that rationalization may, in these circumstances, generate some potentially mobile employment immediately suggests the possibility of greater geographical variability than there is with intensification. This possibility is further increased by a second feature of rationalization – the fact that, unlike intensification, it may actually involve the complete closure of capacity in individual locations. Thus where an industry is undergoing rationalization an individual region/location is faced with a range of possible employment change stretching from minus 100 per cent (complete closure) to some gain (where concentration of capacity occurs). The range of potential employment change for regions/locations when sectors cut back through intensification is smaller. First, no employment gains will take place so the upper limit of regional employment performance is 'no change' (where regions/locations remain unaffected by the production reorganization). Second, complete closure is not part of intensification for, by definition, this production reorganization requires the retention of capacity. The lower limit of regional employment performance will thus be set at that point where no more labour savings can be made using existing production techniques.

The prime difference between the spatial impact of *technical change* and that of intensification and rationalization, is that technical change, in principle, always involves the generation of potentially mobile employment. Rationalization may or may not involve relocation of capacity but technical change, by definition, must involve investment in new production capacity. A positive decision will therefore always have to be taken about the location of the new techniques. This decision may produce a change in the geography of employment in a number of ways. In industries in which markets are growing rapidly, technical change will usually be introduced by firms in the form of additions to capacity. The existing production capacity will remain unaffected (i.e. there will be no major production reorganization on existing sites) whilst the new capacity is potentially mobile. It could be added to the existing distribution of capacity or located in new areas. Where there is no growth in output, the introduction of technical change will be complemented by compensatory scrapping. That is, if new plants are built for the new production process, old factories have to be closed. In terms of the impact of this reorganization on space, there are two obvious possibilities: (a) the closure of plants at existing locations with the investment located at new sites; (b) a change of production technique on site. The same options also exist in industries faced with declining markets for their goods. In these circumstances, however, the capacity that is scrapped will not be completely replaced to meet the now lower capacity requirements of the sector in question.

The range of potential variation in spatial employment change in sectors undergoing technical change is clearly quite wide. Where sectoral output is declining or relatively static it is possible for individual regions/locations to experience, on the one hand, the loss of their entire workforce (from scrapping) or, on the other, some gain in employment from the potentially mobile new investment that is generated. This possible range of regional employment performance is clearly wider than that present with intensification. It is also wider than that for rationalization. Whilst the latter does present individual regions/locations with the possibility of a complete loss of employment (as does technical change), the level of possible gain is much smaller. What also distinguishes technical change from both rationalization and intensification is the fact that it introduces the possibility of employment gains being secured in completely new locations, for it is only in the case of technical change that new plants might be built. Employment gains linked to concentration of capacity in rationalizing sectors will be confined to existing locations. Where technical change is introduced in a context of output growth, individual regions/locations may gain some of the potentially mobile employment. In these circumstances there is less likelihood of any region/location experiencing complete closure (scrapping being less important than in conditions of static or declining output). It is not impossible, however. As we saw in chapter 4, investment in new techniques can occur in the context of even rapidly rising output and still result in a net loss of jobs. This was true over this period for parts of the chemical industry. In such cases, the new investment must clearly, in part, have been used to replace existing production facilities.

Table 6.1 illustrates some of these spatial characteristics of intensification, rationalization and technical change. It is immediately obvious that there are significant differences between them. Most obviously, only with rationalization and technical change will actual closure of capacity occur. Changes in the number of establishments in an industry was indeed one of the pieces of data we used in the initial exploration of sectoral change (see chapter 2). There are other differences, too. There are variations in the amount of potentially mobile employment that is generated: when employment decline takes place through intensification there is none; when it takes place through rationalization there may be some; when it takes place in the context of technical change there is *always* some.

Table 6.1   Spatial implications of forms of production reorganization

Forms of production reorganization \ Output change	Falling	Stable average growth	Rising
Intensification	Employment losses *in situ*		–
Rationalization	Employment losses *in situ* Plant closure Possibility of relatively small local gains as a result of concentration of capacity. No new locations		–
Technical change	(1) Employment cuts *in situ* *or* (2) New locations (i.e. some local gains) and closures	Any combination of *in situ* employment losses, new locations and plant closures to meet capacity requirements	

These arguments certainly emphasize that even in conditions of declining or relatively static output there still exists significant potential for mobile employment, especially insofar as it is investment and technical change that dominate any production reorganization. Declining output in an industry does not inevitably mean low levels of investment and employment mobility. Indeed mobility may form a vital part of the production strategy designed to remedy the contraction in output. It should also be stressed that the regional employment gains that we found in this study occurred in sectors in which employment was declining at the national level. This is an important point and one to be remembered in discussions of employment mobility, for it is often argued that the overall aggregate decline in manufacturing employment has drastically reduced the levels of mobile employment. Obviously a correlation does exist, as it does between output growth and productivity growth (see, for instance, Salter 1969), but neither relationship is quite as simple as it first appears. Clearly in certain instances (e.g. where technical change is being introduced) quite significant levels of mobile employment can be generated even though overall job opportunities are declining.

Similarly, the *range* of regional employment change is likely to vary, depending on the form of production reorganization through which aggregate employment decline occurred. The range is potentially widest in cases of technical change, narrowest in cases of intensification. This, too, has implications for how one approaches the analysis of the geography of employment change. Thus, one common approach to analysing variation in regional employment patterns is to use the 'shift-share' technique. This divides employment change into components. In particular it identifies the structural component – the proportion of the employment change which would be 'expected' given the national rate of employment change in the industry (i.e. on the assumption that employment change takes place at the same rate in each region) – and the differential component – the amount by which the actual employment change differs from what would be 'expected' in the region given the national rate of change. One immediate implication of the argument here is that over the regions in the country the size and variability of the differential component, and the balance between it and the structural component, may vary in the case of national employment decline simply as a result of the kind of production reorganization through which the job loss has occurred. This difference in overall balance between the two components may, in other words, occur without any reference to the characteristics of individual regions and purely on the basis of an analysis of the operation of the dominant form of production change in the industries in question.

Finally, it is only in the case of investment and technical change that new locations may gain employment; in other words that new plants may be established. Although locations may gain employment with both rationalization and technical change, it is only in the latter case that gains can be made by areas with no previous employment in the industry.

* * *

These differences between the forms of production reorganization are apparent in the regional patterns of employment decline in the industries studied here.[1] The regions in question are the eleven Standard Regions of the UK as defined in the period 1968–73 (see figure 6.1). Take first the incidence and scale of potentially mobile employment. Unfortunately, regional data only reveal net changes in regional employment levels and are, therefore, only proxies for the actual processes of job change. Clearly a net sectoral gain in employment in a particular region does not necessarily mean that no individual job losses occurred there. Similarly regions with net employment losses may well have experienced some individual gains. It is impossible, therefore, to identify individual cases of employment gains; figures at regional level are bound often to be underestimates. This problem is compounded when it is *potentially*, rather than actually, mobile employment that is to be identified. Given, though, that net changes in levels of regional employment have to be used, a simple totalling of regional employment gains provides the best, albeit imperfect, indication of the presence of mobile employment. On this basis it is possible to use the data for our sectors, (see note 1) classified according to their dominant form of production reorganization. In order to control for variations which may arise as a result of different rates of output change, those sectors with a high level of output growth (30 per cent and over) – both of them technical change sectors – were omitted. The figures in table 6.2 indicate the differences which exist. First, they illustrate the relative insignificance of regional employment gains in both the intensifying and rationalizing groups of industries, with a slightly higher incidence in the latter. In the technical change sectors with similar levels of output change to those experienced by the two groups of intensifying and rationalizing sectors, potentially mobile employment appears to have been much more important. There were thirty instances of regional employment gains in these sectors, accounting for 15,900 jobs, nearly 16 per cent of aggregate net loss.

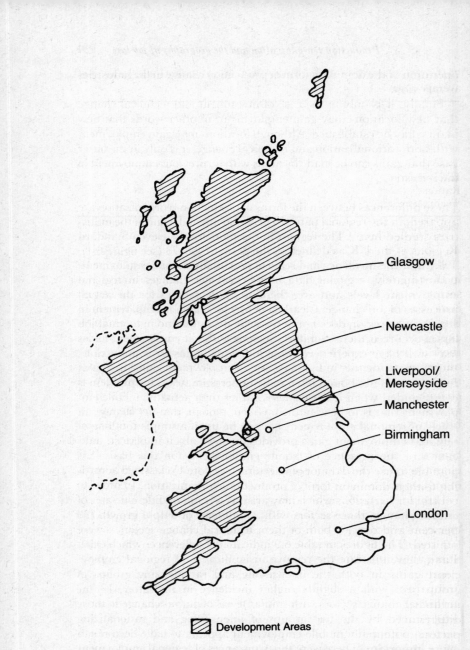

 Development Areas

Fig. 6.1 Development areas in the UK as defined during the study period

Table 6.2 Potentially mobile employment for sectors with negative and average output growth

	Total net regional employment gains:	
	Absolute number	*As percentage total net employment decline*
Intensification	2900	6.3
Rationalization	9900	6.7
Technical change	15900	15.9

Source See note 1

These differences could still, however, be due to minor differences in the rate of output change. In order to explore this possibility, the sectors with either declining output or a rate of growth below 30 per cent were ranked by rate of output growth/decline. Table 6.3 presents this ranking. The figures are the total regional employment gains expressed as a percentage of total sectoral employment loss. Whilst there is clearly no close correlation between these figures and levels of output growth in any of the three groups of industries, the table does indicate the differences that exist between the kinds of production change in terms of the generation of mobile employment. All three groups had cases where regional employment gains were recorded but it was the technical-change group that contained the sectors in which these gains were by far the most important (biscuits and carpets). As the numbers at the foot of the table show, the technical-change sectors both produced the highest average value for this index of mobile employment and showed the greatest variation.

Differences are also apparent between these three types of production-reorganization in the variability of regional employment change. Look first at the intensifying and rationalizing sectors. Figure 6.2 sets out the percentage change in employment in the eleven Standard Regions in each of the sectors in these two groups. There is clearly a much broader range of regional employment change in the group of rationalizing industries than there is in the intensifying industries. Similar differences show up, as would be expected, when differential components are compared. Figure 6.3 presents the pattern of differential regional performance that would be identified using this technique in the intensifying and rationalizing sectors. The figure shows, for each sector and for each region, the differential component as a percentage of initial employment. Table 6.4 presents

Table 6.3 Regional employment gains and sectoral output change for industries with output growth lower than 30 per cent

Total regional employment gains as a percentage of sectoral employment loss

Output change	Intensification	Rationalization	Technical change
%			
+25			Aluminium & aluminium alloys 29.0
+24			Carpets 600.0
+23			
+22			
+21			
+20			
+19	Other printing & publishing 3.3		
+18		Insulated wires & cables 18.8	Brewing & malting 31.8
+17			
+16			Jute 0
+15			
+14			Scientific & industrial instruments & systems 11.2
+13			
+12			
+11		Grain milling 48.4	
+10			
+9			
+8			
+7	Textile finishing 0		
+6	Cycles 11.8		
+5	Men's & boys' tailored outerwear 6.8		
+4			Sugar 4.5
+3			Iron & steel/steel tubes 17.3

+2	Paper & board	Biscuits 2.0	70.6
+1			
0		Bricks	0
−1			
−2		Cutlery 1.6	43.8
−3			
−4	Footwear 15.6	Textile machinery	4.5
−5			
−6	Leather 6.1	Coke ovens	0
−7	Metal-working machine tools		
−8			
−9		Other base metals 1.5	1.8
−10			
−11			
−12	Woollen & worsted	1.2	
−13			
−14			
−15	Weaving of cotton, linen &		
−16	man-made fibres	4.8	
−17			
−18			
−19			
−20	Locomotives, etc.	11.7	
−21			
−22			
−23	Electrical machinery	13.1	
Arithmetic mean	7.3	11.5	62.7
Standard deviation	5.2	14.4	156.4
Coefficient of variation	71.2	125.2	249.4

133

Table 6.4   The size and variability of differential components in intensifying and rationalizing industries

Industries	Mean of absolute values	Standard deviation	Coefficient of variation
Intensification			
Output decline	13.2	12.6	95.5
Average output Growth (0–30%)	6.3	7.0	111.1
TOTAL	8.6	9.8	114.0
Rationalization			
Output decline	19.4	24.5	126.3
Average output Growth (0–30%)	20.5	23.6	115.1
TOTAL	19.8	24.2	122.2

the average values for the differential components in each group, further disaggregated according to the rate of output change. In all categories shown, the average absolute differential component and its standard deviation and coefficient of variation are higher for rationalizing than for intensifying sectors.

Examination of the equivalent figures for the technical change industries indicates that they are different again. Figure 6.4 illustrates, for each of the technical change sectors with declining output, or average growth, the percentage employment changes experienced by the eleven Standard Regions. The whole spectrum of potential regional employment change described earlier appears. In three sectors (coke ovens, jute and bricks) no regional employment gains were recorded. Indeed in one of these sectors (coke ovens) one region (the North West) saw the loss of its entire workforce. Three regions (North West, South West and East Anglia) in fact experienced complete closure (in the coke-oven, textile machinery and cutlery industries respectively). For these individual regions then, the impact of technical change was particularly traumatic. Moreover, any bitterness felt in the regions affected by this loss of jobs will have been heightened in two of the sectors by the knowledge that this contraction occurred alongside some quite significant employment

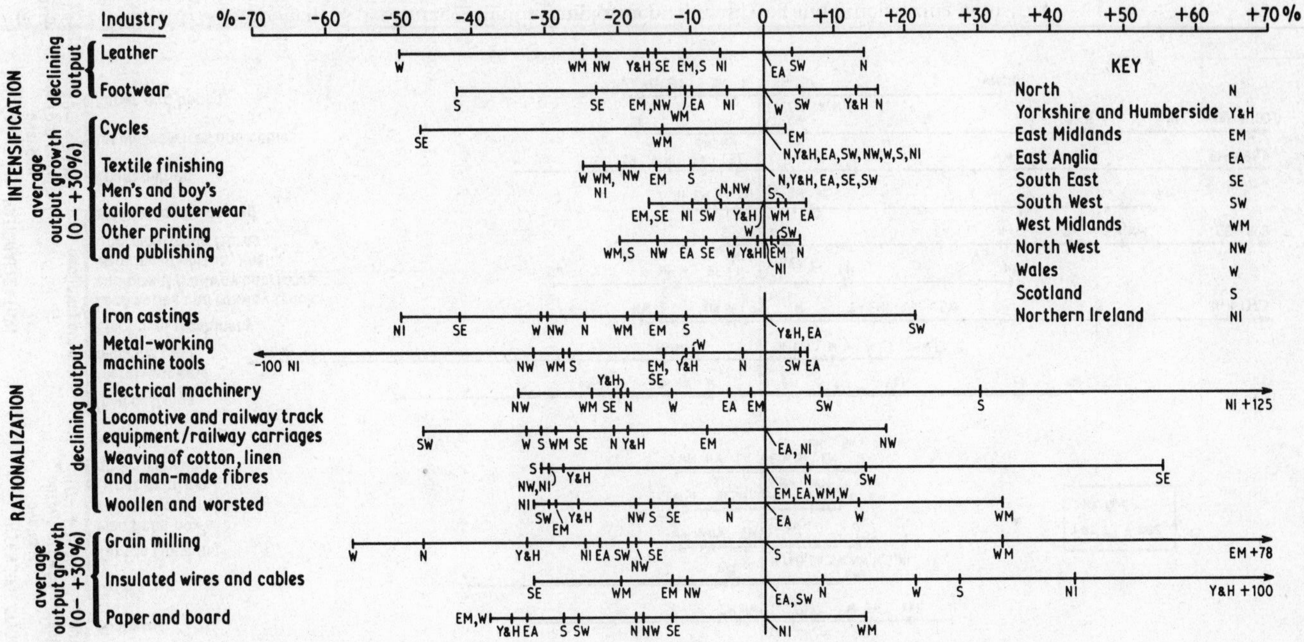

Fig. 6.2 Percentage change in employment, 1968–73, by standard region: intensifying and rationalizing industries

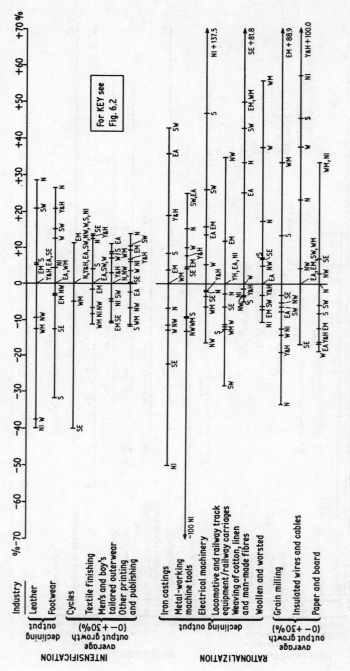

Fig. 6.3 Differential component as percentage of initial employment: intensifying and rationalizing industries

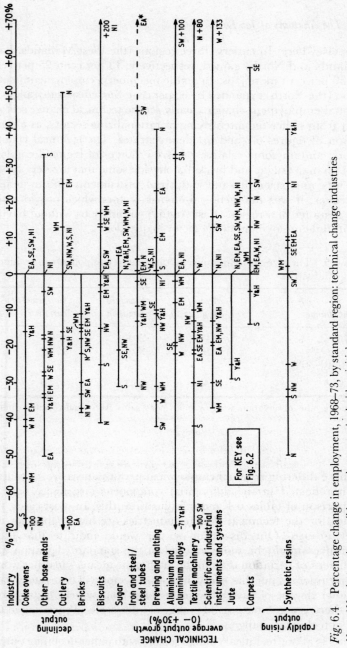

Fig. 6.4   Percentage change in employment, 1968–73, by standard region: technical change industries

Note *No observation possible – employment gained with no initial presence

gains elsewhere. In cutlery, three regions (the West Midlands, East Midlands and North) gained, respectively, 13 per cent, 25 per cent and 50 per cent more jobs. In textile machinery, employment in one region (the North) expanded by 80 per cent. Such disparate ranges of regional employment change clearly set the technical change sectors apart from either the intensifying or rationalizing sectors, as a comparison of figures 6.2 and 6.4 demonstrates. The technical change sectors contain some relatively narrow ranges of regional employment change (sugar and bricks) alongside some that are very broad (biscuits and scientific and industrial instruments and systems). Moreover, it was the technical change sectors which provided the only instance of a region (East Anglia) gaining jobs without having any initial employment in the sector in question.

Table 6.5   The size and variability of differential components in technical change industries

Output change	Mean of absolute values	Standard deviation	Coefficient of variation
Decline	13.0	20.6	158.5
Average growth (0–30%)*	17.9	31.0	173.2
TOTAL*	16.4	28.3	172.6

*excluding the observation where employment gains were made with no initial presence

These differing regional employment performances are, of course, again reflected in the differential component (see figure 6.5). A comparison of tables 6.4 and 6.5 illustrates this. In most cases, the entries for the technical change industries are higher than for the other groups. Our discussion so far would indicate that these differences might be more marked in the standard deviation and coefficient of variation than in the arithmetic means – in other words the argument is not that every individual sector will necessarily have a higher degree of variability in regional employment change, but that there is a greater possible range of inter-sectoral variation in the case of technical change.

This is all for technical change sectors with either declining output or rates of growth lower than 30 per cent. In fact, there was only one

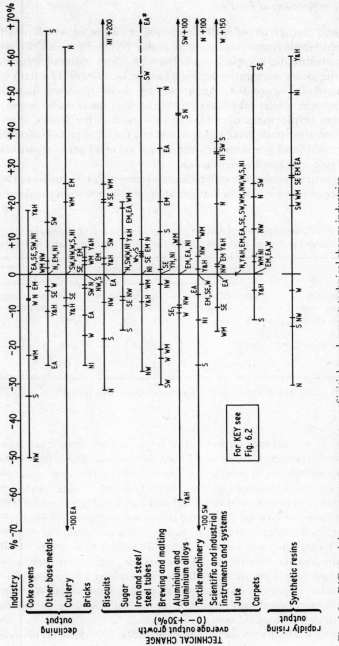

Fig. 6.5 Differential component as percentage of initial employment: technical change industries

Note *No observation possible – employment gained with no initial presence

technical change sector with rapidly rising output for which reliable regional employment data were available (synthetic resins, see note 1), so meaningful comparisons either within this group of sectors or with the other sectoral groupings cannot be drawn. The data are presented in figure 6.4. Again we see some regions expanding employment whilst others are cutting back in the overall context of national employment decline. For five regions (the North, Wales, Scotland, the South West and North West) the rapid growth of output at national level (an increase over the period of 43 per cent) was not translated into employment gains.

The importance of the differential component can be measured in a number of ways. So far we have examined it purely from the point of

Table 6.6   Differential employment change: the amount of national employment change (per cent) that was not distributed according to structure

	Forms of production reorganization:		
Output change	*Intensification*	*Rationalization*	*Technical change*
Decline	34	21	18
Average growth (0–30%)*	30	32	47
TOTAL*	31	23	40

*excluding the observation where employment gains were made with no initial presence

view of its importance for individual regions. This exercise parallels, at an industry level, those performed for the manufacturing and/or service sectors as a whole by other authors (see, for example, Fothergill and Gudgin 1978a and 1979). It is also necessary to look at the balance between the differential and structural components. This can be done in two ways. Table 6.6 shows, for each group of industries and for each category of output change, the total amount of employment change that was not distributed according to structure. Table 6.7 indicates the relative importance of the differential component within individual industries in the three groupings. For each industry the number of regions in which the differential component is greater than the structural component is shown and an average for the different categories of output growth given.

In both of these exercises fairly clear differences show up between

Table 6.7   The balance between the differential and structural components: the number of regions in which the differential component was greater than the structural component

Output change	Form of production reorganization		
	Intensification	*Rationalization*	*Technical change*
Decline	Leather 4	Iron castings 4	Coke ovens 1
	Footwear 6	Metal-working machine tools 3	Other base metals 2
		Electrical machinery 3	Cutlery 4
			Bricks 1
		Locomotives & railway track equipment/ railway carriages 2	
		Weaving of cotton, linen & man-made fibres 5	
		Woollen & worsted 2	
Arithmetic mean	5.0	3.2	2.0
Average growth (0–30%)	Cycles 2	Grain milling 6	Biscuits 8
	Textile finishing 0	Insulated wires & cables 6	Sugar 4
	Men's & boys' tailored outerwear 6	Paper & board 2	Brewing & malting 7
	Publishing 5		Iron & steel/ steel tubes 5
			Aluminium & aluminium alloys 4
			Textile machinery 3
			Scientific & industrial instruments systems 4
			Jute 0
			Carpets 8
Arithmetic mean	3.3	4.7	4.8

141

the three forms of production reorganization as far as industries experiencing average levels of output growth are concerned. The differential component is relatively less important in the group of intensifying sectors than in either of the other two groups. In other words, the loss of employment was more evenly distributed between regions in the intensifying industries. For the industries in which output declined, however, the position is less clear. The differential component in the intensifying industries was relatively more important than in the rationalizing industries or those undergoing technical change. This raises interesting questions on the nature of employment decline in these sectors; questions which we will take up again in chapter 8.[2]

Taken overall, however, there are clear differences in the geography of decline between the groups of industries in which the different forms of production change were dominant. Moreover, these differences broadly coincide with those postulated earlier as arising from the different spatial mechanisms implicit in each kind of production reorganization.

* * *

These empirical analyses are, however, purely explorations of the data concerning the sectors we are examining. *In no way are they a 'test' of the earlier arguments*. It is important to understand why this is so, since the point is symptomatic of our overall argument about methodology.[3]

First, what the earlier argument showed was that the different kinds of production reorganization have the potential for resulting in different geographical patterns of employment decline. What was being considered was what might happen if the different mechanisms were to operate alone and in their 'pure form'. This is unlikely to happen in the real world, however. An individual type of production reorganization is unlikely ever to operate either alone or in its pure form. Its actual occurrence will always be in a particular set of circumstances. For one thing it would be very rare for only one form of production change to occur in a sector. All we have identified in our empirical investigations are the important forms of production change in particular industries. As we have already said, there may well be variations in behaviour within sectors. This is a purely empirical question, though it does raise interesting issues about the usefulness of sectors, even at mlh level, for the analysis of industrial behaviour (see chapter 10). The different processes may also interlock and affect each other. Thus, as was pointed out in chapter 2, drastic falls in output are likely to be accompanied by some rationalization even if, overall, it is the process of intensification which dominates job loss.

At this point it should be stressed again that intensification, rationalization and investment with technical change are only three possible forms of change within industry – the three that were the most important in the industries we examined. They do not exhaust the possibilities. Two other obvious forms of change are: simple expansion of production using the same techniques, and locational shift without any change in the organization of the production process. Of these, the first, by definition, implies an expansion of employment and therefore does not come within the field of concern of this book. The second in principle and in its pure form implies no change in the number of jobs. There may well be, though, savings in labour costs for the company and an increase in worker pliability. Indeed, these may be the reason for the change of location. Examples of such geographical movement are numerous. Much of the movement of older, labour-intensive industries to the Third World has been of this type (see chapter 3), as well as some, though by no means all, of the shift within the USA from the relatively well-organized older industrial areas of the North and East to those smaller towns in those Southern states where 'right to work' means an anti-union attitude and the outlawing of the closed shop.

Such shifts in location can clearly be combined with other kinds of change. In particular they may be combined with intensification. A shift of location in search of a workforce which is less organized or troublesome for management may well be an alternative to intensification of the labour process on site. (In such a shift the emphasis would be less on the cost of the new labour force in terms of immediate wages, and more on vulnerability and docility.) To put it the other way around, a change of location in search of more compliant labour may well accompany intensification. It is, therefore, one of the more obvious possibilities we should look for when examining the actual changes in the industries where intensification was important.

This raises again the issue of the relationship between production change and location change which was briefly considered in chapter 4. In contrast to the three forms we are examining in detail, both the other forms of change mentioned above involve a change in geography but no change in the production process. We shall be considering in the rest of the book some of the different ways in which 'location factors' can be important (or not) in the analysis of the geography of employment decline. But it should already be clear that production change and location change are integrally related. Analytically there is no simple movement from production change to its resulting spatial change. In the example above, intensification on site and moving to a new location in search of a new workforce were alternatives. A lack of possibility for movement may force the company to confront its existing employees and attempt to push through intensification in its existing location. The possibility of finding a new site and a new labour force may, for management, help avoid a confrontation, as the workers at the original location are left jobless and powerless to object.

It is important, then, to recognize that these different kinds of change within industry are often linked, and that they often occur at the same time within different parts of a company or industry or in actual combination in one set of changes within an office or factory.

This, then, is to talk of the interlocking of a number of different processes. There is also the possibility, however, of variation in the operation of the processes themselves. Thus, the different spatial implications that we have identified relate to the *potential* variability in geographical employment performance implied by each form of production change. They are statements of possibility rather than of necessity. While it is clearly possible for sectoral rationalization to involve both employment gains in individual locations as a result of concentration of capacity, and the complete disappearance of jobs in other areas, there is no reason to assume that either, or both, of these have to happen in every case. It is perfectly possible for capacity closure to occur evenly across all regions. Similarly, in the case of technical change, individual locations are only faced with the *possibility* of employment gains from the investment in new production processes, they need not occur. Gross employment gains from such new investment may be turned into an overall net loss of jobs as a result of compensatory scrapping in cases where the production reorganization is confined to existing locations. All locations may perform similarly. Technical change, in other words, *can* result in a greater spatial variability of employment change in a context of overall employment decline compared to the other two forms of production reorganization, but it does not of necessity have to.

The actual geography of decline in any particular industry will be the product of all this potential complexity, and must be analysed as such. Indeed, the explorations of the data so far already indicate this. There were gains in the footwear industry in the North, Yorkshire and Humberside and the South West. Were these the result of the combination of intensification and locational shift, or were certain parts of the industry behaving completely differently from the rest? In electrical machinery, interestingly, the gains from concentration of capacity in the context of overall rationalization were completely submerged at the regional level by the massive losses which took place in the main regions of production (the fact that such concentration did take place is documented in Massey and Meegan 1979a). On the other hand there were gains in other regions (the South West, Northern Ireland and Scotland). Of these we know that the gains in Scotland were due to variation within the sector – there was a classic case of technical change in the production of distribution transformers, with the gains in Scotland being 'compensated for' by closures in other regions. In the technical change group itself, there are three industries in which there were no regional gains at all. This is clearly possible within the 'pure form' – it is one of the potential outcomes. It may imply that the technical change was not such as to induce inter-regional shift – in other words, that the locational requirements did not change enough, or that there were some other countervailing tendencies in operation.

Already, then, the brief examination of industry data in the light of knowledge about the operation of mechanisms of employment decline allows the formulation of questions about the geography of job loss. They are, moreover, different kinds of questions from those that arise from the simple consideration of patterns of employment decline divorced from any notion of the mechanisms producing it. What is clear is that geographically, as well as in terms of what is happening in production, it is wrong to assume that employment decline in one part of the economy is very similar to that in another.

The kind of explanation that an understanding of such mechanisms enables is not, then, simply predictive. The pure forms of the different kinds of production reorganization never actually operate as such. The specific characteristics of the industries and the particular historical conditions will always produce a specific empirical result. Understanding such 'pure' mechanisms is a necessary part of the analysis of the real world, but it is not equivalent to it.[4] The real test of the usefulness of this approach is, therefore, in how it contributes to an explanation of the actual complexity of the geography of employment decline.

* * *

In order to look at this the next three chapters return again to the detailed case-studies and examine how their spatial patterns of employment decline took shape. Each chapter is organized in the same way. First, the argument about 'pure forms' of production reorganization is taken further. All that have been explored so far are the general spatial implications of each of the three forms of production reorganization. For example, we showed that rationalization is more likely to exhibit a greater degree of spatial variation in its employment effects than is intensification. But this simply says that with rationalization some regions/locations are more likely to be more adversely affected than others, than is the case with intensification. It does not say *which* regions/locations, nor why. The questions remain as to why particular factories get closed, why some workers as opposed to others lose their jobs, or, for instance with technical change, under what conditions a change of location is likely. Each chapter starts with an exploration of the different ways in which that type of production reorganization can produce spatial variation in the pattern of employment decline. This shows that not only does each form of production change have different broad spatial implications, but also each has potentially different rules and mechanisms for the creation of geographical variation in employment decline. This provides a framework within which the actual operation of locational considerations in different processes of job loss can be examined. The second part of each chapter takes up again the detailed sectoral studies introduced in part 2, and examines the spatial pattern of employment loss in each. This enables both an analysis of how the forms of production reorganization actually operated to produce (uneven) distributions of job loss in the particular circumstances under discussion, and also an exploration of the geographical effects of intra-sectoral variation in the form of production change adopted.

The industries were deliberately chosen to allow an examination of a range of different questions – they are the awkward rather than the apparently simple cases. The two cases of intensification include regions in which absolute gains in employment took place, but to very different degrees, one of them being the case in which such gains were most important. In the cases of rationalization the two sectors performed fairly similarly in terms of such indices as variability of regional employment change (see table 6.3 and figures 6.1 and 6.2) but, as was seen in chapter 5, are very different in terms of ownership structure, and in the kind of company that is dominant. Finally, the case of technical change is one of the three where that form of production reorganization produced no net regional employment gains: it also allows examination of all the different processes within a single firm.

7
Rationalization: the geography of job loss in the iron-castings and paper and board industries

When it is rationalization through which job loss takes place, the geographical pattern of employment decline is determined by the kind of criteria used to decide where capacity is to be cut. Instead of the usual 'location decision', where to put a new plant, the question here is which factories, or parts of factories, to close. At its simplest, rationalization follows a straightforward scrapping model. That is, in some notional pure form, the abandonment of capacity will take place according to a profitability criterion, with the least profitable capacity being scrapped first. In order to get any further with understanding the geography of decline under rationalization, then, it is necessary to identify the main determinants of the level of profitability. These can be grouped into two types. First, there are those that are 'internal' to the production process: characteristics of the factory itself. Second, there are those that are 'external': characteristics of the factory's location. Among the former − characteristics of production − all kinds of things may be important. In their investigations of shifting patterns of employment amongst US cities, Varaiya and Wiseman (1978) found clear indications of a pattern of scrapping based on age and labour productivity, with serious implications for employment prospects in the older cities of the North-East states. Size of plant may also be important; in a previous study (Massey and Meegan 1979a) we found that, because of economies of scale in both production and management, small outlying factories were often most vulnerable to closure, as companies concentrated their remaining production in their main factories. Clearly, in that precise form, this is an option only open to multi-plant firms. A similar result may well be arrived at, however, in a sector entirely composed of single-plant firms if they are of different sizes, and there exist economies of scale. The second group of influences on profitability consists of those that relate to location. These may include such things as geographical variations in labour type, militancy and cost; they may include rent levels, and the various sorts of accessibility, for instance to market.

In any real case, both these groups of influences (production and geography) are likely to be involved in explaining variations in profitability. The outcome – which capacity is least profitable and which therefore is closed – will depend on the overall effect of the two together. Moreover, the two factors may well interact, different techniques, for instance, being used in different locations. It is nonetheless possible, analytically, to separate the two sets of influences and, roughly, to establish their relative significance in order to clarify the actual role of location factors in employment decline. The implications of the two sets of factors are clearly different. If levels of profitability are heavily dependent on locational characteristics, this may have more general implications for profitable production in the area in question. But a predominance of production characteristics does not necessarily have such implications. This is important because production characteristics, such as age or size of plant, may well exhibit geographical regularity. Geographical regularity does *not* mean, however, that the cause of the phenomenon necessarily has anything to do with location: a geographical pattern does not necessarily imply a geographical cause. Some of the geographical literature, concerned, perhaps, to demonstrate the importance of location, have not kept this distinction clear. This was true, for instance, in the debate over inner-city decline. The fact that in the 1960s and 1970s some of the fastest rates of job loss occurred in inner cities led some to argue that it was the inner-city location itself that was 'the problem', and to talk of 'locational evaluation' by firms. But inner-city location was also highly correlated with production characteristics such as age of plant and machinery. Whether it was geographical or production characteristics that were more important was something which had to be investigated, which probably varied from case to case, but which certainly could not be assumed from the fact of a geographical pattern.

All this, of course, assumes that capacity is scrapped strictly according to a criterion of profitability. Yet, as we saw in chapter 5, the process of rationalization is not that simple. Companies of different types may adopt different strategies, and what is an acceptable level of profit may vary from case to case. Again, although in an oligopolistic situation it may well be that the profitability criterion is followed by each firm, this may not necessarily result in a situation in which, at a sectoral level, the least profitable capacity is scrapped. This may happen, for instance, because certain firms decide to get out of an ailing sector altogether (even though their factories are not the least profitable in the sector as a whole) while another firm may thereby be enabled to stay in production. Similarly, a firm with sufficient strength may take account of considerations other than immediate profitability (for example, degree of workforce militancy) when deciding how much, and which, capacity to close – an option evidently not available for instance, to the single-plant firm.

In addition, there are other circumstances in which profitability may not be the sole criterion for plant closure. These relate more to the broader political and industrial-relations considerations surrounding closure. Thus, for example, a multi-plant firm may be unwilling to consider the closure of a factory in an area which is heavily dependent upon it for employment opportunities. Such a closure is potentially much more sensitive politically than is closure of capacity in areas with a more diversified employment base – and an employer's monopoly position in a labour market can be a powerful weapon against militancy. Further, where profit is the sole consideration, it may not be profit in the production process itself which is important. The possibility of capital gains from the sale of a factory and/or development of land, may dominate questions of the viability of production itself. Even the meaning of the term 'profitability' is open to interpretation. The long debate over whether or not the rate of profit in British industry is falling, and if so by how much, is a good indication of the problems of identifying the most appropriate measure. In a wider sense, too, the questions of what is profit and how to measure labour productivity, even the choice of accounting conventions, are matters for debate. The argument over profit and productivity in the British Steel Corporation (see Manwaring 1981) shows clearly how such things may be highly political.

Instead, therefore, of just moving from geographical pattern to geographical characteristics, and searching for correlations between the two, it is necessary to investigate the actual reasons why certain parts of production in an industry are closed and others not. And the actual criteria which govern these processes are a matter for empirical investigation. They may change from period to period and from industry to industry. A lot will depend on the wider context within which rationalization occurs, and on the state of relations between capital and labour.

It is also important to remember that rationalization is unlikely to be the only form of production change taking place. The capacity which remains will continue to be subject to competitive pressures and some attempts to increase competitiveness are likely to be implemented. The geography of job loss, in other words, will probably be due to more than simply the effect of closures of capacity.

So how does this broad schema help in understanding the geographical pattern of job loss in the two rationalizing sectors we studied in detail?

*   *   *

Nearly 16,000 jobs were lost in the *iron-castings industry* (part of mlh 313) between 1968 and 1973. The regional distribution of this job loss is set out in table 7.1. A first clue to the explanation of the differences in regional performance can be found by looking behind the employment numbers themselves at the output and productivity figures. Table 7.2 shows clearly that the employment changes were, in fact, associated with very different movements in both output and productivity. The indications are that the regional differences in employment decline were due to two main factors. First, there were different degrees of pressure for rationalization in different regions as a

Table 7.1   Regional employment changes in iron castings, 1968–73

Region	Net employment change	Net employment change as percentage of initial employment
		%
North	−1400	−28.6
Yorkshire and Humberside	−1800	−16.4
East Midlands ⎫ West Midlands ⎬	−5600	−11.3
East Anglia ⎫ South East ⎬ South West ⎭	−1600	−11.5
North West	−2300	−25.8
Wales	−1400	−35.0
Scotland ⎫ Northern Ireland ⎬	−1900	−22.9
UK	−16000	−15.9

Source   Data provided by the Council of Ironfoundry Associations

Table 7.2 Regional output and productivity changes in ironcastings, 1968–73

Region	1968			1973			Change in output per head 1968=100
	Output ('000 tonnes)	Employment ('000)	Output per head (tonnes)	Output ('000 tonnes)	Employment ('000)	Output per head (tonnes)	
North	376	4.9	76.7	279	3.5	79.7	104
Yorkshire and Humberside	302	11.0	27.5	298	9.2	32.4	118
East Midlands West Midlands East Anglia	1762	49.7	35.5	1752	44.1	39.7	112
South East South West	384	13.9	27.6	402	12.3	32.7	118
North West	255	8.9	28.7	210	6.6	31.8	111
Wales	261	4.0	65.3	262	2.6	100.8	154
Scotland Northern Ireland	274	8.3	33.0	242	6.4	37.8	115
UK	3614	100.7	35.9	3445	84.7	40.7	113

Source Data provided by the Council of Ironfoundry Associations

result of concentration on different sectoral markets. Much of the variation in output change between regions can be explained by the different fortunes of these different sectoral markets. Perhaps the prime example here is the way output held up in the West Midlands and Wales. This seems to have been due to these regions' concentration on the then relatively buoyant production of, respectively, castings for automobiles and ingot moulds. In contrast, the relatively poor showing in the North in output terms seems to have been due to its specialization in serving the declining markets of shipbuilding, heavy electrical engineering, and general iron and steel and coal industries.

This different movement in terms of output was not the whole story, however. It also tended to be associated with differences in productivity performance. On the whole, the then growing parts of the iron-castings industry (those making castings for the car industry, and ingot moulds) were also those parts which had higher initial levels of productivity and faster rates of increase over the period. In the former, this was because the car industry requires large numbers of identical castings, and it is possible to operate on a mass-production basis. In the other case, ingot-mould production is now being done by continuous casting methods. Thus those regions that did not lose employment because of output decline were nonetheless liable to slow growth, or decline, in numbers of jobs as a result of their increasing concentration on sectors with high and growing levels of productivity. (This resulted from both shifts from low-productivity production to the growing sectors, and from advances in the high-productivity sectors themselves.) An example of this was Wales where the net loss of jobs was entirely the result of advances in productivity (output remaining stable over the period).

This raises again the question of the level of analysis. There were clearly different pressures for rationalization in different parts of the industry and, because of the frequently local nature of the relation between production and market, this meant that rationalization was much more marked in some regions than others. While the North suffered closure on a considerable scale, in Wales the loss of jobs was due more to shifts in the balance of production between markets, and to changes in production, including some fairly significant technical change. Had we been looking only at Wales, the industry would not have been classified in this period as one undergoing rationalization; had we been looking only at the North it certainly would. The geographical patterns of decline *within* the regions are likely, as a result, to be very different.

But there was also a second factor in operation. This was that there was a far higher closure rate among small foundries than among large. In part this was related to the first factor, that of sector, since those sectoral markets that were growing or stable were more dominated by large repetition foundries.[1] Smaller independent foundries are particularly oriented to selling castings to the general engineering industry, and demand there fell faster over the late 1960s and early 1970s than it did for castings as a whole (NEDO 1979b, 10, 11). But the higher closure rate of small foundries was also an independently operating factor, which resulted from the far greater difficulty experienced by small firms in riding out the recession. The NEDO retrospective, for instance, considered

> that small foundries face particular problems because they are *small craft foundries,* as well as having the general problems which affect all small companies. These stem from their dependence on traditional moulder-coremaker skills; from their vulnerability to extreme fluctuations in the trade cycle; from their history of depressed profitability which this has caused; and from their hazardous working conditions. (1979b, 3)

They also clearly often suffered from the disadvantages of a small firm in a basically subordinate, subcontracting relationship with a few larger companies (NEDO, 1979b).

The geographical result of this has been that regions with a higher than average proportion of small foundries have, all other things being equal, experienced a rather greater loss of jobs and a higher number of plant closures than those regions in which production was more dominated by large plants. This in turn has had a number of effects. In terms of productivity, the dominance of a region by small foundries meant that the average initial level of productivity was relatively low. On the other hand, the associated high closure rate would have led, over the period, to a relatively high rate of increase from this initially low level. In contrast, the effect on output of even quite large numbers of closures of such small plants is likely to have been fairly limited. An example of a region where this process might have been important is Yorkshire and Humberside, a region with a preponderance of small craft foundries, a better than national movement in output, an initially low level of labour productivity, but a relatively high rate of increase of that productivity over the period.

It might help to clarify, and contrast, the mechanisms at work if a few individual regions are described. Compare the North and Wales, the two regions with the fastest decline in employment. The high percentage loss of jobs in the North was associated with both the highest level of output decline and the lowest level of productivity increase. It seems that the first explanatory factor above (that of sectoral dominance of the local market) is particularly crucial in explaining the high degree of output decline. The local market was dominated by the shipbuilding, heavy electrical and general iron and steel and coal industries. All these industries drastically reduced their demand for iron castings over the period. Moreover, production for these industries had been in large foundries, but of a jobbing type. The industries (particularly shipbuilding and heavy electrical engineering) generally specify large, discrete orders which are not amenable to mass-production techniques. The large scale of individual jobs did mean, though, that the level of productivity in the region was high (it was in fact ranked first in output per head at the beginning of the period). The low productivity increase, however, is explained partly by the fact that the capacity closures were not accompanied by shifts to mass production of castings for growing markets. In addition, the low presence of mass-production plants also meant that there was less scope for increasing productivity significantly in the remaining plants. The North fell from first to second place in the ranking of output per head over the period.

Whilst falling output dominated job loss in the North, it was rising productivity that underlay employment decline in Wales; here output remained stable. Again sectoral dominance of the market for iron castings appears to have been important. In this case, however, the dominant market sector (ingot moulds) was not declining. Moreover, this area of production is on a scale (per job) which allows high levels of productivity and has the potential for significant increases on the initial levels. That this occurred in Wales is shown by the region moving from second to first place in the ranking of output per head over the period.

So how can this analysis be interpreted in relation to the schema outlined earlier? First, the very different relations between output, productivity and employment in the different regions emphasize again how inadequate it is simply to equate employment decline with decline on any other measure.

Second, examine the main reasons for the regional differentiation in the overall decline of the sector. The first was that the foundries in different regions tended to face different market conditions. This is certainly a geographical factor, but of a particular sort. Given the generally intra-regional nature of the market in iron castings, the differentiated production characteristics are themselves a reflection of specifically regional characteristics. The greater (or lesser) rationalization in a particular region was due to factors characteristic of the region – a major castings market in a declining/growing industry – other than those associated with the actual companies or factories being considered. It is not a location factor as such, but rather a characteristic of regional economic structure – a local negative multiplier effect. The second factor was the higher rate of closure of small foundries. Although the effect of this was similarly systematic in its geographical distribution, it was clearly a production characteristic and not a geographical one. The fact that a region loses employment heavily because it has a high presence of small foundries expresses nothing more than that. In itself it says nothing further about the competitiveness of the region other than that those plants lost jobs. Of the two main factors determining the geographical distribution of job loss, therefore, one was primarily a locational consideration and one was not. However, the interaction between the fortunes of regional markets and the distribution of small foundries, and in particular their concentration into a few regions, had a further effect primarily through the power relations between firms. NEDO in a survey of small foundries done in the 1970s

> concluded that the location of a foundry . . . can have an important effect on foundry profitability.
>
> Our questionnaire survey showed us that the biggest concentration of 'craft' foundries was in the West Midlands and in Yorkshire and Humberside, and our detailed studies showed that this level of concentration affected the price structure of individual foundries. Thus foundries with little local competition seemed to get away with relatively inefficient operations because they could afford to charge more; whereas in traditional foundry areas, competition was so intense that it affected the survival prospects of all the local foundries. (1979b, 24)

Put another way, in periods of declining demand foundries that are the sole suppliers for their local areas can take advantage of their monopoly position and charge higher prices. In complete contrast, in those regions where there are lots of small jobbing foundries competition increases and the power of the customer firm in the subcontracting relationship becomes much greater.

The difference in closure rate between large and small factories also raises the question of the influence of organizational structure on the form of rationalization itself. As already intimated, many small foundries are owned by small companies; they are not small units within wider organizations (see, for instance, Farrant 1977, 465). Their higher rate of closure is not due simply, therefore, to lower levels of immediate profitability. It is also a result of their lesser ability to survive a given low level of profitability in a downturn. The industry works closely to customer specifications and in some areas this means that standardization is very difficult. The machine-tool and mechanical engineering markets in general require small-batch production. This does maintain demand for small craft foundries[2] but it also gives them less scope to cut costs and limits their ability to carry, what may be only temporary, losses. Therefore, the structure of capital ownership in the sector considerably influenced the pattern of scrapping away from a 'simple profitability' criterion, and influenced it in such a way that the pattern itself reinforced that structure.

There was another aspect other than straightforward employment loss, to employment change in the iron-castings industry over this period: a faster decline amongst skilled workers than others. As we saw in chapter 5, AUEW membership in the industry declined, especially its skilled membership (NEDO 1974d), and unskilled and semi-skilled workers increased in relative importance, see Farrant 1977; NEDO 1974d; Foundry Industry Training Committee 1978. These sources indicate that the main factor behind this change was the increasing relative importance of large repetition foundries, and the fast decline of the small jobbing firms (see also NEDO 1979b). Other factors included the impact of mechanization within the mould and core-making stage (see chapter 5), though again mainly within larger firms (NEDO 1979b), and a tendency for individual foundries to become increasingly specialized. Given the different reasons for employment decline in different parts of the country, this change in skill balance is unlikely to have been the same in all regions. There are no adequate figures available, but regions with a high proportion of small and/or jobbing foundries at the beginning of the period are also likely to have had relatively high proportions of skilled workers, and to have experienced a loss of many of them over the period. This would have been the case in Yorkshire and Humberside and the North. Other regions, however, which experienced lower levels of job loss, because, perhaps, of the compensatory growth of larger, new and mechanized foundries, may have also suffered a loss of skilled jobs, but in these instances there would have been some employment created for less skilled workers in its place. This may have been the case in the West Midlands. A net figure of employment decline certainly does not tell the whole story.

* * *

The influences on the form of rationalization in the *paper and board industry* were rather different from those in iron castings. First, over the sector as a whole output grew over the period whilst employment fell by an even higher proportion (20 per cent) than in iron castings. Second, geographical factors were of very limited importance in explaining geographical variation. Third, while organizational structure was again significant, its different nature meant that its effects were also different.

Table 7.3   Regional employment changes in paper and board, 1968–73

Region	Absolute change	Percentage change
North	−400	−18.2
Yorkshire and Humberside	−1300	−35.1
East Midlands	−300	−37.1
East Anglia	−200	−33.3
South East	−3500	−13.3
South West	−1800	−26.1
West Midlands	+300	+14.3
North West	−2700	−17.4
Wales	−1200	−37.5
Scotland	−4100	−28.5
Northern Ireland	0	0
UK	−15200	−20.0

Source   Census of Production (see note 1, chapter 6)

The distribution of the national loss of 15,200 jobs in paper and board is set out in table 7.3. As in iron castings, one of the major factors contributing to the geographical variation in employment decline was intra-sectoral differentiation in production. We have already indicated that the paper and board industry consists of a number of different production processes making different commodities. These were subject to different rates of decline over the period, and the fortunes of particular geographical areas therefore reflected the initial composition of employment in terms of these sub-sectors. However, the case is not simply the same as that in iron castings. In iron castings there was both a systematic geographical distribution of the constituent sub-sectors, and a geographical reason (local markets) for that distribution. In paper and board there was little systematic pattern to regional variations in sub-sectoral composition. On balance, therefore, it seems correct to disaggregate the sector before analysing the pattern of rationalization, especially as the different sub-sectors were subject to different rates of scrapping, with one or two even continuing to expand (see chapter 5). Moreover, in all sub-sectors a small amount of labour was lost as a result of measures to increase productivity. The aggregate regional figures in table 7.3 are thus the result of this complicated pattern of geographical and growth variations between sub-sectors.

At this point, in order to avoid such complexity, we shall focus on the newsprint sub-sector, the one which declined most heavily over the period. Newsprint production at the beginning of our period took place in six mills, of which four were in the South East, one in the North West, and one in Yorkshire and Humberside. Moreover, these six mills were owned by three large companies. The structure of the sector in terms of both numbers of plant and of ownership was therefore very different from that in iron castings. And so were the influences on the pattern of rationalization. With such a concentrated ownership structure, and such a discrete pattern of factories, the outcome (which capacity would be closed and which retained) depended heavily on inter-firm differences and strategies. Because of the difficulties of below-capacity working (see chapter 5), it was almost inevitable that certain mills would have to close down altogether while others remained intact. It was unlikely, therefore, that capacity reductions would be shared evenly between existing locations. Neither did regional characteristics play any role at all in the determination of comparative levels of profitability. In the event two mills were closed, one in Yorkshire and Humberside and one in the South East. Some concentration of capacity occurred in the South East with production being transferred from the closed mill to one nearby.[3]

In the standard terminology, Yorkshire and Humberside, for example, thus 'performed' badly. Employment fell by a higher proportion than nationally; but this differential pattern of closure in no way reflects the relative competitiveness of *regions* for the production of newsprint. What it reflects is relative competitiveness between different *companies*, and different strategic decisions made by these companies.

Apart from closures, there was also some loss of labour as a result of attempts to increase productivity in the finishing process (see chapter 5). This was occurring in all parts of the sector, and mainly involved women. For the UK as a whole,[4] the loss of jobs done by women was smaller in absolute terms, but higher proportionately, than losses of jobs for men. The relevant indices for 1973 (1968 = 100) were 71 for women and 83 for men (Department of Employment 1975a). This balance of job losses is likely to have varied between regions. The loss, through productivity increases, of women's jobs in finishing will have occurred in all regions, even where production was retained. But losses of jobs through closure, though involving both men and women, would involve far higher numbers of men. The composition of employment loss in any particular region will, therefore, depend on the combination of processes ('pure' rationalization and cost-cutting) at work.

8

Intensification: the geography of job loss in the outerwear and footwear industries

In chapter 6, we argued that in situations where only intensification is occurring, the 'pure model of geography' would consist of a simple pattern of employment reductions on site. At its simplest, the same strategy might be pursued in factories everywhere. The pattern of job loss would therefore be a straightforward and equal proportionate decline across the country. In practice, however, this is unlikely to be the case. It is much more likely that there will be some differences both between firms and between plants. Such differences may relate either to factors internal to the firm or plant (production character-istics) or to geography. Among the former, production, factors it may be that intensification produces greater job losses in more labour-intensive factories, or that some parts of the industry are under more pressure than others to reduce costs. It may also be that differences in the state of management-union relations either provoke intensification or enable resistance to it. As far as geographical factors are concerned, it may be that there are spatial variations in the pressure on costs, and therefore in the need for cost-cutting measures. Or again the industrial-relations environment may vary spatially, with workers in particularly vulnerable situations being subjected to greater pressures for speed-up.

But it is also unlikely, as we saw in part 2, that intensification will be the only form of production change occurring. Variations in be-haviour may relate to differences in organizational structure. Thus certain firms, because of their size and/or structure may not experience the macro-economic pressures to the same degree, or in the same manner, as the bulk of those within the sector. Very small firms may be forced to close, for instance, while very large ones may be able to avoid the pressures and may possibly expand their market share. Finally, intensification may be mixed with other forms of production change even within each firm in the sector. In a situation where demand/output actually does fall, for instance, some rationalization is likely to occur alongside the on-site reductions in labour within continuing production.

* * *

All of these factors were operative in the case of the *men's and boys' tailored outerwear* industry. At regional level, the distribution of employment change is given in table 8.1. As that table shows, the range of percentage changes over the regions of the country is comparatively small. It is, in other words, not inconsistent with the potential effects of intensification. There is, nonetheless, some indication that something other than intensification was occurring. In particular, three regions show small net gains, indicating the existence of at least some mobile employment. Moreover, from other data sources we know that although the aggregate establishment figures (showing a slight gain over a period in which there was a 6 per

Table 8.1 Regional employment change in men's and boys' tailored outerwear, 1968–73

Region	Net change in employment	Net change as percentage of initial employment
North	−800	−5.8
Yorkshire and Humberside	−900	−3.0
East Midlands	−900	−16.4
East Anglia	+100	+5.6
South East	−2500	−16.2
South West	−200	−8.3
West Midlands	+100	+1.7
North West	−600	−5.5
Wales	0	0
Scotland	+200	+2.9
Northern Ireland	−400	−9.8
UK	−5900	−5.9

Source Census of Production

cent fall in employment) are highly consistent with the importance of intensification, these are net figures and certainly conceal greater, though still relatively small, gross changes.[1]

What else, then, was happening? In fact, two things were going on. First, some firms were continuing to take on more employees, and in some cases this involved opening new factories. Such increases in employment seem largely to have been confined to medium-sized and larger firms which were, in this period, better able to weather the economic storm. With reference to the discussion in chapter 6, it does seem that many of these new locations, therefore, represented expansions of capacity rather than transfers in search of more pliable labour. There is, however, evidence that some such shifts of location did occur, these being more directly related to the process of intensification, reorganization of the workforce being undertaken as part of the move (Birnbaum, Eversley, Clouting, Allard, Hall, Woods, Allen and Tully 1981). In all these cases geographical considerations were necessarily in operation since positive location decisions were involved. The evidence indicates that the main considerations governing location decisions were those of labour cost and labour availability (NEDO 1974a, 47). It is notable, for instance, that all the regions that (in aggregate) were stable or increasing in employment terms had wages below the national average; particularly wages for women. Finally, given that these were the dominant locational considerations, there was one further option open to firms with sufficient capital backing and therefore locational flexibility: to set up production facilities in the Third World (NEDO 1974a, 54) – a process that, as we have seen, continued over the period and contributed to the aggregate decline.

Second, however, there were also some closures. Although this changed in later years (see National Union of Tailors and Garment Workers 1978), it seems that in this period these occurred especially amongst small firms. The pattern was also, however, affected by locational characteristics, and particularly by geographically differentiated cost increases. It seems that these two factors probably combined to produce the heavy losses in the South East, for instance, where especially high cost increases (both wage and non-wage) were a heavy burden on the typically small firms involved in the industry in that region.

Questions of availability and cost of labour were also a geographically differentiating factor within the process of intensification itself. The South East and the East Midlands appear to have suffered particularly badly in this respect – the latter more from the declining availability of female workers than from wage levels – and also larger towns in relation to small ones. All the regions with an above-average level of wages and salaries per worker (North West, Yorkshire and Humberside, North and South East) experienced losses of employment.[2] It should also be noted that the level of wages was closely related to the degree of presence of the industry within a region, with low presence being associated with relatively low wages, and vice versa. This fits in with the fact, referred to earlier, that those firms which were able to expand or establish capacity were doing so in regions that did not have a significant history of employment in this sector. The labour sought by the clothing industry as a whole is mainly young, low-wage, female, unorganized and non-traditional clothing workers:

> The industry recruits largely female labour in competition with the light engineering industry, distribution and the clerical trades. The industry requires as a high or a higher degree of skill as any other employer of female labour without paying higher wages. (NEDO 1974a, 47)

In the men's and boys' tailored outerwear industry, therefore, locational considerations appear to have been of real significance in producing geographical differentiation within the national pattern of employment decline. This happened in a number of ways. First, certain firms were choosing new locations, and were therefore involved in positive location decisions. Second, geographical factors were important in determining the pattern of decline itself, particularly as a result of spatial variation in the pressure on costs. Geographical factors do not, even so, provide a complete explanation of the geographical pattern of employment decline. Organizational structure, and particularly the factor of firm size, was also important in determining variations in levels of growth and decline.

* * *

The *footwear industry* exhibits many of the same features as the outerwear sector. Unlike outerwear, however, footwear over this period suffered an absolute decline in production; sectoral-level output fell by 4 per cent. This inevitably produced a greater pressure for, and in fact a greater number of, actual capacity reductions, including closures, than occurred in outerwear (although the major period of closures was after 1973). There was thus a noticeable element of sectoral-level rationalization alongside the intensification of continuing production. At the same time, however, and in spite of this aggregate decline, there was new investment, and new plants were established. Indeed, of all the industries we looked at where intensification was important, footwear was the one with the highest level of net regional employment gains as a percentage of national employment change. Once again there appears to have been a fairly clear difference in behaviour between large and small firms. As well as the many extremely small firms in the industry, often single-plant and employing, at most, a couple of hundred workers, there are a few large, multi-plant, and international, producers. The behaviour of the two types was very different.

The smaller plants were, in general, more liable to close than the large ones, and the East Midlands and the South East may have lost a higher percentage of jobs than the national average as a result of the differential geographical distribution of this production characteristic. Conversely, some of the major companies continued to expand, and to establish additional new capacity (a process which can only have increased the competitive pressure on the smaller firms); and this, it should be remembered, was in a context of decline, not just in employment but also in output. Further examination of this process revealed an interesting phenomenon: what may be the development of a different use of space by the larger firms in the industry from that typical of the rest. Many of the traditional areas of footwear manufacture were experiencing relative shortages of local female labour for closing. The established sexual division of labour between clicking and closing (see chapter 3) meant that even though it might have been possible to recruit male workers locally (Economists Advisory Group undated, 139) the necessary women workers were not available at the right wages. This relative shortage of women closers caused the siting of that part of the process (closing rooms) in new locations 'well away from the main factory . . . The difficulty in obtaining women closers . . . has been met by normal responses to market forces, that is by taking the work to where labour can be obtained and by offering a higher than average wage' (Economists Advisory Group undated, 134, 201). These new investments were frequently in Development Areas, such as Wales and, most particularly, the Northern region (their higher than average plant size is indirect evidence of this process).[2] This process of production and extension of multi-plant firms also occurs at the intra-regional level. Moseley and Sant give an example from East Anglia (where employment fell by the same proportion as nationally, but where the average factory size was again well above the national); they write:

In 1971 the proportion [of workers in the industry who were female] was almost three-fifths. This, together with the growth of other sources of female employment, especially in the service sector, has helped to give Norwich a high female activity rate compared with surrounding areas, but, at the same time, has made it necessary for growing firms in the shoe industry to look outside Norwich for small pockets of labour. (1977, 70)

In this case, the retention of 'close linkages with parent factories' (p. 70) meant that almost all these branches were located in neighbouring small towns. It is not clear from the above whether this intra-regional expansion has led to the division of the process of production as it has with the major firms at an inter-regional level, but it is clearly a response to similarly locationally differentiated conditions. Moreover, where it has been happening (and it is not a brand new phenomenon), this splitting of the process of production into stages, and their different location according to their various labour requirements is, particularly under recessionary conditions, an option only available to the largest firms, with the most capital behind them, and to the most competitive companies. It is possible, therefore, that an increasing differentiation is beginning to occur within the industry in which firms, on the basis of size and strength, can adopt a different spatial division of labour, and, through being able to make a more effective use of geographical differentiation, further push home their advantage. Once again, on the theme of production change and location change, it is interesting to note that here the new locations are the result of changes in the spatial surface (i.e. the differential rise in the cost and availability of labour) and not the result of changes in the type of worker required, as in cases of technical change.

To sum up: the process of employment decline in the footwear industry was less simply a case of intensification than in outerwear. In particular, this was due to the combination of an absolute decline in production together with the continuing ability of major companies to invest. The result of this was that the national net loss of jobs was distributed about the country relatively unevenly (see table 8.2). The approximate comparisons in table 8.3 show how, even at the regional level, the decline of employment in footwear was far less evenly distributed than in outerwear.

So far, however, we have only looked at the influence of forms of production change other than intensification. But deviations from the sectorally typical form of behaviour only partly explain the geo-

Table 8.2   Regional employment change in the footwear industry, 1968–73

Region	Net change in employment	Net change as percentage of initial employment
North	+800	+16.3
Yorkshire and Humberside	+300	+12.5
East Midlands	−5200	−13.3
East Anglia	−700	−10.1
South East	−2000	−22.7
South West	+400	+4.7
West Midlands	−500	−10.6
North West	−1800	−12.6
Wales	0	0
Scotland	−800	−42.1
Northern Ireland	−100	−4.5
UK	−9600	−10.1

Source   Census of Production

graphical distribution of employment loss in this industry. There was also differentiation in the degree of job loss as a result of variations in the degree of intensification itself. Three factors seem to have been responsible, two of them (labour availability and labour cost) being locational characteristics, the third (plant size) being a production characteristic that was also geographically differentiated in its distribution. Labour availability was clearly an important factor, as it was in clothing. It operated at both inter-regional and intra-regional scales, as did the factor of labour cost. Together they seem to have been responsible for greater pressures on firms in the East Midlands (Economists Advisory Group undated, 35) and the North West, and relatively to have benefited the Development Areas. The Economists Advisory Group suggested 'that firms in the East Midlands, where

Table 8.3   Variability of regional employment change in footwear and outerwear

	Range of percentage changes	Range of absolute changes
Men's and boys' tailored outerwear	−16.4 to +5.6	−2500 to +200
Footwear	−42.1 to +16.3	−5200 to +800

alternative work is more readily available, are more vulnerable to the increasing cost of labour than those in development areas' (undated, 196). Intra-regionally the differences in cost pressures seem to be reinforcing a long-term trend in this industry: a shift away from large and middle-sized towns to smaller settlements. In 1950 there were 54,200 workers employed in London, Leicester, Northampton and Norwich. This amounted to 50 per cent of total employment amongst firms in the British Footwear Manufacturers' Federation. By 1975 the number had dropped to 17,700 and accounted for only 30 per cent. This trend is clearly continuing (Department of Industry 1977, 45). The two factors together were probably influential in the higher than average rate of decline of employment in the South East. The final factor, plant size, was a production characteristic with a systematic regional variation, rather than a locational characteristic, *per se*. Regions where the average factory size was larger than the national average[2] did perform relatively well (the North, the South West and Wales), while the predominance of small plants in the East Midlands and the South East seems to have had a negative effect on the aggregate performance of these regions. Here, however, it is difficult to disentangle the effects of closures and new investment from those of differences in the degree of intensification of the production process.

In conclusion, then, in both these industries the pattern of employment decline resulted from a combination of losses through intensification, closures, new plants and movement. Both organizational structure and geographical factors were significant in determining the form of each of these, and the balance between them. In reference to our questions in chapter 6, it was the combination of a number of mechanisms, not the differential operation of one, which produced the relatively high 'differential components' in these sectors.

9
Investment and technical change: the geography of job loss in the fletton-brick industry

The locational considerations involved when employment decline takes place through investment and technical change are far more complex than in cases of intensification. For one thing, technical change, by definition, always involves taking a positive decision about the location of the new production process. The nature of that decision will depend on the level of output change, on the difference between the locational requirements of the old and new production processes, and on changes in the spatial surface (the available locational possibilities) since the old production process was established. When new technical processes are introduced in a context of output growth, it may be that they are embodied entirely in additional capacity, with all existing production remaining unchanged (or anyway being subject only to small-scale changes). A location decision will therefore, obviously, have to be made about this additional capacity. With static output new production processes will replace old, in order to maintain the same overall capacity levels. In this case, both a positive location decision about the new capacity, and a decision about which existing capacity to scrap, will be involved. The latter is likely to involve the kinds of considerations already indicated under the discussion of rationalization in chapter 7. The positive location decision will also probably entail consideration of whether or not the replacement capacity will be installed on the same site as the capacity which is to be scrapped. This will inevitably depend on a whole range of considerations; for instance, on whether the technical changes in production have altered the locational requirements of the industry. They may mean that a different kind of labour is needed, or that the industry is freed from a requirement that previously tied it to a particular area. It may also, of course, be that the original site has ceased to be a good location, and that new investment presents an opportunity for change. A change in location could be a device on management's part for avoiding trouble with existing unions, especially if the proposed changes in production involve major shifts in labour requirements, and even more especially if the technical change is itself a response to militancy. One important thing to remember here is that a particular 'physical' technology (the system of machinery, etc.) does not of itself determine labour requirements. The number of workers, their organization in relation to the machinery, and their wage levels, all have to be negotiated. It may often be possible for management to achieve lower 'manning' levels at a new factory than in an existing plant where an actual change in employment has to be negotiated with the present workforce. A geographical shift may therefore make the production change not only easier but also more effective, from management's point of view. Once again we see a way in which production and location change may be interdependent. Again, in the late 1960s and the early 1970s, with land prices rising quickly, it was sometimes possible for firms to gain substantial amounts of money from the sale or development of an existing site, especially if it was in a major urban area. Such a consideration could also be an important element in the location decision. Of the industries we looked at, it was probably most important in the case of the brewing industry, where a number of firms moved out of central London. It is in situations such as these, when technical change takes place in a context of locational shift, that the notion of 'in-transit losses' in employment is relevant (see Massey and Meegan 1979a). For the number of jobs lost at the original location is likely to be greater than the number gained at the new site. Finally, in a situation of output decline, new capacity embodying new techniques will always be replacement capacity and scrapping will have to be at a level sufficient not merely to compensate for the new production, but also to reduce capacity below the initial level. But even here, with output falling, there will be potentially mobile employment, and a positive locational decision will have to be made.

This process of new investment together with compensatory scrapping may occur either within a single firm or within a multi-firm sector. The net result will be similar in the two cases in the sense that the new investment, by stealing a competitive advantage, is likely to

170 The Anatomy of Job Loss

force some other capacity out of production (though remember that this may be anywhere within the relevant market area – the resultant closures may occur in a different country from the one where the new investment was made). The two situations may differ, though, in their impact on individual firms. Thus technical change may be introduced by one firm that, perhaps because it is doing well competitively, treats it as a straightforward addition to capacity. The new investment is therefore not complemented by any closures on the part of that firm. But if aggregate demand is growing less than the additional production, closures will have to take place elsewhere, probably as a result of market forces, with the most vulnerable capacity in the industry being closed.

*   *   *

The *brick industry* provides a very clear example of some of these processes in operation. Once again, we shall concentrate on the production of fletton bricks. As we saw in chapter 4, technical change in this sector was very much a 'leading-firm' phenomenon, and was bound up with the strengthening of that position through takeovers. By the end of the period one company (the London Brick Company) accounted for the whole of fletton production, and its investment and scrapping strategy is clearly recorded. In this example we are looking at a fairly simple case, where company and industry were more or less equivalent. As we saw in chapter 4, this was a case where the technical change embodied in new investment had the purpose of cutting costs because of the problem of demand. It is necessary to analyse, therefore, not only the locational characteristics of the new investment, but also the geography of the compensatory closures. Finally, even within the context of one company, other changes in production were going on at the same time with the continued attempt to cut costs on existing sites.

Within the overall fact of employment decline there are, then, three distinct processes going on: 1) the location of new investment; 2) the closure of some works to compensate for the new investment; and 3) cutbacks in jobs in other works as a result of cost-cutting measures. Each of these three processes involves locational considerations in very different ways. All three contributed to the geography of decline in the industry. Let us examine each in turn.

The fact that the siting of new investment involves a positive locational choice implies the operation of 'location factors'. In the case of fletton bricks two huge new works were constructed, and indeed expanded, during the period. A number of different considerations determined their location. In order to achieve sufficient increases in labour productivity to justify them, the works had to be on a massive scale to take advantage of potential economies (see Monopolies and Mergers Commission 1976; see chapter 4 above). This restricted the number of possible locations and also implied that they would have to be situated with access to sufficiently large parts of the national market. Both works were in fact located at Whittlesey in the Peterborough area (see figure 9.1) with good access, not only to the company's established markets in the south, but also to their expanding ones in the North (London Brick Company 1970, 19). The same considerations of transport costs and regional markets, together with the fact that there would have to be compensatory scrapping, also favoured a location where production was already taking place. This factor was reinforced by the advantages to be derived from having a number of works grouped together. Such advantages included, in particular, the possibility of shipping half-made bricks to kilns in other works (see p. 175). Although clearly a geographical consideration, this is a location factor of a different sort, being related entirely to the geography of the systems of production already established by the firm. The existence of land owned by the company, and specifically of used pits in which the new works could be located, was a further incentive to location within existing areas of production. Finally, of course, there was the very basic locational consideration of raw material. By far the most important input to brickmaking, and one which is costly to transport, is clay. The Oxford clay used by the London Brick Company in making flettons has two major advantages. First, it uses 'a process based on the unique qualities of the clay that enables us to produce bricks on a vast scale more cheaply and with less labour than by any other process' (London Brick Company 1968, 21). Second,

> it is worth remembering that over three-quarters of the fuel needed to burn fletton bricks is contained in the Oxford Clay from which they are made, with the result that fletton brickmaking has the lowest fuel cost in production of any manufactured building material. In fact, in our case fuel only represents 5 per cent of the total manufacturing cost. (London Brick Company 1973, 18–19)

Both characteristics are obviously of major importance at a period of both pressure on costs and rapidly rising fuel prices. Moreover, this raw material aspect of production is identical with that in the previous generation of plants, and therefore technical change did not imply any changes in raw-material location factors. This was true

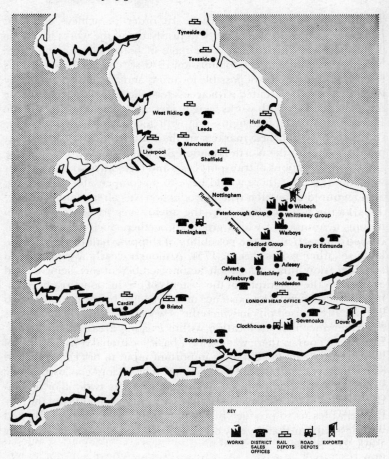

Fig. 9.1   The geography of production and distribution in the London Brick
Company, 1973
Source   London Brick Company 1973, 2

also of the labour employed: although less labour was used it was of a
similar type. This does, however, raise an interesting question concerning, once again, the relationship between production change and
location change. While the technical change in fletton-brick production did not necessarily imply any alteration, such as de-skilling,
in the labour required, it is nonetheless true that the industry was
under cost pressures, and that it had been having some difficulty

finding what it thought of as adequate labour at a suitable price. The 1970 London Brick Company annual report reflected the dual problem for the company of the necessity to pay higher wages to attract labour and of the impact of higher wages on overall costs. A low wage rise in the last year of the Labour Government period of incomes policy had:

> caused growing resentment amongst our employees and made management's task in recruiting and retaining labour more difficult. The new negotiations were preceded by a series of unofficial strikes and there appeared a real danger that the unions would lose control of their more militant members. Whilst, in the final outcome, the increases were well below the original claims put in by the unions, they did represent a substantial advance in the existing rates and by lowering the differential between those paid on piecework and day-work did help the lower paid. The new rates improved our competitive position in the labour market and we were thus helped in recruiting the additional labour required to increase production in the latter months of the year. (p. 20)

Given this, it might have been beneficial for the company to locate the new investment where labour was cheaper and more available, a strategy often pursued in other industries, such as clothing (see chapters 6 and 8). But, because of all the other locational requirements and constraints outlined above, this was not possible. The geographical delimitation of the market and production system for bricks, and the dependence on Oxford clay, meant that production could not be moved to the Third World, or even to a British Development Area. Locationally, it was stuck. Given this, it is interesting to note the strategies that the London Brick Company did adopt. First, since it could not move geographically in search of labour, it found a new reserve of labour where it was – chapter 4 details the increasing use made by the company of immigrant workers. Second, although there is no direct evidence in this particular case, it is worth noting that this is precisely the kind of situation where geographical inflexibility can itself be part of the pressure which provokes changes in production. The lack of ability to shift to more amenable locations may be a contributory cause of production change on site. The new investment was therefore made in existing areas of production, but it did clearly involve a positive location decision. There was potentially mobile employment, and geographical factors – both in relation to the firm's existing system of production and of a more conventional geographical kind – determined the ultimate decision.

But, second, these new investments had to be accompanied by closures, and here the rationalization model already described is relevant. The selection of works for closure was made, above all, on the basis of internal production costs and productivity – in other words, on purely production characteristics. Numerous quotations and examples could be cited in demonstration: the London Brick Company's annual report in 1969 stated

> The lower level of demand and consequently [*sic*] increase of stocks during 1969 forced us to cut overall production by 11 per cent, but we were able to do this by closing down the least efficient kilns and works so that while the closures increased the pressure on our overheads, they did also bring some reduction in overall operating costs in the latter months of the year. (p. 19)

In the same year the smaller of the two Marston works was closed, because, given the level of demand, it was too expensive to run. It 'was not only unmechanized, but was laid out in such a way that it would have proved extremely difficult and costly to convert . . . . We therefore took advantage of the period of lower demand to close [it] down' (p. 19). In the following year

> In the Peterborough area, where the older, smaller units tend to be situated, a weeding-out of the higher-cost works has been carried out with a consequent reduction in costs. Later in the year, as stocks were lifted, several kilns at operating works were re-lit, but no effort was made to re-open marginal works which, in terms of cost, would have lowered our overall production efficiency. (p. 19)

In 1972, production at Yardley, Peterborough was discontinued, the works being a 'higher-cost' one on account of its lack of mechanization. Clearly, the internal nature of production, not in itself a geographical factor, was of prime importance in accounting for the geographical distribution of closures.

Nevertheless, geography did exert some influence on the pattern of closures. First, the highly cyclical nature of demand for bricks can often make it worthwhile expanding production to extra works during upturns. In this case this took place in 1971–2, followed by re-closure in 1973. The system of production in grouped works in different regions enabled great cost savings. Thus the annual report 1971 reported

> a series of measures were taken to re-light kilns and re-open closed works. Cost would have risen unduly had we sought to re-

introduce production to certain of the older, higher-cost works, so ingenious methods were devised to feed their kilns from existing plants. Unburnt bricks, mechanically loaded and unloaded, were transported by road on articulated vehicles specially adapted for the purpose. In this way, the concentration of our works in the Bedford and Peterborough areas was utilized to gain higher output from the larger and more efficient works. (p. 15)

A similar operation was undertaken in 1972, but by autumn 1973 declining demand both put an end to this procedure and led to the closure of some of 'the older and less efficient works which had been temporarily re-opened in 1971 to meet the higher call for bricks at that time' (London Brick Company 1973, 14).

This was again a 'geographical' influence related to the regional organization inside the firm. But more straightforward geographical considerations were also important, and led to modifications to the simple internal production-cost criterion for rationalization. Three factors were important in this way: cost of transport of the output to market, the availability of labour if the existing workforce was dispersed, and the quality of clay. The two quotations which follow illustrate all these considerations. They are taken from the National Board for Prices and Incomes report on fletton production, the first being from an appendix entitled 'A total systems approach to the problems of brick production and transport costs':

In LBC [London Brick Company] there are groups of brickworks at four different locations (Peterborough, Bedford, Bletchley and Calvert). The cost of production at each works is different, the average for each group is different and the cost of transport from each location to each customer's site is different. Even vehicle capacities vary, depending on which works the bricks come from, because of the varying densities of the finished bricks.

An added complication arises from the fact that the zone which is naturally served from the Peterborough area normally contains more demand than the works have capacity. Therefore it is not always possible to adopt the simple rule that customers should be supplied from the nearest available works. Similarly in times of low demand it is not necessarily the best policy to shut down the least efficient works first, since a closure in the Peterborough area might impose extra transport costs on the system such that a closure of a more efficient works in the Bedford area might be a better policy when all costs are taken into account. (1970, 40)

For LBC, with about thirty works, curtailment of production in the face of reduced demand presents a difficult choice between conflicting requirements. Some works cost more to operate than others and ought, on that account, to be closed. However, due regard has also to be paid to the location of works, since transport costs form a high proportion of the delivery price of bricks – on average about a third. Again, in closing down a brickworks and dispensing with the labour force, a firm has to have regard to the prospects of reopening that works and the likelihood of being able to re-man it. Finally, the clay used is not the same everywhere and customers may demand bricks made from clay of a particular colour which is obtainable only from one works which might otherwise be closed. Since costs vary only with relatively large changes in output at any works, reduced production results in higher unit·costs and lower profitability. (1970, 3)

Finally, the major changes in terms of new works and compensatory closures were accompanied by a third process: the continuing improvement of productivity at remaining sites. This included other forms of lower-level technical change at existing works – important mechanization of many of the works took place (London Brick Company 1969, 19; 1970, 20; 1971, 16, 17). It included the standardization of bricks both in general ('standardization of this kind is of great benefit in a mass production process such as our own' London Brick Company 1971, 20), and between the main company and those it had recently acquired (London Brick Company 1969, 19); and it involved various forms of intensification of the work process ('many small schemes were evolved for the re-organisation of work and re-allocation of tasks at different works that made useful contributions to overall productivity' London Brick Company 1968, 22). The first of these would almost certainly have involved cuts in labour, the second two might have been mechanisms directed more towards increasing output, but were likely, nonetheless, to cause labour reductions in the longer term.

On the whole, the pattern of these changes followed that indicated in the discussion of intensification, with some such changes being made on almost all sites. But the fact that on-site changes in production took place in the context of the dominant process of technical change and rationalization did mean that they were co-ordinated with these processes. In other words, the fact that a number of different changes in production are going on together may itself influence how each of them operates individually. Groups of works were assessed and a combined decision made as to which should be closed, which improved, and so on. Thus, for instance, to expand an earlier example, Marston Valley Brick Company, which was acquired by the London Brick Company in 1968, had two plants, and decisions about changes were made considering the two of them together. The smaller of the works, at Marston, was both unmechanized, and laid out in such a way that it would have proved extremely difficult and costly to convert. On the other hand, the larger works at Ridgmont, which had already been partly mechanized, was capable of much greater production and efficiency if the necessary investment in money and 'know how' was applied. The company 'therefore took advantage of the period of lower demand to close down Marston works and to concentrate our efforts on completing the mechanization and modernization of the larger plant at Ridgmont' (London Brick Company 1969, 19). The next year's annual report commented on the completion of this programme:

> Not only has [Ridgmont] now become the second largest brickworks in the world, with an output comparable to the previous total production of Ridgmont and Marston works combined, but with the benefit of complete mechanization, costs have been held and productivity raised. (London Brick Company 1970, 20)

During the next year 'by concentrating our resources on modernizing and expanding production at Ridgmont and closing down the unmechanized works at Marston, more bricks are now produced at lower man hours per thousand than previously' (London Brick Company 1971, 17). Once again, therefore, the pattern of job loss was a response both to geographical factors and to factors internal to production.

The pattern of job loss in the fletton-brick industry was thus the result of three different things: closures, new plants and on-site cutbacks. Technical change, with its associated closures and new plant, certainly dominated, but other losses occurred through increases in productivity at existing works. In each of the three contributory elements of the overall pattern, geographical and locational factors played a different role. They were clearly and straightforwardly important in the location of new investment. In the decision as to which plants to close, they were combined with more purely production characteristics, but locational considerations were still important, particularly in regard to access to the market (since capacity was being closed down). In the losses of jobs resulting from changes in the production process on site, geography was least important, and when questions of location were significant they tended to relate, above all, to the internal geographical structure of the firm.

It must be stressed again that these characteristics are not meant to be simply generalized. What they are meant to emphasize is the danger of considering employment decline as a single, and fairly simple, process of job loss.

Part 4
Conclusions

10
The anatomy of job loss

There are, then, many ways that jobs can be lost, many ways in which the demands of production for profit can lead to employment decline.

The methodological aim of this study has been to take an important, and an apparently simple, phenomenon, employment decline, and to disentangle some of its complexity. We have tried to show how the causes lying behind this phenomenon may be many and varied, and we have examined some, but by no means all, of the possible mechanisms. We have also tried to show how these different causal mechanisms may in turn have different implications, in terms of both economic processes and geographical patterns.

The argument started from the point that employment changes are, arithmetically, the net result of two other movements: changes in output and changes in productivity. In relation to the industries studied here, in all of which employment was declining, this means that the loss of jobs could be due to either or both a downward movement in output and an upward movement in productivity. This point has been amply illustrated in practice in the industries considered in the preceding chapters. In spite of the fact that we were mainly examining industries at the lower end of the output-growth spectrum, considerable contrasts emerged. In the industries where rationalization was dominant, while iron-castings output fell by 4 per cent and employment by 18 per cent, in paper and board, where output over the whole mlh actually grew by 2 per cent, employment fell by an even higher proportion: 20 per cent. There were, amongst the industries studied, even occasions where such differences occurred within one sector but between regions. The iron-castings industry presented a clear case of this. While it recorded the highest rate of job loss in Wales, this region had the second best ranking in output terms; the loss of jobs was entirely the result of increases in labour productivity. In the Northern region a lower percentage loss of jobs (in other words a relatively better employment performance) was in contrast associated with the worst fall in output – completely the opposite picture to that of Wales.

So output decline (and profits decline – though the numbers are hard to come by at this level of definition) and employment decline are clearly different phenomena and should be treated as such. Employment decline is not equivalent to a failure of accumulation. To assume such an equivalence is to assume also a common interest between labour and capital.

But the real point is that behind these different output/employment relationships are different mechanisms – different strategies for changes in production in order to maintain profitability – any of which may result in a net loss of jobs.

As we have tried to show, each of these mechanisms is part and parcel of the process of production for profit. Intensification and technical change are both responses, in the most general sense, to the fact of competition between firms within an industry and the various forms of pressure which that can produce: to cut costs, to produce a more technologically sophisticated product, to gain greater control over the workforce. Both are also ways of maintaining profits to make continuing production in that industry worthwhile from the company's point of view. Rationalization may be sparked off by the failure of these strategies, as investment is shifted elsewhere in the search for more lucrative returns (whether these be from another sector of production, from property speculation, or from playing the money market). The need for each form of production change, in other words, is stimulated by, and defined by, the process of production for profit. Each too, therefore, is a means of sustaining or restoring profitability.

But although the different forms of production change we have looked at are distinct kinds of responses, they are also closely linked. Cost-cutting measures may be attempted before rationalization and closure is resorted to. Technical change in one industry, or one part of an industry, may cause closure elsewhere. The competitive battle of cost-cutting may force other companies out of business altogether. We have been looking at some of the responses of UK-based industry during the late 1960s and early 1970s – at the response of industries in one country to a changing international situation. This was the period when much of UK industry was beginning to feel the effects of the end of the long boom, of relative uncompetitiveness, and of the changing international organization of production. The way this fed through to the different industries, and the spatial levels at which it operated, varied from case to case. Direct international competition within an industry was perhaps clearest in the case of outerwear, but it was also important in newsprint production. In these industries the cost-cutting (in the case of outerwear) and the cutbacks (in the case of newsprint) were the response of UK-based industry to a changing wider situation in the sector itself. In contrast, in brickmaking, where international competition was not a direct factor, the pressures for change were filtered more through the slowdown of the UK economy as a whole. In iron castings, as we have seen, the impact of this national economic slowdown produced different pressures and responses even between different regions of the country.

Such variations and links between the different processes need not, of course, be organized spatially. The main lines of competitive advantage and disadvantage may be between different kinds of companies. Continued expansion by strong firms may force closure on weaker ones – 'British industry' is not a coherent entity. The clothing industry once again provides a good example. Geography was clearly important. Companies operating in very low-wage countries had a clear cost advantage, and it was that which in general caused problems for companies producing in the UK. But not all companies were equally affected, and the ability of some to continue to expand increased the pressures on the rest. (Nor, of course, should it be assumed that 'British industry' is the same as 'companies producing in Britain'. Some of that 'foreign competition' was from production owned and controlled by UK firms which had themselves been able to move their production to cheaper-labour areas.)

The different kinds of production change leading to job loss are therefore linked; all are integral to the wider system of competitive production for profit. But to say that is not to say that they are inexorably determined by some abstract 'logic of capitalist development', or by the demands of the macro-economy. The production process is a social process involving relations between different companies, between different groups of workers, and, above all, between management and workforce. The external pressures of, say, the changing international economic situation, do not of themselves determine what will happen in the office or factory. The actual outcome of those pressures will depend both on the character of capital and labour and on the state of play between them. The strength and organization of labour is clearly important. A militant workforce may be what provokes, or what prevents, changes in production. The character of capital can be equally important. As we have seen there are sections of capital and management in British industry which are both ill-equipped and disinclined to embark on major changes.

Similarly, one crucial element in the analysis has been the nature of, and changes in, the labour process. Our detailed studies included a number of changes in production which 'conformed to expectations' concerning the long-term development of the labour process under a capitalist economic system. The notion of 'labour process' is being increasingly suggested for use in studies of industrial location and regional development. The studies presented here enable some comments to be made on how such concepts can be used in practice. In many studies, changes in the labour process are characterized in terms of major waves and phases, as, for instance, 'scientific management and Fordism' succeed 'modern industry', and are in turn superseded by 'neo-Fordism'. One thing that is immediately clear from our studies is that the actual identification of such forms, and in particular their association with different parts of capital, is a far from simple matter. Some fairly obvious associations can be made (see, for instance, the footwear and outerwear case studies), but the overall picture is extremely complex. Not only are there big differences within sectors (Elger 1979), which can easily be dealt with, there are also variations within one overall production process. Such diversity is, of course, one of the conditions for the presently increasing tendency for production to be split up between different locations. This geographical disaggregation of the production process is not always possible, however, and in such cases there can be no simple correlation between labour process and location. The enormous contrasts within newsprint production are an obvious example. Further, the actual shifts between labour processes do not, of course, take place in great leaps, either within existing industries or through the development of new industries. The process of change is constant, and often incremental. The causes of such differences and changes must therefore be specified, and related to particular characteristics, to specific pressures and stimuli. Calling something an 'immanent tendency' is not an adequate specification of cause in any particular real situation. The actual process of change is in each case specific and particular. At any one time there may be moves in completely opposing directions (there was some evidence that this was the case with 'group work' in the industries studied here, particularly clothing, with some companies adopting it as a strategy and others abandoning it). The actual reasons for changes in particular labour processes, the nature of those changes, and the degree of their success for management, can not, therefore, be explained on the basis of 'the logic of capitalist development'. As a number of our case-studies made clear, the whole process is very much the product of a continual battle between management and labour. As such, the outcome is always to some extent in doubt.

* * *

Moreover, it is not only within the individual company or workplace that the state of play between capital and labour is important. Levels of pay settlements, the 'availability' of labour, the ability and willingness of a workforce to resist the imposition of changes, depend also on the state of those relations at a wider level. The period we have been examining was one in which productivity bargaining and the attempt to 'reorganize British industry' and update production techniques were national issues; ones, too, which caused divisions within both capital and labour. We have seen, for instance, how one element of the government's attempted solution to national economic problems – to cut back on wage increases – rebounded to the detriment of weaker firms in consumer-goods sectors. The outcome of such strategies at a wider level influences the balance of forces in the office and on the factory floor.

Indeed, of course, the very fact of job loss itself both changes the state of play between capital and labour and leads to very different kinds of conflict. The very fact of employment decline, and of increasing levels of unemployment, can weaken the bargaining power of labour and force it to accept more losses. Indeed, the different mechanisms of job loss can interact. The threat of rationalization and the awareness of closures occurring in other parts of an industry, can increase management's chances of pushing through other forms of production change that are designed to increase productivity but which may worsen the working conditions of employees and/or themselves lead to further job loss. Not only increased pressure in the face of worsening economic conditions but also increased ability due to the shift in the balance of power towards management and away from the workforce may mean, therefore, that there are more attempts to change existing production processes in times of retrenchment than there are in periods of growth.

Within an individual company, each of the different kinds of production change we have discussed (and there are plenty of others) tends to relate rather differently to management/worker relations. While changes of the intensification type may often be a response to low-level conflict (such as absenteeism, as in the outerwear case-study), it is actually less likely to be attempted when a workforce is well organized and militant (which, of course, is precisely why a locational shift to another kind of workforce may be seen as an alternative). Quite the opposite is likely to be the case with rationalization; the criteria for closure may well include the strength of organization of the labour force, with the most militant being the most vulnerable. Technical change is different again. Not only may the stimulus to technical change, and its timing, be conditioned by, say, an inability to hold down wages sufficiently (as, possibly, in the brick industry), or by struggles within the workplace, but so also may its form and its geography (whether the new investment is made on the old site or elsewhere).

Moreover, because the different types of job loss are related in different ways to the overall system of production for profit, they also tend to lead to different kinds of conflict, over different issues, and posing different problems for the workforce. Essentially, the different kinds of production change raise, as issues, different aspects of the social relations of production in a capitalist society. With intensification, although it clearly varies from case to case, in general the battle is essentially over control of the existing work process, over established rules and procedures, over the organization of daily life in the workplace.

With rationalization, especially where it involves the closure of whole factories, the battle is very different. Perhaps one of the least-challenged rights that derive from the private ownership of the means of production, is the power *not* to produce. The question is how that should be challenged. As we have seen, rationalization may occur for many different reasons, and under many different conditions. Probably those cases that make most headlines are where the capacity closed down is still profitable. Such a strategy seems easy to challenge for its 'irrationality'. In fact, of course, it is not irrational, as we have seen. A shift to a form of investment with an even higher rate of profit is excellent capitalist rationality. Moreover, to argue that a closure is 'wrong' simply because the firm got its sums wrong (the plant does really make a profit), or because it is agreed that production there is still profitable, is implicitly to accept that lack of profitability *is* an adequate justification for closure. Similar distinctions and difficulties arise in relation to different company structures. When factory closure also entails the bankruptcy of a company, the case seems irrefutable. It seems less so when the plant is part of a much larger, and overall profitable, industrial empire. Certainly these different conditions under which rationalization can occur, make a lot of difference to what kind of resistance, and how much, can be raised. Yet all these different cases are reflections of the same overall process, the search after profit. To challenge the kind of rationalization we have been looking at here, it is necessary to challenge the criterion of profit itself.[1] A number of different kinds of challenge have been developed. One is to conduct a 'social audit'; this takes account not just of profit and loss to the company, but also of the social costs involved in closure – costs that will fall on the State (loss of tax revenue, liability to extra unemployment and social security payments, etc.), and wider social costs falling on the community. The implication of taking into account both private and social costs and benefits is that private profit cannot be the sole criterion for whether or not production takes place. That, in turn, may mean challenging private ownership. A rather different version of this approach has been proposed in the USA, with attempts to get legislation passed to force the company itself to pay some, at least, of the social costs which its closure will incur (see, for instance, Bluestone and Harrison 1980; New American Movement 1981; Coalition to Save Jobs 1979). Both of these strategies remain within a calculation concerning the individual plant, and the second is most applicable in cases of multi-plant companies which are closing or moving only part of their operations. Another approach is to argue that the products being produced, while not necessarily profitable, are socially useful, or that the plant and the skills of the workforce could and should be turned over to making socially useful products. The Lucas Aerospace Alternative Plan is probably the best-known such initiative (see, for example, Wainwright and Elliott 1982).

In cases where it is technological change that is the occasion for job loss, the difficulty is that technology itself may come to be seen as 'the enemy', and the defence of jobs turn into a Luddite intransigence. But as we have seen, even at the level of the individual plant it is not the simple fact of productivity increase that is the cause of job loss, but the relation between productivity increase and the rate of growth of production. The real questions, as with rationalization, are much broader. The issue is not whether to implement technological change or not, but what kind (see, for example, Council for Science and Society 1981). Technological change can eliminate boring jobs, or it can reduce work to mindless repetition. It can result in unemployment or it can create new opportunities. Recent technical change in the printing industry has done the former, but it could provide the chance for a wider, freer press – for instance through having publically available and cheap printing facilities. Once again the question is, on what criteria production is to be justified and organized.

The different forms of production change can also have the effect of dividing the workforce in various ways. The divisions provoked by intensification are most likely, as we have seen, to be between different groups of workers within one plant. It is unlikely for this management strategy to pit one factory against another. But conflicts and competition between workers in different factories are very possible in both the other forms of production change. Both rationalization and technical change can lead to situations in which groups of workers in different regions can be played off against each other.[2] In other words, rationalization and technical change, unlike intensification, enable space itself to be used as a means of dividing the workforce. There are also, moreover, differences in the way in which this can happen in each case. In rationalization, the potential divisions will be over the question of which factory is to be closed. There have been many recent examples of workers in one factory being 'accused' of having a lower productivity than those in others, and therefore being threatened with redundancy. Recent arguments over closures by the British Steel Corporation (consequent upon both rationalization and technical change) have sometimes implicitly degenerated into questions of *which* works was to be closed, rather than over the shape and role of the steel industry as a whole. In some recent cases attempts have been made to overcome these problems. For instance, the last proposed round of capital reorganization in the electricity-generating machinery industry in the UK had all the elements of a battle between those in the North East of England (in one company) and those in the North West (in the other) over fears of redundancies should rationalization ensue. An attempt was made at shop-floor level to overcome this divisiveness by establishing a Power Engineering Committee to cover the industry as a whole. To mitigate the problems of declining demand the committee urged the nationalized Central Electricity Generating Board (CEGB) to maintain a steadier ordering pattern and moved towards the development of alternative products, including, for instance, those based on the joint production of heat and power. To help overcome the competition between the two groups of workers, it was suggested that in future orders should be distributed according to employment needs, rather than through competitive bidding.

The way worker may be pitted against worker in a situation of technical change combined with locational change is rather different from cases of rationalization alone. With technical change, employees in the region where the existing technique is located may see new production with new techniques being established elsewhere. In a period of output growth, this may not involve compensatory scrapping, but in a period of decline it will be combined with closures of existing factories. In the 1960s and 1970s in the UK, there were many cases of companies closing factories in conurbations in the central regions of the country and opening new ones, based on new production techniques, elsewhere, particularly in the Development Areas. Moves of that kind helped produce a hostility towards regional policy and the regions in receipt of it, amongst those in the inner cities of the Midlands and South East who saw their jobs disappearing.[3] That combination of production and location change was an important element in shaping the policy debate as 'inner cities versus regions', and thus in weakening the arguments against overall levels of unemployment.

* * *

One of the reasons why different kinds of production change imply different dangers in terms of dividing the workforce, is that they have different geographical implications. The conclusion both of our arguments and of the empirical studies, is that it is necessary to analyse the 'mechanisms behind the numbers' before an adequate explanation of the geography of employment decline can be constructed. We have examined three such mechanisms; there are others, and we have referred to some of them. The general point is that it is necessary to understand production for it to be possible to understand geography.

But to say that does not mean that there is some unique correlation, and necessary distinction, between these different processes and their resultant geographical distributions. As we have stressed, the processes will never operate in a 'pure form', and the industries in which they occur will vary widely. But correlation is not necessary to explanation. What we are arguing here, is that it is important to analyse these different processes of change within production, both because they are the means by which the changes in the geography of employment occur and because it is through them that these changes can be linked to their fundamental causes, which lie in the organization of production. Nonetheless, as argued in part 3, each of the different mechanisms of change does have different broad locational implications and its own rules for geographical differentiation. Rationalization will, by definition, see more closure of capacity; technical change will always produce at least some potentially mobile employment; different processes will have different impacts in terms of the kinds of workers affected.

Further, 'location factors' – that is, in a broad sense, the influence of geography itself – vary both in their degree of importance and in the way in which they operate, depending on the overall process in which they are embedded.

We have, for example, made a distinction between geographical and non-geographical influences on the spatial pattern of employment change. Although very rough and ready, this is an important conceptual distinction to bear in mind, particularly when studying employment decline. Whereas in situations of employment growth there is always a positive locational decision (even if implicit), this is not so in a situation of job loss. A range of different instances occurred in the empirical studies presented here. In cases of rationalization or intensification it is possible for geographically differentiated patterns of employment change to result from processes in which location as such does not figure at all. Of the four cases examined, this was more or less true of one: paper and board. In the other three industries, non-geographical characteristics of production combined with specifically geographical characteristics to determine the spatial pattern of employment change. The same was true of the rationalization and intensification that occurred alongside the major technical change in the brick industry. But in cases of such technical change itself, there is always (definitionally) a positive location decision to be made. The same, of course, applies to the positive location decisions made by firms that continue to expand in otherwise declining sectors. This phenomenon was very clear in both cases of intensification where only the larger firms were able to take advantage of the changing relation between the requirements of production and the spatial surface (the locational opportunities available), and secure more advantageous locations (simply because being better able to survive they could increase their share of the market and even continue to expand).

This leads to a second point. For not only did the industry cases provide examples of the possibility of location factors varying in importance between different situations, they also illustrated how such factors can operate in different ways, in different combinations, with other, non-geographical variables. This again will depend on what is happening in production. In situations of technical change, location factors may be important in determining the geography of the new investment but not have any influence on which capacity is closed. The range of different possibilities was made particularly clear in the analysis of changes in the brick industry in chapter 9. Again, the same locational factor can have different implications for the behaviour of different firms within the same industry. This was the case in clothing and in footwear where increased costs forced closure on some small firms, increased the pressure for intensification in others, but for larger firms, surviving more easily, merely influenced the location of their new investment.

To argue, then, as we just did, that to explain the geography of employment change it is necessary to understand what is going on in production, is not to say that the two spheres are distinct: first one analyses production and only then does one analyse its spatial form. The two are, in fact, inextricably linked. One of the recurring subthemes of our argument is the integral relation between production change and locational change. Put another way, it is not just that geographers need to understand something of what happens in production, but that economists and those studying production also need to see that a company's locational strategy can be as much a part of its production planning as the, perhaps more obvious, changes in organization on the shop-floor. Not only may geographical factors be bound up with production change in different ways, but locational possibilities and geographical changes can also influence what happens in production. We saw in chapter 3 how variations between different regions of the UK in the job market for women produced differential pressure for cutting back on labour costs. In some cases it provoked a change of location. In others, that kind of locational response to geographically differentiated conditions of production may not be possible. This was true, as we saw, of the brick industry. The lack of geographical flexibility in that case forced other responses on the company: it adopted cost-cutting measures and, most importantly, sought out a cheaper labour force on site; finally it opted for major technical change. Had it been able to shift location and lower costs that way, the changes in production might not have been so necessary.

* * *

All these considerations raise questions about methodology, and in particular about some of the approaches at present frequently adopted for the analysis of the geography of employment. Take first the approach known as 'components of change analysis'. This disaggregates employment change into its gross components, such as plant birth, death, expansion, contraction, immigration and emigration. It is argued that 'conceptually, the significance of component analysis of spatial manufacturing change lies in the possibility of quite different forces occasioning different trends in different components over the same period' (Keeble 1976, 116). Our studies contain some examples where such a distinction may be important. But they also contain cases where the simple identification of components would not necessarily lead in the direction of explanation. One example has already been referred to in the discussion of rationalization, where it was pointed out that reductions in capacity do not always show up as complete closures. Production can easily be reduced on a site, particularly a major one, without a closure being recorded. But what then would be the basis for making any conceptual distinction between contraction and closure? Both could be the product of exactly the same forces. Of course, it could be that this is accepted, and closures and contractions classified together. But then what of the fact that some contractions in employment may be the result, not of a cut-back in production at all, but of on-site increases in productivity with the same or even increased output being produced? In other words, not only may the same stimulus produce similar responses in a number of different components (which could then be classified together in any *explanatory* categorization), but also each of the components may relate to a whole number of different processes. And these in turn may represent responses to very different pressures, and have different implications for the economic health of the region concerned.[4] Such components, in order to figure in any explanation, would have to be further disaggregated. The question is: do such components relate to explanation at all? What is the theoretical status of 'a closure' or a 'contraction'? We would argue that, although such classification may be a useful way in to analysis through descriptive disaggregation, it *is* only descriptive. In order to explain, it is necessary to go directly to the forces and mechanisms actually in operation.

Similar questions are raised as to how one should interpret the results of shift-share analysis, in particular in cases of employment decline. First, assuming that a division has been made between national, structural and differential components, it is clear that the differential component may be a result either of the geographical/ locational characteristics of the area in question, or simply of the internal production characteristics of the industries *in* that area. In the latter case, although possibly related in some more general sense to location – for instance to the location decisions of a previous period

– the characteristics are not in an immediate way geographical. The distinction is important. 'Geographical' characteristics may have implications for the more general competitiveness of the area in question, an assessment which may have a bearing on the location of future investment there. But if it is production characteristics that have resulted in this systematic locational pattern then no such implications follow. The non-structural component, in other words, may refer to 'local' characteristics, but these need in no way be 'locational'. As is commonly acknowledged, they may, indeed, rather refer to other dimensions of industrial structure. Both of the rationalizing industries discussed in chapter 7 present clear examples of this.

Moreover, once this distinction has been made, and the genuinely geographical elements of the differential component have been separated from those of production, there may still be differences in implications and interpretation between the various geographical factors. Even the few detailed studies presented here have indicated the existence of a variety of types of location factor, each with different implications for the interpretation of the economic health of an area. Each, too, as with the distinction between geographical and production factors, is differently amenable to influence through policy. First, there are the obviously geographical characteristics of a particular area: level of wages, availability of labour, geology. Large negative differential components accounted for by factors such as these may – although this will depend on the locational demands of prospective incoming industry – have implications for the future economic competitiveness of the area. In that sense, they represent a genuinely locational component. Second, however, decline in a region may be greater than nationally, i.e. there is a negative differential component, as a result of a local negative multiplier effect. A case of this was presented in the discussion of iron castings. Here the reasons for relatively high levels of decline lay in the economic structure other than in the industry concerned. In the case of the iron-castings industry in the Northern region of England the above-average employment decline was a result of the region's concentration (i.e. high structural component) in other industries that were collapsing. In that case, the high rate of job loss was clearly a result of the region's structure, with consequently different kinds of implications for any future incoming industry. Third, and with different implications again, there are those location factors, exemplified here by the brick industry, that relate primarily to the existing geography of a particular firm – to the geographical organization of its system of production. These points are not new, but they emerge perhaps more clearly from studies of decline than from studies of growth, since the role of location *per se* in decline is more complex and variable.

Finally on this issue there is the problem of making the distinction in the first place between the national, structural and differential elements in employment change. Two aspects of this have been illustrated by the analysis in the preceding chapters. First of all there is a difference implicit in the very means by which employment change takes place. The fact that rationalization is a much 'lumpier' process than intensification, and that it is likely to be less evenly distributed over space (see chapter 6), implies that differential components are likely to be higher in relation to structural components than they are in cases of intensification. Thus, there may well be differences in the degree of geographical variation in employment change which result entirely from the mechanism through which that change occurred, and without there being any corresponding degree of geographical variation in the conditions of production.[5]

What the argument indicates is the danger of using shift-share techniques as explanation, of equating a statistical disaggregation with causal mechanisms, of arguing that the method

> identifies two main influences: (i) that change *resulting from national economic trends* working through the particular mix of industries (or 'industrial structure') in each area; and (ii) the remaining variation which is change relative to the national average and is *not caused by* differences in the mix of industries. (our emphases) (Fothergill and Gudgin 1979, 160)

Like components of change, shift-share components are useful descriptive statistics. They may indicate where to look for explanation but they cannot do the job of explanation itself.

Similar problems of interpretation may apply within any one form of production change. Here, the organizational structure of the industry and the nature of the production process may be crucial factors. An industry with five plants, each employing a hundred workers and distributed between five regions of a country, is faced with the problem of excess capacity. Twenty per cent of capacity must be scrapped. The high level of capital-intensity and the continuous-process nature of production mean that it is impossible to run plants much below full capacity. Equal proportionate decline across regions is therefore not to be expected. One plant is therefore closed, one region loses all its production and employment, the other regions retain all theirs. This is not a crazy example; it is very much what happened during the rationalization of the paper and board industry (chapter 7). The 'expected' levels of employment loss in such a case are in fact, therefore, most unlikely! What sense does it then make, in terms of explanation, to divide the employment loss from that closure into national, structural and local components?

The danger of all these kinds of techniques is that they can encourage a tendency to reduce questions of causal mechanisms to ones of quantitative description.

One effect of examining mechanisms rather than aggregate numbers, is that it raises in acute form questions of disaggregation and of sectoral definition. In our own case, detailed (mlh level) sectoral categories were adequate for the initial working identification of important forms of production change; but it was clear with the more detailed studies that there was much significant and systematic variation within industries – and not just as a result of product differentiation. Indeed in chapter 2 it was noted that of the approximately sixty industries we were examining in the larger project, it was in many cases not possible to make any statements about particular forms of behaviour in sectors as a whole. We were perhaps lucky to find as many examples of relatively coherent behaviour, or at least cases where particular forms of production change were clearly important, as we did.

What the studies have done, however, is indicate much about the variations within industries (even at mlh level), and about possible alternative, or additional, lines of disaggregation of the economy. Within the sectors, the importance of company size and structure stood out clearly. In outerwear and footwear the differences between large and small firms, and in the social nature of capital, were a more significant differentiator within each industry than was the product differentiation between them in influencing the nature of a company's response in terms of both production reorganization and location strategy. There were similar differences within iron castings. Again, among the characteristics that were influential in conditioning the kind of production change undertaken during this period, three emerged as particularly significant: the place of the industry in the overall structure of the economy, the nature of the dominant labour process, and the organizational structure of capital. Footwear and outerwear were clearly affected in specific ways by the recession as a result of their position as producers of consumer goods. Iron castings and bricks, on the other hand, responded to the general level of industrial investment and production rather than to aggregate consumer income. These differences were combined with others. In the cases studied here, the kind of production process and the organization of capital were closely linked. The low level of development of the labour process in footwear and outerwear is integral to the fact that they are old consumer-goods industries that continue to be dominated by small and old-fashioned capital. Putting all these characteristics together may enable more coherent divisions of the economy to be defined. It is clear, for instance, that industries such as these, traditionally large employers of female labour, and not primarily within Development Areas, have suffered in cost terms from increased pressure in the market for female labour in other parts of the economy. And here the nature of the capital involved becomes of crucial importance, especially in relation to locational strategy. As was pointed out, while small firms and their workers suffered fairly dramatic cutbacks, some of the larger firms were able to continue to expand by taking advantage of other potential sources of female labour, particularly in the peripheral areas of the country. The inter-regional effect of this was, of course, to contribute to the famous convergence of manufacturing employment levels between Development Areas and the rest of the country during this period. In footwear, the initial distribution of the industry was biased towards non-assisted areas, so that even a spatially undifferentiated decline would have affected these areas more seriously. But decline was not undifferentiated. Both the distribution of net losses at regional level and the distribution of net gains resulted in a shift of employment balance towards the Development Areas. In the case of outerwear, there was a much heavier initial representation in the assisted areas but these regions both suffered less than their share of losses and took more than their share of net regional employment gain. Both industries were thus, in aggregate, part both of the convergence of the period and of the growth in Development Areas of jobs traditionally done by women. But this aggregate result was, in fact, the outcome of two different processes in which the larger individual companies in the sector pursued strategies more akin to those of similar firms in other sectors, such as light engineering, than to the small individual proprietorships within the same industry. The initial definition of categories for the study of industrial location is clearly an issue which deserves more study.

It would be wrong, however, to suggest that, because certain constellations of these characteristics correlated with particular forms of behaviour in the late 1960s and early 1970s, they will always do so. Empirical findings in a particular time and place are not the basis for constructing immutable laws. The attempt to construct such laws at all is, indeed, extremely suspect. In this sense, the impetus of our work is different from that concerning, for instance, closures, which has appeared in recent geographical literature. Thus, O'Farrell writes:

> There is no existing body of theory which outlines the causal variables of plant closure. The present study is innovatory in that it attempts to systematically test a series of hypotheses relating survival or closure of an enterprise to its date of establishment, projected employment size, manufacturing group, organizational type, nationality of major shareholders, and regional and town size location. (1976, 434)

We take a different approach. While many of the variables we use in explanation will be the same as in such studies – the influence of the degree of capital intensity, or age-specific cost pressures, or size of firm – we do not expect there to be any potentially discoverable 'laws' governing their influence. The impact of age, of capital structure, of labour processes, and so on, will vary according to economic and political circumstances. To take one example: even in the few years since the end of our study period the relationship between small firms and technical change has altered considerably. Many of the newer developments in automation have been specifically geared to adoption by small companies; the 'technical page' of the *Financial Times* in recent years has carried numerous examples. The aim of this study has not been to produce law-like conclusions which can then be 'applied' in other times and other places. The aim has been to go some way towards elaborating some of the mechanisms of job loss, in a way which may be useful in understanding other situations. The period from the late 1960s to the early 1970s turns out, in fact, to have been an extremely instructive one. Understanding what was going on then throws a lot of light on what has been happening since.

11
Implications and issues

Since the end of our study period employment decline in the UK has continued, indeed in many ways it has become worse. In what way, then, do the analyses here, and in particular the approach to analysis, aid the understanding of what has been happening since the mid-1970s?

One notable feature of this period has been the decline of regional policy. This is not just part of the withdrawal into 'monetarist' politics since the mid-1970s; it is a longer-term trend than that: commitment to regional policy was declining relatively for much of that decade (see, for example, Cameron 1979). In other words, as national unemployment has increased, and the areas that are hard hit have covered more and more of the country, the tendency has been for the government increasingly to abdicate responsibility for the geographical distribution of what jobs there are.

To a large extent the rationale put forward for this withdrawal has been technical. It is argued that an active regional (or other spatial) policy is less feasible because there is very little mobile, or potentially mobile, employment available to be steered towards areas of high unemployment. The reason given for this is that manufacturing employment is declining. This overall conclusion is not in dispute – there is certainly less employment where the location can be influenced or planned – but the situation is more complicated than appears from this argument.

First, manufacturing employment has been declining in the UK since 1966. In other words, it has been declining for most of the period when regional policy has been in operation, including the period in which it is claimed to have been most successful. Employment decline in itself, then, is not an adequate argument for withdrawal by the government from any socially oriented spatial or locational policy. The case-studies presented here confirm that, even in industries where employment is declining, there may still be potentially mobile investment and employment. Indeed, one of the industries that contributed most to the decentralization of jobs to the peripheral regions during the second half of the 1960s was clothing, an industry that at the same time was losing employment nationally at a rate of over 3000 jobs a year. Our studies here of outerwear and footwear give some indication of the sources of this mobility in the context of decline. There is certainly less mobile employment in a period of national decline, but there is some.

Second, however, our case-studies have also indicated that this potentially mobile employment is more likely to occur under certain circumstances than others. Given the overall reduction in mobile investment, it is particularly important that these circumstances are understood. The fact that there may be *some* potentially mobile employment even under conditions of overall employment decline is indicated by the basic point that employment and output need not move in the same direction. While output continues to rise, even while employment falls, new investment will be possible, in combination with employment losses (either total or partial) at existing locations. Whether or not the mobile employment is generated will depend on the actual mechanisms in operation, in other words on what is happening to production. Taking first the range of logical possibilities, it is clear that definite differences exist between the three mechanisms examined here in terms of their likelihood of generating potentially mobile employment. In a pure case of intensification no such employment would be generated and locational policies are therefore unlikely to be of use. In rationalization it is unlikely, but some production and employment may well be shifted around as part of a reorganization within a multi-plant firm cutting back (for example, concentrating on major plants, see chapter 7). In paper and board, for instance, the newsprint closure in the South East was accompanied by the transfer of some of the closed plant's production to another mill in the same region. This, however, is not mobile employment in a full sense; it is restricted mobility. Its destination is already determined by a site that already exists. Indeed the very fact of mobility is predicated on knowing this destination. This is mobile production, and possibly employment, but not mobile new investment. Thus, although geographical shifts in employment patterns may result, the movement is likely to be less amenable to influence by the normal instruments of regional policy. Although the now defunct subsidies on labour might possibly have had some impact in such a situation, subsidies on capital will not. With major technical change, however, as defined here, there will always be genuine potentially mobile employment, alongside new investment, and potentially open to influence by the full range of policy instruments. Other forms of change are possible as well. Even in a period of decline, perhaps even more so, companies may move, without any changes in production, to areas where costs are lower.

But these are deductions from the pure form of the mechanisms. In fact, of course, the real situation is always more complex, and even in the brief industry studies presented here a number of other reasons become evident indicating why there might still be mobile employment within a sector even when the overall number of jobs is declining. There are three reasons that are important to mention. First, in all the industries studied in detail there was some increase in production, including the opening of new, or reopening of old, capacity as a result of the 1972/3 upturn, or 'mini-boom', within the overall context of decline. This, however, is not often likely to prove to be real potentially mobile growth. In cases, as in the brick industry, where old capacity is brought back on stream, there is no potential mobility. In labour-intensive and non-oligopolistic sectors, it may be that small firms come in and out of existence with the fluctuations of the cycle (the sweatshops in the clothing industry are a good example). Again, however, these are unlikely to be susceptible to policy influence, nor anyway to be of much value to any regions to which they might be diverted. They represent precisely that flexible margin to capacity that produces all the problems of cyclical instability that have already been the focus of attention in the regional policy debate.

The second source of potentially mobile employment is that which results from the different rates of growth/decline in different parts of an industry, even one defined at the level of an individual mlh. Within both of the rationalizing industries we studied in detail (paper and board and iron castings) there were parts of the sector in which new capital investment, and consequently potentially mobile employment, were being generated. This, the result simply of different conditions in product markets in different parts of the industry, produces new investment and employment that is potentially amenable to influence by the currently operated forms of regional policy.

In footwear and outerwear there was a third type of situation. Here, potentially mobile employment was again generated in certain parts of the industries, but in this case the distinction was based, not on the type of product or product market, but on the type of firm. There was a clear distinction between large and small capital in their response to recession, and it was almost exclusively the larger firms that, in conditions of overall absolute employment decline, generated some potentially mobile jobs, both through new investment and as a result of such firms' greater locational flexibility. Such employment is certainly amenable to influence by regional policy, though the very fact that it is mainly big capital that generates such potential mobility means that its movement reinforces the problems of external control in the recipient assisted areas.

The fact of aggregate employment decline does not remove altogether the relevance and possibility of spatial policies, whether these be focused on the regions or on inner cities. There is still the possibility of exerting some degree of social control over industry's locational strategies. What is clear, however, is that this possibility will vary from industry to industry and from time to time, and that different forms of potentially mobile employment have different implications. Conversely, the different mechanisms of employment decline are open to influence by different kinds of policy instrument. While the potentially mobile employment resulting from intra-sectoral differences (i.e. real growth) and from technical change may be subject to locational influence, the only kind of policy (within the spectrum currently applied) that is relevant to rationalizing industries is that of employment protection, such as the Temporary Employment Subsidy.

It may be, then, that locational policies in a period of employment decline have to be more selective and more sensitive to individual circumstances and variations, and in particular may have to consider more closely the link between production and location (all of which might be possible, for instance, under some kind of enforceable Planning Agreements system), but it is also clear that they are technically feasible. The real problems are political: given the overall context of employment decline, the trade-off between one geographical area and another is far clearer. In cases both of simple locational transfer and of location shift in a context of technical change, one region's gain is clearly another region's loss (and the gain in employment numbers is rarely as great as the loss). A 'greenfield' development in one area often means dereliction in another. But that, in turn, merely reinforces the case for a change in the type of regional policy. The inadequacies of a spatial policy based on incentives, with each region or area competing to offer more than the others to the few mobile firms that are around, become particularly glaring when employment is in decline and unemployment rates are so high in so many regions. It is another way in which the relative power of capital is increased through its own generation of job loss.

*   *   *

Indeed, while they are in no sense a representative sample, it is interesting to note that, while all were declining nationally in job terms, the net effect of the changes in the industries we studied was a shift in the balance of their employment towards the Develop-

Table 11.1   Employment change 1968–73

	Development Areas	Rest of UK
	%	%
Intensification sectors	−8	−9
Rationalization sectors	−15	−21
Technical change sectors	−8	−14
TOTAL	−10	−15

ment Areas. First of all, the four major Development Areas together (the North, Wales, Scotland and Northern Ireland) had a slightly higher share of initial employment in these sectors of employment decline than they did of manufacturing employment as a whole (22.6 per cent and 19.7 per cent respectively). However, given this initial employment structure, the Development Areas did far better in terms of actual employment change in each of the three forms of production reorganization; they had a lower percentage net loss of jobs than the rest of the UK (table 11.1). Further, as we have said already, although we are only dealing at a very unsatisfactory level of aggregation, so that many conflicting movements are caught in one net figure, it is nonetheless interesting to note that there was also a consistent pattern to the regional gains and losses when totalled across individual industries, and that this pattern was maintained within each individual type of production reorganization (see table 11.2). In comparison with their initial share of employment in the twenty-nine industries, the Development Areas as a group had a generally lower share of net regional losses and consistently, and very notably, a higher share of net regional gains in each of the three forms of production reorganization.

Table 11.2   Employment change in the Development Areas

Development Areas' share of	Initial employment	Regional losses	Regional gains
	%	%	%
Intensification sectors	16	16	48
Rationalization sectors	18	16	46
Technical change sectors	30	24	53

There were, of course, considerable differences in performance between the individual Development Areas. Table 11.3 gives the figures by region and illustrates both the consistency of the overall pattern of convergence and these inter-regional differences. One region that deserves immediate comment is the North West, which includes the Merseyside Development Area (see figure 6.1). It is not possible formally to apportion the employment change in our study between different parts of the Standard Region, but it does seem clear from the evidence we have that a considerable proportion of the North West's substantial loss of employment occurred in Merseyside. Merseyside, of course, is a very different kind of Development Area from the others, being primarily a conurbation, and having very different reserves of labour. It is not surprising that, in the years of regional convergence, its performance was out of line. However, in the four main Development Areas the different forms of production reorganization identified in these studies made a significant contribution to their relative manufacturing employment gains between 1968 and 1973 – and this occurred in industries that were losing employment at national level.

This kind of shift in manufacturing employment, from central regions to peripheral regions and from conurbations to smaller towns, is of course one common to a number of advanced capitalist economies, though varying in nature and scope from country to country. The so-called 'Frostbelt to Sunbelt' shift in the USA is another example. In their recent analysis of this phenomenon, Varaiya and Wiseman point to many of the same factors which we have identified

Table 11.3   Employment change by region

| | Share of national employment | | Employment change |
Region	1968	1973	1968–73
	%	%	%
North	6.6	7.2	−6.7
South West	3.7	4.0	−6.7
East Anglia	2.0	2.1	−8.2
Wales	5.9	6.2	−8.3
East Midlands	8.6	9.1	−9.3
Scotland	8.6	8.7	−12.4
Northern Ireland	1.6	1.6	−13.9
UK	100.0	99.9	−14.0
West Midlands	11.7	11.6	−15.0
Yorkshire and Humberside	16.5	16.2	−15.7
South East	19.8	19.2	−16.3
North West	15.0	14.0	−20.0

here. They write: 'all this suggests that the widely observed inter-regional "shifts" in manufacturing employment may have as much to do with changing technology and vintage as with investment flows' (Varaiya and Wiseman 1980, 15). They point out that disparities in employment growth are 'not wholly created by disparities across areas in gross investment. It is the interaction of investment, technology and the process of capacity retirement that has worsened the outlook for so many jobs over the period 1966–76' and they go on to show both that new investment is, in aggregate, more capital-intensive than old, and 'how substantial growth in investment per worker can be associated with dramatic decline in manufacturing employment'. Varaiya and Wiseman use their results to argue against the importance of simple locational shift, of 'corporate flight' from north to south in the USA. Unfortunately, however, because they are working at the level of aggregate manufacturing numbers it is not possible for them to look at the actual processes of change, at the way in which 'investment, technology and the process of capital-retirement' are related on the ground. In particular it makes it impossible for them to analyse the many different potential roles of location and locational change.

It seems likely, in fact, that a complex of different mechanisms is in operation in the USA, as in the UK. First of all, there clearly are simple locational shifts, in search of cheaper, more pliable labour, and without any changes in the process of production. Such shifts certainly do not account for the total disparity in rates of employment change between the different sections of the USA, but they clearly happen. Many instances have been documented (see, for example, Bluestone, Harrison and Baker 1981). Indeed they are probably more significant in the USA than they are in the UK. For one thing, the variation in locational opportunities is probably greater in the USA. This is not only an economic, it is also a political question. The fact that legislation about the closed shop is operated at State level, together with the USA laws prohibiting secondary boycotts, has produced much greater variation in the USA in what is known as 'business climate' than exists in the UK (on the legislation, see Harrison 1981). For the same reason union organization on this issue has taken a different form from that in the UK. Bluestone, Harrison and Baker report, for instance, on new contracts between the United Food and Commercial Workers (UFCW) and several meat-packing firms that prohibit the companies from closing a plant and then reopening it on a non-union basis within five years (1981, 82). Once again the form of job loss influences the kinds of conflict and response that it provokes.

However, there are certainly also many cases in the USA where locational change is connected with changes in production. Recent changes in the tyre industry provide a good example. Goodyear's shift from conventional tyres to radial tyres, and at the same time from Akron, Ohio, to Lawton, Oklahoma is one of the more infamous cases (see again Bluestone, Harrison and Baker 1981). Varaiya and Wiseman's (1978 and 1980) confirmation of the generally increasing capital intensity of new investment also means that jobs will often be lost 'in transit', on the way from North to South. At the same time, the combination of the international economic slowdown in the 1970s, the decline of the undisputed economic dominance of the USA, and its secular shift away from manufacturing industry, has meant that straightforward rationalization has also been occurring in a number of American industries. Varaiya and Wiseman argue that this scrapping of capacity is, at the aggregate level, on an age-related basis (the oldest plant and machinery are closed down first). This, too, hits Northern cities more than those in the South and West (Varaiya and Wiseman 1978, 14). In the USA, too, the loss of manufacturing jobs from the cities of the North East seems to be the product of a range of different combinations of production change and location change.

* * *

But all this is to talk only of long-term trends. Not only are there differences between countries, for instance in the balance of kinds of production reorganization, there may also be significant shifts over time in the nature and mechanisms of employment decline.

So, while manufacturing employment has fallen throughout the period, and unemployment has risen, there have, in fact, been major changes in the UK economy since the mid-1960s. The period that we have been studying in detail was one of relative economic decline for the UK, but it was before the real international collapse of 1974. In the late 1960s and early 1970s the politics of economic recovery were designed in an overall context of growth. In government policy terms in the UK, this was a period of modernization, of productivity schemes, of relatively high investment, of attacks on unofficial shop-floor organization and agreements with union leaders. There was an emphasis on science and technology, on bringing British industry up to date. It was in this context that the decline in manufacturing employment began.

Since then employment has continued to fall and unemployment to rise. Over the period as a whole both trends have indeed accelerated. 'Hidden' unemployment has also risen, as the active workforce as a proportion of the total potentially economically active population has fallen. Job loss has become more general. It has spread to most parts of manufacturing industry, and is beginning to affect services. Indeed, it is increasingly clear that many of the processes we have studied in the context of manufacturing industry are now well in progress in a growing number of service sectors. Geographically, too, job loss has become more general. By the autumn of 1981 the once prosperous 'central region' of the West Midlands had an unemployment rate of 13.4 per cent, above that in Scotland, for long a Development Area. Intra-regionally, also, the process has become more general. Not only have 'inner cities' been added to 'the regions' as problem areas of high unemployment, but suburbia and small-town England is beginning to be hit by redundancies too (Townsend 1981).

Employment decline, in other words, has both continued and worsened. But it has also changed its form. Some initial indication of this can be gained by looking at other aggregate statistics. Perhaps the most dramatic is what has happened to output. While from the mid-1960s onwards the rate of growth of output certainly fell in relation to the years of the long post-war boom, it was still positive: manufacturing output increased by 15 per cent over our period. Since 1973 it has been very different: between 1973 and 1980 manufacturing output in the UK fell by 13 per cent. Profitability, too, has been hit. A study for the Bank of England reported that:

> The main conclusion is that, although not surprisingly levels of profitability vary quite markedly between sectors, the downward trend in real profitability observed at the aggregate level during the 1960s and the early 1970s, and the recent fall to a very low level, are common to all of the industrial groupings presented in this article. (Williams 1979, 395)

That these figures reflect a more straightforward decline rather than a loss of jobs through changes in the organization of the production process is indicated especially by the figures for productivity growth. Between 1968 and 1973 the rate of growth of productivity, and its ratio to the rate of growth of output, was particularly high. Since then its growth has been much slower. Indeed, between 1973 and 1975 and between 1979 and 1980 labour productivity in manufacturing actually fell (Monthly Digest of Statistics). Overall, between 1973 and the late 1970s the underlying rate of growth in labour productivity in UK manufacturing fell to less than half the pre-1973 rate (Treasury 1979). Finally, some idea of the reason for that slower growth of productivity can be found in the figures for investment in manufacturing industry. Fixed capital expenditure, after rising steadily from the mid-1950s to 1970, fell back. The average level for the six years 1968–1973 was, in fact, slightly above that for the subsequent six years, and the three highest years of all (1969, 1970 and 1971) were in our study period.

There is, then, in those aggregate numbers, some indication that the configuration of job loss may have changed. Not only is UK manufacturing industry in a position of relative uncompetitiveness and decline, other changes have also taken place. First, as we have already mentioned, since 1974 the decline in the UK has taken place against a very different background, one in which the international capitalist economy has been growing much more slowly, if at all. The context within which the attempt to resuscitate the British economy has taken place has therefore been much tougher. Second, the politics of that attempted resuscitation have also changed. From the active attempt to modernize there has been a shift since the mid-1970s to a less 'interventionist' position towards industry. There is less emphasis on technological renewal than on more directly shifting the balance of power between capital and labour. Job loss, as we shall see, is both precondition and consequence of such a political shift. Both economic and political conditions have changed.

What that means is that employment decline in the late 1970s and early 1980s is very different from that which took place a decade before. The kinds of production change through which job loss is occurring have probably shifted quite dramatically over the period.

In particular, all the evidence suggests that rationalization is now a far more important cause of job loss. The collapse of manufacturing output, referred to above, is one piece of evidence for this. The same change in output performance can be found also at individual-industry level. At the beginning of this analysis we pointed out how, even though every single industry we studied was declining in em-ployment terms, only thirteen out of thirty-one were declining in output terms. Table 11.4 shows what has happened since then. Between 1973 and 1980 annual production has fallen in twenty-four out of the thirty-one industries; in only seven has it increased. And in some of the industries the declines in output have been really dramatic. In the textile-machinery industry production in 1980 was 30 per cent of what it was in the (relatively peak) year of 1975. Figure 11.1 shows that much the same picture applies to other major sectors of the economy. As we saw in chapter 5, output decline does not in itself mean that there will necessarily be rationalization. But it certainly increases its likelihood. And there is other evidence too. Since 1973 the number of bankruptcies and company liquidations in England and Wales have increased, reaching a peak first in 1976, then falling back only to rise sharply again in 1980–1 (see figure 11.2).

All this is confirmed if we look at more detailed evidence for the industries we have studied here. The two industries that were already dominated by rationalization have continued to be so; in fact in both cases the process has accelerated. In the foundry industry the collapse of output has continued (see table 11.4). A recent forecast by the industry's Sector Working Party put output in 1982, a supposedly peak year, at 3,170,000 tonnes, a figure still 25 per cent below the 1964 level. Closures have continued apace, and not now just amongst small foundries. Both BL's and Ford's foundries have been threatened (Gooding and Garnett 1981; Harper 1981), and demand in some of the previously buoyant sectors of the industry's market has slumped like the rest.

In newsprint the collapse has been of headline-making proportions ('Bowater newsprint plant closure halves UK capacity', *Financial Times* 20 August 1980; 'Collapse of Britain's newsprint industry', *Financial Times* 11 March 1981; 'Reed to halve newsprint capacity', *Financial Times* 10 March 1981). The picture for much of the 1970s was similar in most parts of the paper and board industry. Between 1970 and 1976 in only one sub-sector did production grow: by 27 per cent in

Table 11.4   Output change by industry, 1973–80 (1975 = 100)

Industry	1973	1980
Grain milling	99.1	99.7
Biscuits	107.9	102.9
Sugar	135.2	125.2
Brewing and malting	93.7	100.6
Coke ovens	115.7	63.3
Chemicals	127.3	109.4
Synthetic resins, etc.	123.7	106.0
Fertilizers	103.1	104.7
Iron and steel/steel tubes	133.1	68.4
Iron castings	116.9	62.6
Aluminium	110.5	112.0
Other base metals	111.2	78.4
Metal-working machine tools	98.0	72.6
Textile machinery	85.6	30.0
Instruments	91.0	107.9
Electrical machinery	93.7	81.6
Insulated wires and cables	109.9	89.0
Cycles	126.6	75.2
Locomotives, railway-track equipment, etc.	109.9	150.3
Cutlery	106.5	74.5
Cotton weaving, etc.	120.7	69.1
Woollen and worsted	138.9	82.2
Jute	120.2	96.1
Carpets	112.6	65.8
Textile finishing	105.1	77.9
Leather	101.4	70.9
Tailored outerwear	107.2	76.4
Footwear	106.7	86.4
Bricks	129.9	82.1
Paper and board	131.4	103.3
Other printing and publishing	107.6	109.8
All manufacturing	108.4	94.8

Source   Data supplied by Central Statistical Office

tissues. Production in all the other sub-sectors recorded declines, ranging from 0.4 per cent in corrugated case materials to 56.9 per cent in newsprint. Production in the industry as a whole fell by nearly 17 per cent. After a lull in 1977 when no mill closures occurred, and only two paper machines were shut down, the industry appears to have embarked upon another major phase of rationalization. Fifteen paper mills were closed between the beginning of 1978 and mid-1980. These

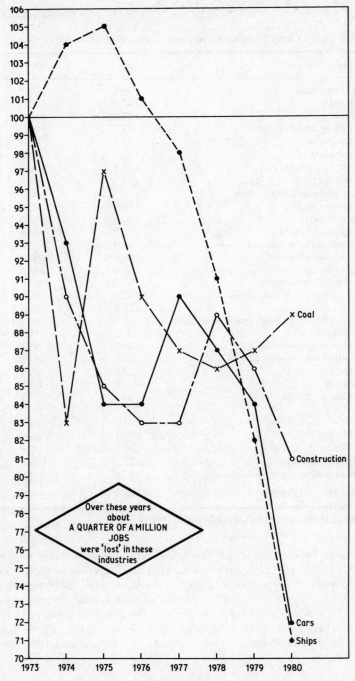

Over these years about A QUARTER OF A MILLION JOBS were 'lost' in these industries

Fig. 11.1   Output collapse 1973–80, selected industries (1973 = 100)

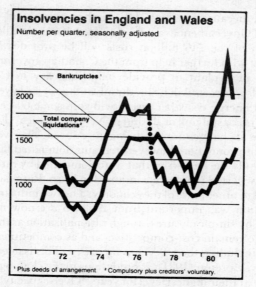

Insolvencies in England and Wales
Number per quarter, seasonally adjusted

Fig. 11.2   Insolvencies in England and Wales 1971–81
Source   *British Business* 23 October 1981, 345

closures were accompanied by the shutting down of ninety-three paper machines, a staggering figure when one considers that the seven years from 1971 to 1977 had only seen the scrapping of eighty machines (Hall 1980a). Data on the introduction of new machines are not readily available, but such new investment does not appear to have been important, especially in the newsprint sub-sector (Hall 1980b). Not only has there been little recent investment in new capacity at existing newsprint mills, the early part of 1980 also saw the cancellation of the plans of Wiggins Teape and Consolidated Bathurst to build a £100 million newsprint mill at Fort William in Scotland (Hall 1980a). Bowater's closure of its newsprint mill at Ellesmere Port accounted for nearly 80 per cent of the company's UK capacity in newsprint and just over 50 per cent of total newsprint capacity for the UK as a whole (calculated from figures given in Hall 1980a). The closure resulted in the loss of over 1000 jobs. The problems have primarily been an exacerbation of those already evident in the late 1960s and early 1970s. And the latest news from the newsprint industry reflects those pressures as well. Having cancelled the proposal for Fort William, Consolidated Bathurst has turned its attention to Bowater's mill at Ellesmere Port. The former project was abandoned because of 'high UK timber prices and insufficient promises of Government assistance' (Fisher 1981). At Ellesmere Port £10 million of the £46 million costs will be provided by the UK government with further help from the Canadian government for the conversion of a plant to provide pulp. The key to Consolidated Bathurst's lower costs will lie in 'the advantage of far lower Canadian timber and energy costs because it will ship some 60 per cent of its pulp from its coastal mill at Bathurst, New Brunswick' (Fisher 1981). Technological changes are also being introduced. The overall picture in newsprint production, however, remains dominated by closure.

It is not only the industries that were dominated by rationalization in our study period that have continued to be so. Rationalization has also spread to other parts of the economy. The two industries in which intensification was important from 1968–73 are now more clearly dominated by simple closure through rationalization as they have lost the battle to remain cost-competitive, and as competition from other countries (including the USA) has increased. This is documented for footwear by Moreton (1981). Liquidations in the clothing industry as a whole are at their highest level for years. 'Over-capacity' and closure are hitting a whole range of industries, which although losing jobs in the late 1960s and early 1970s, were doing so primarily as a result of other forms of production change. Indeed, of the industries that we have studied in detail, brick-making appears to be the only exception. There is certainly over-capacity, as figure 11.3 shows all too clearly, but it has not, as yet, produced massive rationalization. The reasons for this include both the technical nature of the production process and, presumably, the competitively secure position of the one dominant company, the London Brick Company. It will be interesting, however, to see how long the situation can continue – it is not unlike that of paper and board in the mid-1960s just before it embarked on its process of rationalization.

Two things emerge. First, the kinds of production reorganization that most typify an industry will change over time. This reinforces our earlier point about the dangers of trying to derive general empirical rules of behaviour. Economic and political circumstances have changed, and so has the response of industry. It seems that in a number of cases the attempt to compete – for instance through intensification or technological change – has been abandoned. Second, rationalization has clearly become more important throughout the economy. In particular, rationalization seems to be far more significant at present as a cause of job loss.

But rationalization is by no means the only process occurring, even

Psst . . . anyone want to build 50,000 houses?

You might think that this collection of bricks in a Bedfordshire field would build a lot of houses. Indeed it would. This vast pile is 12 ft deep. It is the creation of the London Brick Company, Britain's biggest brickmaker, but the company is far from pleased about it. Bricks are an extremely slow moving product these days. The picture shows just a part of a stockpile of 70 million

bricks covering eight acres of fields round the company's Stewartby brickworks. And that's not all.

At the company's 13 other works in Bedfordshire, Buckinghamshire and Cambridgeshire there are another 420 million unsold bricks covering nearly 50 acres. Its entire brick mountain would make 50,000 houses or a new city the size of Derby. And that's not all.

In Britain as a whole, according to the latest statistics, for the first quarter of the year, the brick stockpile is 1,152 million – a postwar record, and enough to build 100,000 three-bedroom detached houses. (There's also a vast pile of unwanted cement, 1,100,000 tonnes of it.) And that's not all. The figures for stockpiled bricks do not include millions more in the yards of builders' merchants or builders themselves.

. . .

Unemployed building workers now total 425,000. But the London Brick chimneys keep smoking. It is more efficient to keep brick kilns going through a slump. A London Brick spokesman said: 'Running a brick bank is something we have practised through a number of recessions.' But never a brick bank quite like this.

Fig. 11.3 Impending rationalization?*
Source Sunday Times 12 July 1981

* Authors' note:

Rationalization is no longer impending – before this book went to press the process was under way. In the second half of 1981 London Brick announced the closure of its big Ridgmont works in Bedfordshire (1100 jobs), the Kempston works in the same county (330 jobs), and two smaller brickworks near Peterborough (300 jobs).

(a)

West Midlands bosses find they have the upper hand

If the Government wanted evidence that its tough monetary policy was having an effect on Britain's workforce, it need look no further than the West Midlands. In the country's industrial heartland – with a disproportionately high 46 per cent of employment in manufacture – modest pay settlements are being agreed as the recession deepens and the number of layoffs mounts.

. . .

'Job security rather than the level of inflation is likely to be the main concern in the forthcoming pay round.'

The dramatic change in mood of a workforce traditionally noted for its independence and militancy is

explained by Mr. Chris Walliker, director of manpower at Delta Metal and chairman-elect of the regional CBI: 'The speed and severity of recession surprised everyone. Suddenly orders dried up, cash flow was hit and stocks run down.'

Indeed plant closures and redundancies in recent weeks amount to a roll-call of the high and mighty, with Lucas Electrical announcing a cut of 3,000 jobs, GKN Forgings 2,100, GKN Sankey 930, Cadbury-Schweppes 700, and Renold 800. Cutbacks in the automotive industry, which accounts for one in six jobs in the region, are gathering pace with redundancies sought at

Wilmot Breeden, Associated Engineering and Automotive Products.

'Complaints about the weakness of James Prior's Bill to curb the power of the trade unions reflect the remote Westminster and Whitehall view of industrial relations. The reality is that employers already have the power to pose workers unions – the power to pose workers with the choice between a realistic pay deal and short time working or redundancies.' That hard headed view, expressed by the personnel director of a leading Midland engineering company, typifies the tough stance many employers are now adopting in pay negotiations.

. . .

Developments at BL Cars, where the militant shop stewards traditionally set the pace for pay claims, have also had an impact upon the Midland industrial relations climate. Mr. Geoffrey Armstrong, the employee relations director, claims 'a significant

> 'I have never known Midlands workers so docile.'

change' in workers' attitudes and that many of the controversial changes in working practices have already been implemented at the company's 34 plants.

(b)

Chemical companies 'tearing up' deals

By our Labour Staff

Companies throughout the chemicals industry were demanding by 'tearing up' union agreements the General and Municipal Workers Union said yesterday.

Some of this demanning resulted from plant closures arising out of the way companies responded to the recession. In other cases companies used the impact of the recession to lower manning levels in an attempt to improve productivity.

The latter response appeared to be one the Government had sought from companies. However, the union said yesterday, it objected on two grounds to the way the industry was trying to do this.

Mr. David Warburton, the union's national officer, said companies had been doing this with no consultation with their unions. In many cases companies presented the unions with new manning levels and told them that if they did not like these they should put the issue through disputes procedures, he said.

Secondly, the union believed that in many cases an individual company's financial performance did not warrant the kind of job cuts it was making.

Delegates at the annual GMWU chemicals conference voted yesterday for a policy banning overtime in the industry. This will be put to the union's executive and regional officials.

(c)

Fear of unemployment – and the recession – have had their effect on the much-publicised militancy of the Coventry car workers. Talbot, like several companies, has been emboldened to press ahead with new manning levels and work practices at its Ryton assembly plant in spite of union opposition.

'Two years ago such a move would have been unthinkable. Now the workers know it would be foolish to pick a fight. With so much unemployment, the company holds all the cards,' says one senior shop steward.

Fig. 11.4   The impact of rationalization

Source   (a) *Financial Times* 9 July 1980; (b) *Financial Times* 6 March 1981; (c) *Financial Times* 28 January 1981

(a)

Office staff laid off by 'one in four companies'

By James McDonald

One company in four is making office staff redundant because of the recession, according to a national survey by the Alfred Marks Bureau. The survey was conducted in March and April among 381 employers of office staff.

It found nearly half the sample reported office employees consciously working harder to keep their positions, and that three-quarters of the sample had a lower staff turnover than in April 1979, before the recession.

Mr Bernard Marks, chairman of the bureau, said employers had been forced to reorganize their businesses. 'In addition to the 25 per cent who have already made redundancies 43 per cent have reduced staff by natural wastage and 9 per cent by offering voluntary redundancies.'

Increasing numbers of applicants were applying for every job offered, almost doubling the April 1979 figure in some areas.

More rigorous recruitment procedures were adopted by employers. The average interview-time had been extended.

With fewer positions open, more qualified staff were accepting less senior jobs. According to 44 per cent of the sample this had led to a much higher general quality of office staff.

New technology was not a major factor in staff reductions. The survey found that although 34 per cent of the companies installed a word-processor after April 1979, only 13 per cent said it reduced staffing levels.

now. Indeed, the very obviousness of the closures happening all around has made other forms of change in production more likely. The clear threat of job loss through rationalization has, as suggested earlier, increased management's ability to push through other changes in the organization of production. This has been particularly true of intensification. The new, tighter disciplinary procedures introduced into the British car industry (and in that of the USA) in recent years (in Ford, BL and Talbot; see figures 11.4 and 11.9) are an example of this. So is the imposition by BL management of new work speeds, including those which eventually led to the Longbridge 'riot' at the end of 1980. The press-cuttings in figures 11.4 and 11.5 from the *Financial Times* of 1980 and 1981 are only a few of many that could have been picked out. An even more recent *Financial Times* special survey of the UK motor industry, for instance, documents numerous examples. Note in particular that these effects are not confined to manufacturing. In figure 11.5 the reports of 'self-imposed' intensification among office staff (Alfred Marks Bureau 1981) and the management-

(b)

Barclays staff urged to work harder

By Nick Garnett

Barclays Bank is instituting an average 5 per cent improvement in productivity across its operations, largely through requiring staff to work harder.

The move has brought an angry response from the Barclays Group Staff Union which said yesterday that the bank had not consulted the union and had previously denied that it was considering such changes.

The bank uses a system called the Clerical Work Improvement Programme based on a measurement of work over a 140-hour, four-week period.

Index

Of this, 100 hours of tasks are taken as the basis of calculations with the balance covering supervision, holidays, sickness and other periods when work cannot be measured.

The bank has been using an index of effectiveness of 100 measured against a basic staff figure. It wants this index improved, which the staff union says will mean a 10 per cent productivity rise in small branches and 5 per cent in medium sized ones.

The bank said yesterday there had been a substantial drop in the rate of resignations in the past three years and as a result the relative experience of staff had increased. This allowed a greater level of effectiveness.

No redundancies

The work load was rising and the bank would continue to recruit staff but it was essential that productivity rose. There was no question of redundancies.

The bank's move is part of a general trend within the clearers to cut costs. This has been most marked by Midland's announcement of 2,000 redundancies.

Barclays' staff union said it would consider whether to institute money claims against the bank if it could not get the bank to change its policy.

It said that a 25-man office would be reduced to 23½ and its seemed that no replacements would be provided until staffing had fallen to the new figure.

Fig. 11.5   Intensification in the service industries
Sources   (a) *Financial Times* 5 August 1981; (b) *Financial Times* 20 August 1981

imposed changes at Barclays Bank show that the same pressures exist among service workers. These processes indicate again the importance of identifying different kinds of job loss. In these cases the constant threat of rationalization, of output decline as well as employment decline, further strengthened management's hand in introducing other kinds of changes in production. What is referred to as 'a changing, more responsible, attitude on the shop-floor' and 'a new mood of realism', as if this represents some realization by workers of what constitutes sensible behaviour on their part under a capitalist system, is often a straightforward submission to the fear of unemployment.

Biffen looks on bright side of jobs loss

By Ian Aitken, Political Editor

Mr John Biffen, Trade Secretary, yesterday urged fainthearted colleagues in the Conservative Party to look on the bright side of the present economic crisis. Though harsh in terms of short-term personal misery, he said, high unemployment had brought some significant advantages to the country as a whole.

. . .

. . . he went on to list four areas of the domestic economy in which the consequences of high unemployment had been welcome. They included a reduction in over-manning, a sharp fall in the number of strikes, a lower level of pay settlements, and the halving of the rate of inflation from its peak of just over 22 per cent.

. . .

Fig. 11.6   The politics of rationalization
Source   *The Guardian* 11 August 1981

Such changes have wide implications. In the USA, Metzgar (1980) has written of how the increasing importance of job loss has raised new questions across the whole spectrum of industrial relations, which may lead to a more fundamental renegotiation of terms between labour and capital. In the UK, the rise to power of a political rhetoric of 'free-market economics' was in part enabled by the very fact of job loss. The recession created the opportunity for it, enabled talk of 'tough medicine'. Job loss, or the very real threat of it, has been one of its weapons. By the early 1980s, some of the impact of this was clear. Unemployment was bringing down trade-union membership; the level of strike action had fallen back, even taking account of the lower numbers in work; absenteeism was down. The economics of unemployment were the centrepiece of a political battle; a senior minister even admitted as much (figure 11.6). A measure of the effects

---

Slump 'scares ill workers'

High unemployment has made people so afraid of losing their jobs that they may be going to work even when ill, according to a report published today by the Office of Health Economics.

Latest statistics for days lost through sickness show that for March 1981 the figures are 21 per cent below the average for the same month over the past four years. The drop coincides with a one million rise in unemployment between 1978 and 1981.

Fig. 11.7 'Slump "scares ill workers"'
Source *The Guardian* 10 August 1981

of the threat of job loss, in terms of daily life at work, was given in a survey by the Office of Health Economics (1981), reported in *The Guardian* (10 August 1981, figure 11.7).

So the increased levels of rationalization have also enabled more intensification. What, then, about technical change? Certainly some has taken place. There has even been a (much-heralded) case of it in one of the more technically backward sectors of British industry, one of our intensifiers: Hepworths, of men's and boys' tailored outerwear, introduced computerization into their patterning and cutting system. It is an interesting development in a number of ways, reflecting many of the points discussed in chapter 4. It is being introduced by one of the two largest producers in the sector (a classic leading-firm phenomenon), and is the first of its kind to be used in the menswear industry (Dibben 1981), although effort is being made by the Garment Technology Group to introduce equivalent changes into smaller companies (Woodcock 1980, see figure 11.8). As figure 11.8 makes clear, the cost-savings derive from two sources: savings in material and a lower wage bill. The latter, in turn, depends on breaking down the traditional sexual division of labour in the industry, by replacing men ('skilled cutters') with 'girls' (*sic*) who, in spite of the fact that they use a 'specially developed code' and operate

Clive Woodcock examines the role played by new technology in the traditionally-minded clothing industry

Computer Charlie makes a better tailor of Hepworths

A year old cutter named Charlie with 150 years of experience is helping a British clothing manufacturer to improve productivity on its made-to-measure suit output by 250 per cent.

The bespoke cutter is in fact a computerised patterns system developed by the clothing manufacturer and retailer, Hepworths, adapting advances in microprocessor technology to the special needs of the clothing industry, in an attempt to control the ravages of high cost inflation and compete against imports.

The achievement of Hepworths in devising this system, however, is only one aspect of how technology can help the survival of the fragmented clothing industry, much of which is still made up of smaller to medium sized firms. Those firms cannot sustain the cost of research

but has 150 years of experience.'

The introduction of the system has meant that a team of girls is now doing jobs which were traditionally a male preserve. Made-to-measure suits have always relied on expert measuring of the customer and the skill of the bespoke cutter, almost invariably a man in the past, to produce the bits and pieces.

A four-man team of Hepworths clothing production and computer specialists spent two years developing the system, adapting the Camsco bespoke package to their requirements, establishing a link with the group's main computer and devising a sophisticated code language to enable one computer to talk to another in clothing technology.

How Hepworths' customers wanting a made-to-measure suit are measured as usual at the branch,

them on to the appropriate length of cloth and cut the cloth before machining. Use of the new system has resulted in very significant savings in cloth use and labour costs, together with very considerable improvements in quality.

The girls operating the Camsco computer system can be fully trained in eight weeks to do a job which reduces to 20 minutes, operations which previously took an hour or more. Some of them are former machinists from the factory floor.

The other team which has taken over the traditional male cutter's role use electric shears for the cutting process and receive 12 weeks' training to acquire the necessary accuracy, compared with a seven-year apprenticeship for a traditional bespoke cutter.

Nearly 30 per cent of Hepworths'

has taken place in Britain is encouraging to the Clothing Industry Economic Development Committee, which recently expressed concern that most technological developments in the industry were taking place abroad, though it added that growth in productivity would not be held back in the coming decade for lack of technological advance.

This view arises from the fundamental issue that clothing manufacturers, in general, do not make the optimum use even of current technology and management techniques, which means that many opportunities for greater profitability are not taken up.

The industry is highly labour intensive, a major reason why it is so susceptible to competition from low wage countries, but at the same time probably less than half of its output

and development necessary to make advances of this kind and often it would not be worth their while to do so anyway.

But benefits matching those obtained by Hepworths from advanced technology can also be achieved by those other firms in a more appropriate form and at much lower cost simply by applying existing technology rather than venturing into new fields.

These two aspects of advance have been clearly illustrated recently by the Hepworths' development and a two-year project carried out by the Garment Technology Group in applying current technology.

The Hepworths' system was developed by its own employees from the American Camsco Markamatic 5000 system at a cost of £250,000 and has been in use for a year. The group's production director, Mr Ron Sheffield, produced the description of Charlie as a skilled measure cutter who is one year old

the statistics are transferred to Leeds and fed into the company's main computer. These are then passed on to the new system – nicknamed Charlie by the girls who operate it – in the specially developed code.

Charlie automatically adjusts the customer's individual measurements from a basic chest pattern, providing for a longer leg length, sloping shoulders, heavier waist, thicker thighs, centre or side vents or whatever else is needed.

A team of six girls, working in two shifts, on a video screen then arrange and rearrange in jigsaw fashion the 25 or so individual parts which go to make up a suit. In five minutes they produce a pattern representing each individual order.

Charlie checks that all requirements of the customer's order have been met, takes the miniature pattern on the screen and then traces out a life-sized paper pattern.

The paper patterns are used by another team of girls who place

made-to-measure suits, which account for about half of the total suit output, are now produced under the new system, but it is hoped to increase this proportion to four out of five. About 50 traditional cutters have either taken voluntary redundancy or moved to other jobs in the factory. Another 100 are still employed using traditional methods of cutting suits which cannot yet be programmed into the system.

Other clothing manufacturers have computers working on ready-to-wear suits, but Hepworths have led the field in applying them to bespoke tailoring, a lead which has led to interest in the system from Japan which could possibly lead to a licensing arrangement in the future.

The system enables the company to provide the customer with a better fitting suit than before, but it does not claim that it will bring down prices, only enable it to peg the effects of inflation and to give better value.

The fact that this development

– and that mainly in menswear – lends itself to mass production engineering techniques. The remainder of the industry requires greater flexibility and fast response to deal with varying degrees of style and fashion in production.

For that reason, the encouragement of greater use of existing technology could probably produce wider and larger benefits even than the technological advances achieved by Hepworths in their particular field. An illustration of what can be done is provided by the project carried out by the Garment Technology Group, which has resulted in annual savings of at least £250,000 by the ten clothing firms involved.

Technical audits were carried out in the ten firms as a result of which agreed recommendations were implemented by the companies in collaboration with the group.

Fig. 11.8   Technical change comes to men's and boys' tailored outerwear
Source   *The Guardian* 8 July 1980

technologically advanced machinery, are not classified as 'skilled'.

There is other, wider, evidence of major technical change, particularly in recent years, and also evidence that, as with intensification, technical change is sometimes made possible by the threat of rationalization. The new products at Plessey's plant at Edge Lane, Liverpool (figure 11.9) were introduced with a warning 'that this and other investment planned for the site will have to be accompanied by big changes in working practices and productivity . . . there was a secure future for the remaining employees, if the plant could make the new range of products efficiently' (David 1981). Once again the different forms of employment loss clearly interact.

But in spite of all these individual pieces of evidence it seems unlikely that technological change has been as important in British industry since 1973 as it was in the years before. For one thing, as we have seen, average annual, fixed capital expenditure in manufacturing industry has been lower, as has the rate of growth of productivity. And in spite of its increasing use, numerous articles and government and other reports bemoan the relatively slow rate of introduction, in recent years, of advanced technology (ACARD 1979; Allen, Bati and Bragard 1981; Large 1981; Policy Studies Institute 1981). In some cases, changes have even taken place in the opposite direction, chapter 5 reported the closure of BL's Rover car plant at Solihull in 1981: this was a plant that on completion, only five years before, had been described as 'a workers' palace':

> The plant incorporates revolutionary new ideas for motor-car production, designed to give Rover more flexibility and higher quality control than any other production unit in the country. . . .
>
> With a million square feet of assembly space under a single roof the new assembly plant has given Rover's engineers an unprecedented opportunity to try out the best of the new production techniques which have been developed in the rest of Europe. (Jackson and Richardson 1976)

Production has now been shifted to one of BL's older factories, at Cowley (near Oxford) where in turn productivity has been increased through both intensification and technical change. Nonetheless, in terms of the 'tendencies of the capitalist labour process', this is something of a step in a backwards direction. In other industries, too, modern factories are being closed. Townsend (1981) reported that in electrical engineering the closure of modern branches in the provinces has been more prominent than the closure of conurbation premises. This, of course, might reflect some of the criteria mentioned in

THE STATE OF BRITISH INDUSTRY

2: Productivity

Making the gains stick

By John Elliott, Industrial Editor

Productivity improvements at Liver-Ford's traditionally militant Hale-wood plant have helped cut these operating costs by some 6 per cent this year.

British Steel Corporation's Scunthorpe plant has recorded a 20 per cent productivity improvement. ICI's Mond division believes it is set for a 7 per cent overall productivity gain. Plessey is pushing its annual sales per employee up from £14,000 three years ago to £22,000 (with a 1990 target of £55,000) this year at its Edge Lane plant in Liverpool. It is achieving £27,000 at a highly automated circuit board factory in South Shields.

These are just a few of the examples which demonstrate the considerable gains in British productivity as managers – and relatively quiescent workforces – down. 'It's just a question of sur-together sweep away many of the vival' is a phrase one constantly

inefficiencies of the 1970s. But it may be too early to tell how many of these improvements will endure if – and when – the upturn comes.

Almost every company in manufacturing industry has a story to tell of increased efficiencies, often far exceeding anything it would have thought possible even a year ago. Companies which began to modernise before the recession have often gained the most.

From the boardroom downwards employees have been drastically slimmed down, overheads cut, and shop floor operations improved – often with the help of investment in automated and electronic plant.

Restrictive practices have been reduced, labour flexibility increased, and unprofitable companies and products have been shut

hears from management and shop stewards.

'Middle management has switched from despair to enthusiasm to a degree that I can't fault' says Mr Bill Hayden, Ford Europe's manufacturing vice-president.

'Mrs Thatcher's had no influence on my thinking but she's contributed to the workers' realisation that if they don't do a solid day's work they're out because the Government won't save them' says Mr Arthur Rothwell, the Halewood general operations manager.

. . .

A lot of changes – in a technologically changing company like Plessey for example – are being achieved by massive investments in new products and processes. The technology will protect some of the productivity gains, even in tra-

ditionally militant areas like Liverpool, although a company like Plessey has not always found the massive changes easy to introduce.

The recession has coincided with the rapid spread of microelectronics. A surprising number of companies are managing to maintain modest investments in key productivity initiatives like installing advanced machine tools.

For example, Thorn EMI's gas meter factory in Trafford Park Manchester – called Parkinson Cowan Measurement – is investing £1m a year, half of it in automated production machines. It is achieving productivity gains of at least 8 per cent when redundancies and other economies are taken into account, enabling it to develop the export markets as its dominant customer – British Gas – has cut back.

Fig. 11.9 Technical change under threat of rationalization
Source The *Financial Times* 24 July 1981

chapter 7 – for instance pulling in to major sites (where capacity has certainly been reduced even if no total closure has been involved); but it does also mean that older plant and equipment may be being retained at the expense of new. Nor is money going into research and development for future technological change. A report from the British North America Research Association (Schott 1981) showed how 'total UK industrial R and D [has] fallen in absolute terms since the later 1960s' and detected 'a circular relationship between economic activity and innovation, with the relatively poor economic performance of the two countries [the UK and the USA] through the 1970s both causing and being caused by a relative lack of innovation' (Lorenz 1981). Elliott commented that in a review of the progress of the (Conservative) Government's economic policy in August 1981, a statement from NEDO:

> cast doubt on the current optimism of Government ministers and some industrialists that productivity will be boosted significantly and permanently.
>
> It acknowledged that there have been gains. By March, manufacturing productivity stood over 11 per cent higher than would have been expected on the basis of productivity and output trends in the pre-recession period of 1977–9.
>
> 'Similar gains in production have, however, occurred before: indeed they characterize each of the last three recessions.
>
> The gain this time is larger, as the fall in manufacturing output has been larger: but otherwise it is not noticeably different.
>
> The record after these earlier recessions does not generate optimism that the long-term trend of productivity will have been improved once growth resumes.'
>
> The statement did not take into account the optimism that a larger productivity gain will emerge because cuts have been made into inefficient practices and because some workers' attitudes may have been changed by high unemployment.
>
> Instead, the paper based its warning on the lack of positive investment. (Elliott 1981)

Taking all this evidence together, it does seem likely that there has been a shift in balance over the 1970s between the different causes of employment decline, and in the kinds of changes in production through which job loss is taking place.

This has major social, economic and political implications. First, it means that to the extent that productivity is being increased it is happening more through intensification of existing processes (and possibly also through differential rationalization) than through significant technical change. People are being made to work harder (those, that is, who still have jobs) but the equipment and technology with which they work is not being brought up to date at the same rate.

Such increases in productivity depend more on a trial of strength, both within industry itself and at the political level, than on any real modernization of productive capacity.

The 'foundations for future growth' are being laid more through political changes in the balance of power between capital and labour than through changes in the technology of production. The title of the article reproduced in figure 11.9, 'Making the gains stick', was therefore very apt. Such a strategy for economic recovery is not only 'on capital's terms', it also depends on things remaining that way. It represents a very different kind of interaction between the economic and the political in the 1960s. Moreover, precisely because of the slower rate of growth and the actual decline of output, to the extent that technical change in production *is* pursued, it is even more likely to lead to yet further losses of jobs. Not only does the balance of kinds of production change alter with shifts in the economic and political climate, so also do their social effects.

One of the other implications of all this is that the geographical distribution and the effects of decline will also be different. Thus, if there has indeed been an increase in the relative importance of rationalization, a number of implications follow. It is likely, for example, that the amount of potentially mobile employment, and particularly of employment associated with new investment, will be far lower than in the period 1968–73. The individual points of growth which may occur under rationalization are related to the concentration of existing capacity on existing sites, rather than to the establishment of new locations. Again, with intensification there is little likelihood of potentially mobile employment. It is with investment and technical change that potentially mobile employment is most likely to be generated, and this seems to have become relatively less important. Moreover, given that in the most recent period technical change is likely to take place in a context of both employment decline and falling output, the likelihood of its being introduced on existing sites, rather than on new ones, is probably increased. And the breakdown of figures for capital investment does provide corroborative evidence. While the total level of investment has gone down slightly, the balance between investment in plant and machinery on the one hand and investment in new building work on the other has shifted quite significantly. While that in plant and machinery has remained relatively stable, and indeed rose in 1978 and 1979, the amount of investment in new building work has fallen quite dramatically (data supplied by the Department of Industry). Not only, therefore, may technical change be relatively less important as the occasion for employment decline, but also the geographical impact of technical change may be different. One other reason for this apart from the fact of output decline, may well be the greater ease of reorganization on site, in the face of a humbled workforce.

This in turn has important implications for regional policy. One thing it means is that any given level of operation of an incentive-based regional policy has far less chance of success in influencing the distribution of employment now than it did in the period from the mid-1960s to the early 1970s. The impact of regional policy has indeed declined over the 1970s. Its reduced effectiveness has been attributed both to the decline of manufacturing employment and to a plateau effect implicit in the operation of such a policy (Moore, Rhodes and Tyler 1977). We would not dispute these reasons (although it should be repeated that manufacturing employment has actually been declining for most of the period of the operation of regional policy), but it is not only decline, it is also the nature of decline that influences the potential impact of regional policy. In particular, if it is correct that mobile technical change has, over the 1970s, become less important as a mechanism of employment decline, one would expect the degree of locational shift and the potential impact of regional policy to decline similarly. In other words, a shift in the economic and political climate may well have brought about changes in the balance of mechanisms of production reorganization and a consequent change in their geographical implications.

By going behind the aggregate numbers on jobs to look at how, why and where employment decline is occurring, it is clear that job loss is not one single, or simple, process. It is the manifestation of a whole range of different kinds of 'industrial problem'; it reflects many different struggles going on on different fronts, different arguments, different issues, different terms of debate. The changing form of job loss over the decade of the 1970s has been an important component of wider shifts. It both resulted from bigger changes at the economic and political levels of society, and was part of their precondition. The years from the mid-1960s to the early 1980s have not, therefore, just seen one long decline in manufacturing employment. There has, over that period, been a significant shift in the nature, the geography and the political implications of that decline.

Notes

2 Forms of production reorganization and job loss

1 The 1968 Census of Production and the three annual Censuses in 1970, 1971 and 1972 covered all establishments employing twenty-five or more workers. Estimates were made of data relating to small establishments (and unsatisfactory returns). In 1973, to meet EEC regulations on the collection of statistical information, the size threshold for Census coverage was lowered to establishments employing twenty or more persons. The degree of estimation of data for small firms was accordingly reduced. We do not feel, however, that this seriously affects the comparability of the data over the study period.

2 For an interesting and detailed discussion of the problems involved in interpreting the net output figures in the different Censuses of Production, see Sorrell (1971) and Mitchell (1978).

3 Shipbuilding was accordingly excluded from our national-level output and productivity analyses.

4 For each industry the movement of the Census of Production capital expenditure data was plotted in constant (1970) price terms. Capital expenditure on plant and machinery was deflated using the broadly industry-specific deflators suggested by the Central Statistical Office (1977) for deflating capital assets in current cost accounting. The 'Blue Book' deflators for gross domestic fixed capital formation (see Table 17, Central Statistical Office 1975) were used to deflate the capital expenditure series for both

new building work and land and existing buildings. The use of a single industry-wide deflator for these data was felt to be less problematical than it would be for those for output and capital expenditure on plant and machinery because of less marked inter-sectoral variations in the price of land and buildings. In an attempt to minimize the problems of investment 'lags', capital-expenditure data from the Census taken immediately preceding the survey period (1963) were also included. The Census years covered were thus 1963, 1968 and 1970 to 1973. It is perhaps worth noting in this context that the study period includes the year 1970 in which UK manufacturing investment in constant prices reached a record level (Treasury 1976). There is a good chance, therefore, that the study period encompassed a substantial number of major investment shifts.

3   Intensification

1   One way of looking at intensification is as elaborated by Palloix (1976). If the production process is schematized in terms of the labour required to produce a commodity, and the expenditure of labour during the working day, a distinction can be made between T: the length of the working day; tn: necessary labour time (i.e. the time required to produce the worker's wages); and tr: labour time actually devoted to production. The basic aim of intensification as we have defined it is to expand the ratio tr/T. In Palloix's terms it 'involves reducing the amount of time during which labour power produces no value' (p. 50), in other words where labour power is not converted into labour. It reduces the 'porosity' of the working day. In the second case, tn is reduced. In both cases, costs are reduced and the rate of exploitation $(tr - tn)/tn$ is increased.

In some analyses, this distinction, between true intensification (reducing porosity) and increasing productiveness (mechan-ization of work itself), is related to the distinction between absolute and relative increases in surplus value in modern indus-try (see especially Palloix 1976). As Elger (1979) points out, this is at variance with Marx's usage, though in purely technical terms Palloix would seem to be correct. There are two points to note: first, there is some point in making the distinction, by whatever terms one wishes to characterize it, because the two different ways of increasing the output of the production process as a whole can have rather different implications for relations between labour and capital. In particular, true intensification is likely to have definite limits and require more control over workers. Just as the other form of absolute increase in surplus value, lengthening the working day, is limited both by the fact that there are only twenty-four hours in a day and by worker resistance (for instance, the battle for the eight-hour day), so does this. Palloix wrote: 'the limits to the production of an extensive surplus are determined by the resistance of the working class to the intensification of the rhythms of work' (1976, 50). Second, contrary to what is implied in some analyses, the two forms would almost always seem to occur together, although the balance between them can vary substantially. In the detailed studies in this chapter, absolute increases in surplus value were probably more important, for instance. Both forms of increase can also be achieved through some forms of what we call here 'technical change'; in particular, the introduction of Fordist techniques of production, subordinating workers to the continuous movement of systems of machinery, involves both relative and absolute increases in surplus value. As Palloix points out 'this form of production of an extensive surplus (absolute increase in surplus value), linked to mass production, is necessarily related to the production of an intensive surplus' (1976, 50). In such cases, however, the production of relative increases in surplus value is probably more important.

2 This increase in labour costs must, of course, be less than savings made elsewhere. What is involved is essentially a shift between *types* of labour cost. Thus Stanton divides labour costs into three types:

> (1) basic cost: approximately, the wage plus social security charges, employer's subsidies and training expenses; (2) excess-hire cost: the increment of basic cost due to 'carrying' labour not needed in a production period, inversely related to the degree of capacity utilization and of labour flexibility; (3) control cost: expenditure necessary to ensure that the worker performs at full intensity, both all day and over a long production period (1979, 121).

Intensification in the form of reducing porosity is thus an attempt to reduce (2) (excess-hire cost) but which may involve an increase in (3) (control cost). See also 'The capitalist labour process' (Brighton Labour Process Group 1977).

3 The TMU is a time standard defined as one hundred-thousandth of an hour, or six ten-thousandths of a minute.

Therbligs were elementary body-movements used in early time and motion study. Their name is (approximately) their inventor's (F. B. Gilbreth) spelt backwards.

4 Once again, we must stress that this characterization does not imply that intensification was the only form of production reorganization going on in these sectors. To take an example actually from these industries: the motor-bike part of mlh 382 also saw during this period straightforward closures (i.e. rationalization) as a result of demand changes for British bikes and a failure of one of the Small Heath product ranges and some attempt, though short-lived and not major, at more thoroughgoing modernization of the production process in a newly-built plant (for a useful survey see Rogers 1979). Apart from the forms of intensification already mentioned, reduction of product ranges was an important part of the strategy of enabling faster throughput in this part of mlh 382, while a research centre was established, and at least some encouragement given, for more 'scientific' approaches to management (see Louis and Currie 1978).

5 The basic calculation was for the percentage of total pay made up by payment-by-results and compared with the same figure for all manufacturing. For some industries (leather and cycles) Order-level equivalents had to be used, and for some (textile-finishing and leather) the calculation was only possible for full-time manual men aged twenty one and over.

6 This similarity is not simply coincidence, as the analysis shows, but neither does it indicate that all intensifiers are of this type: old consumer-goods industries, dominated by small capital, and with unitized labour processes (see chapter 10).

7 We have tried to avoid constant references to source material at each point in the text; only major points are referenced. The main data sources used in this section are: Economists Advisory Group (undated); NEDO (1971a,b; 1973; 1974a,b,c; 1975a,b; 1976; 1978a,d).

8 Consumer-goods industries were thus, along with all industry, at a 'total-system' level, contradictorily wanting their own workers' wages to be cut, but hoping for an increase in wages overall in order to ensure an expansion of the potential market for their products. Thus, between 1963 and 1968 wages per head in both outerwear and footwear rose at the all-manufacturing average, thus putting pressure on costs. After 1968, wages in these industries fell behind the growth in manufacturing as a whole (calculated from Wood 1976).

9 That is, competition in that period from Third World and Comecon countries (now there is also cost competition from the USA). There was also 'fashion competition' from countries such as Italy, but this was quantitatively less important.

10 Though with the increasing possibility of automating small-batch production with numerical control, this may change. Thus the Monopolies and Mergers Commission report concluded that: 'A substantial degree of automation in the closing room was possible in the next few years through the development of numerically-controlled sewing-machines which would be within the financial reach of fairly small footwear manufacturers' (1973, 6).

11 It should be pointed out that in both these sectors *some* very large firms do exist. As will be seen in chapter 8, their behaviour was in fact different. But from the point of view of this chapter, small companies, and intensification, were dominant.

12 Female activity rates:

	1961 %	1971 %
East Midlands	37.6	43.3
Yorkshire and Humberside	37.8	41.7
GB average	37.4	42.7

Source   Department of Employment 1974; quoted in Moseley and Darby 1978

13. The terms 'excess costs' and 'standard costs' also partially mirror Palloix's distinction in time-terms between (T−tr) and (tr) (see note 1 to this chapter).

14 These two documents represent assessments of, and encouragement to, possible change, rather than evidence of the change itself (though they do include case-studies). The evidence for implementation is based on the other sources mentioned.

15 This lack of control, in the sense used here, is even greater in the case of home-working, a form of work organization which is very common in the clothing industry. Many of the forms of intensification described here are applicable to home-workers, in particular the payments schemes and the small work-aids; some are inapplicable.

4   Investment and technical change

1 As already stated in chapter 2, we are not including consideration of sectors where investment in new techniques took place primarily as simply additions to capacity. Such investment would, in

itself, not lead to a loss of jobs. The focus of attention in this chapter is on cases where investment, technical change and employment decline all occurred together.

2 It should be remembered that these statistics are all at mlh level. As there are considerable variations within mlhs (see later) aggregate statistics should not, on their own, be related together to imply actual processes. Such inferences of processes must always also be based on other evidence. Part of the problem with the argument that employment decline implies low levels of mobile employment is that it is based on inferences at this aggregate (sectoral) level.

3 Competition also, therefore, governs the nature of technical change. It is not necessarily the boring or physically debilitating jobs which are 'automated-out', but those which will lead to the greatest cost-savings or the removal of a militant section of the workforce.

4 Much of this argument about the perception of investment concerns what is going on within individual firms. Exactly the same result in terms of jobs will occur whether the new investment and the replacement takes place within one firm or whether the investment in new capacity by one firm replaces, through competition, capacity in another. In the second case, however, the 'problem of perception' will be muted.

5 This difference in level and stability of price is in turn based on the social conditions under which the two 'raw materials' are produced. The joint report by the Fraser of Allander and Overseas Development Institutes puts it as follows:

> By and large, raw jute is produced by many thousands of peasant farmers in areas remote from the end-users of the product. These peasants have been known to respond to price stimuli in a contrary way and they are notoriously difficult to organize. Jute is an annual, so each season it is planted afresh. It is never possible to predict the total harvest from the acreage planted since the yield is liable to severe fluctuation according to weather conditions. Since much of the land given over to jute can equally well produce rice, acreage under jute depends partly on the price of rice. The total supply of raw jute, therefore, depends on the largely uncoordinated decisions of thousands of peasants and on the weather. . . .

> The contrast with polypropylene could not be more complete. A relatively small number of international oligopolists is

responsible for the entire output of this raw material. Even oligopolists, of course, can miscalculate and there have been mismatches between capacity and demand in the short history of polypropylene. But essentially the supply is predictable from year to year. (McDowell and Draper 1978, 18, 19)

6 This point will be taken up again in the final chapter. For the moment it should be stressed that the comparison is based only on the thirty-one industries, which themselves are not a 'representative' sample from the economy as a whole.

7 The sectors are those in which companies employing less than 100 people accounted for 80 per cent or more of total employment. The figures on sales relate to each sector's principal products.

8 The ability of some of the original jute firms to diversify into polypropylene was also in some measure due to the trade protection provided for jute cloth. This meant that they had larger internal funds than might otherwise have been available. Without that, the production of polypropylene goods might have been dominated by the major petrochemical companies with access to the feedstock, as has occurred in the USA (Odling-Smee 1977, xvii).

9 The following account of problems in the brick industry is extremely condensed. It does not include the refractory-goods part of mlh 461, nor can it go into detail about the many different kinds of bricks produced. The focus is on the area in which technical change occurred: the fletton interests of the London Brick Company. Fletton bricks are those made from Oxford clay, found in a band stretching from Dorset northeast towards Lincolnshire, and particularly extensive in the eastern midlands of England.

10 There was, however, some consideration of trying to offset declining profits by internationalizing the production operations of the London Brick Company (1969, 22).

11 Although some on-site cost-cutting did continue throughout the period.

12 The London Brick Company does argue in its Reports (e.g. 1972, 14) that the new investment might be justified also as extra capacity. This argument, however, as the Monopolies Commission quote indicates, is based on the assumption that the company can increase its market share, rather than that the market will increase in size overall. In either case, therefore, at sectoral level this was replacement investment and would have required compensatory scrapping in other companies if not in

London Brick itself (see note 4). In the event the company itself
undertook much of the scrapping.

13 The latter was also dependent on changes in transport (the
company's 'fletliners') to expand the market area (London Brick
Company 1969, 20; 1971, 19). There was thus a mutually enabling interaction between production and spatial distribution to
markets. (This kind of interaction can also be seen in the brewing
industry where changes in the product – subsequently much
objected to by consumers – were stimulated by alterations in the
process of production, in part required by the need to transport
the product to a wider geographical market, which was required
in order to take advantage of economies of scale.)

5 Rationalization

1 This question of the social characteristics of capital is frequently
underestimated. It is considered in more detail in Massey (forthcoming).

2 For a discussion of US data on differences in behaviour towards
plant closure (though not only in a context of rationalization) and
opening by firms of different types of ownership, see Bluestone and
Harrison (1980, chapter 2).

3 The influence of workforce militancy on the implementation of
rationalization is discussed in chapters 7 and 10.

4 The figures in this table relate purely to iron castings as does the
bulk of the subsequent discussion. Mlh 313 also includes pig-iron,
to which many of the same arguments apply, but the focus in this
chapter and in chapter 7 is on iron castings as such. Unless otherwise stated, figures from this point on refer only to iron castings.

5 As usual, the possibilities for technical change are socially as well as
technologically determined. It is 'possible' for the melting stage to
be done on a direct-reduction basis, and for mould- and core-
making to be done on a continuous basis.

6 The Industrial Reorganization Corporation was involved in these
ventures, giving loans to both Peter Dixon & Sons and the Reed
Paper Group (now Reed International) in 1968, and encouraging
the financial reorganization of blade-coated paper manufacture.

7 Formed in 1967 following the amalgamation of the tissue interests
of Associated Tissues Ltd, the Inveresk Group and Peter Dixon &
Sons (Holdings) Ltd.

6 *Forms of production reorganization and the geography of job loss*

1 The Census of Production does not give a breakdown of the regional distribution of either employment or net output in cases where to do so might link specific data to individual firms. The coverage of Census regional data consequently varies both by industry and by region according to the relative importance of the 'information disclosure problem'. Thus, for example, the total number of possible regional observations for employment change between 1968 and 1973 in the fifteen industries in the two groups of intensifying and rationalizing sectors was 165 (fifteen industries by eleven Standard Regions). Only 114 entries were directly calculable, however, using the 1968 and 1973 Censuses of Production. Ninety-eight thousand, six hundred jobs were not allocated to individual regions in 1968, nearly 8 per cent of total employment. The position was worse for the sixteen technical change industries with only eighty-three regional employment changes being directly calculable out of a possible total of 176. In 1968, 172,900 jobs (17 per cent of total employment in the technical change sectors) were not allocated to regions. In 1973 this figure increased to 336,700 jobs (36 per cent of total employment). It was decided to apportion this 'unallocated' employment to individual regions on the basis of the regional distribution given by a complete series of unpublished Department of Employment statistics kindly provided by Stephen Fothergill and Peter Tyler, formerly of the Centre for Environmental Studies. Even these data had to be used carefully. In the first place, they covered both employed and unemployed workers. Secondly, the figures for 1968 were only available on the basis of the 1958 Standard Industrial Classification and it proved impossible to make precise adjustments to allow for the changeover to the 1968 Classification. For this reason, the 1969 data had to be used to apportion the 'unallocated' Census of Production data for 1968 (in conjunction with the 1968 Department of Employment statistics for those industries in which the change in Standard Industrial Classification had not been too serious). Finally, it was also necessary to make an adjustment for the change in the method of data collection that had occurred over the study period. Data for 1971 were available on the basis of the two methods that have been used (the count of National Insurance cards and the Census of Employment) and a conversion factor was therefore calculable which could be applied to the data at the beginning of the study period to make them broadly comparable with those at the end (for

a discussion of the problems involved in constructing a continuous series of regional employment numbers using Department of Employment statistics see Fothergill and Gudgin 1978b, and Tyler 1979). The statistical exercises in this chapter are based, therefore, on a data set involving some estimation. We nevertheless remain confident in its general accuracy. Indeed for only two sectors did it prove impossible to apportion the unallocated data with any degree of confidence. These two sectors (general chemicals and fertilizers) were accordingly excluded from our regional analyses. It is not felt, however, that the exclusion of these two technical change sectors affects any of the findings of these analyses. On the contrary, it is felt that their inclusion, were it possible, would strengthen in particular the findings, presented in chapter 11, on the relative performance of Development and non-Development Areas. It should also be noted that, as a result of rounding, some of the national-level employment changes in our regional analyses differ very slightly from those given in previous chapters. The complete data set is available from the authors.

2 This is *not* to imply that only such cases need further investigation. All the results, including those which descriptively conform with those which would be produced by the operation of the 'pure' form of the mechanism, require actual empirical investigation before any statements on causality can be made. Neither high nor low 'correlations' in themselves imply anything about causality.

3 These considerations concern the nature of the argument itself. They are quite separate from practical problems such as the inadequacies of the data.

4 In this, then, we agree with Sayer who discusses the non-equivalence of structures and empirical events, and the necessity of understanding the former in order to be able to analyse the latter, using the concept of 'the combination of internal and external or necessary and contingent relations' (1980, 4).

7   *Rationalization: the geography of job loss in the iron-castings and paper and board industries*

1 Repetition foundries produce large numbers of similar castings, jobbing foundries concentrate on small-batch and/or one-off jobs.

2 It is perhaps important to stress that this process is not likely to continue until there are no small foundries left. Indeed the NEDO (1979b) survey was undertaken to ensure that this does not

happen. It seems that small companies will continue to exist within the specialist, jobbing part of the sector. What seems to be happening is an increasing dichotomization between large repetition and small jobbing foundries (see Farrant 1977, 465), with more production also being done 'in house' by very large firms in other sectors that use castings (NEDO 1974d). This is a good case of the point, often made, that monopoly capitalism does not imply the elimination of all non-monopoly production (see, for example Poulantzas 1975). Linear extrapolations are inappropriate.

3 It is possible that the fact that there were two mills close together influenced the firm in its decision on closure, though we found no direct evidence on this.

4 The Department of Employment's set of Continuous Employment Estimates for the UK (Department of Employment, 1975b) does not give separate figures for mlh 481.

8 Intensification: the geography of job loss in the outerwear and footwear industries

1 The reduction in the degree of estimation of smaller establishments in the Census of Production over the study period (see note 1, chapter 2) might also be reflected in this increase.

2 Based on calculations from the Census of Production. This is likely to be important, of course, in sectors with a relatively high presence of small firms.

10 The anatomy of job loss

1 There will, under any method of organizing an economy, always have to be changes between sectors of production, and factories cannot go on for ever. It is not necessary, however, for the criterion for such changes to be profitability at individual plant or company level.

2 In both cases, this applies at the within-firm rather than the between-firm level. In rationalization, therefore, it only applies to multi-plant firms.

3 They were not the only kind of moves to produce such hostility; so did locational shifts made simply in search of cheaper labour, and associated with no changes in the production process.

4 More generally, not only may one cause produce, according to circumstance, a number of different effects, but the same effect may be produced by a number of different causes.

5 There is always, of course, the possibility that the mechanism of employment change (the kind of change in production) is itself influenced by the degree of geographical variability in conditions, though this is unlikely to be the case in a 'choice' between intensification and rationalization.

References

Aaronovitch, S. (1981) *The Road from Thatcherism: The Alternative Economic Strategy*, London, Lawrence & Wishart.

ACARD (1979) *Joining and Assembly: The Impact of Robots and Automation*, London, HMSO.

Adam, J. S. (1974) *A Fell Fine Baker: The Story of United Biscuits*, London, Hutchinson Benham.

Alfred Marks Bureau (1981) *Survey of Secretarial and Clerical Salaries*, London.

Allen, R., Bati, A. and Bragard, J.-C. (1981) *The Shattered Dream: Employment in the Eighties*, London, Arrow Books.

Beynon, H. (1973) *Working for Ford*, Harmondsworth, Penguin.

Birmingham Community Development Project (1977) *Workers on the scrapheap*, London and Oxford.

Birnbaum, B., Eversley, J., Clouting, T., Allard, D., Hall, J., Woods, K., Allen, R. and Tully, R. (1981) 'The clothing industry in Tower Hamlets: an investigation into its structure and problems 1979/80 and beyond', London, mimeo.

Blackaby, F. (ed.) (1979) *Deindustrialization*, London, Heinemann Educational.

Bluestone, B., and Harrison, B. (1980) *Capital and Communities: The Causes and Consequences of Private Disinvestment*, Washington, D.C., The Progressive Alliance.

Bluestone, B., Harrison, B. and Baker, L. (1981) *Corporate Flight: The Causes and Consequences of Economic Dislocation*, Washington, D.C., The Progressive Alliance.

Braverman, H. (1974) *Labour and Monopoly Capital*, New York, Monthly Review Press.

Brighton Labour Process Group (1977) 'The capitalist labour process', *Capital and Class*, 1, Spring, 3–42.

Brimson, P., Massey, D., Meegan, R., Minns, R. and Whitfield, S. (1980) 'Small firms: the solution to unemployment? An examination of employment in small firms in the South East of England', *South East Regional TUC Discussion Paper*, December.

British Footwear Manufacturers Federation (1969) *Footwear Industry Statistical Review*, London.

British Paper and Board Industry Federation (undated) *Facts About the UK Paper and Board Industry: Newsprint*, London.

British Wool Textile Industry Press Office (1971) 'The British wool textile industry today', 7 December.

Brown, C. J. F. and Sheriff, T. D. (1978) 'De-industrialisation in the UK: background statistics', *National Institute of Economic and Social Research Discussion Paper*, 23.

Brutton, M. (1975) 'Mellor's industrial revolution: miniaturised mass production at Broom Hall. A businesslike alternative', *Design*, 316, April.

Burawoy, M. (1979) *Manufacturing Consent: Changes in the Labour Process Under Monopoly Capitalism*, Chicago, University of Chicago Press.

Business Statistics Office (1978) *Historical Record of the Census of Production, 1907 to 1970*, London, HMSO.

Business Week (1980a) 'The shrinking standard of living', 28 January.

Business Week (1980b) 'The re-industrialization of America' (special issue), 30 June.

Business Week (1981) 'America's restructured economy', 1 June.

Cameron, G. C. (1979) 'The national industrial strategy and regional policy' in Maclennan, D. and Parr, J. B. (eds) *Regional Policy: Past Experience and New Directions*, Glasgow Social and Economic Research Studies, 6, Oxford, Martin Robertson.

Canning Town Community Development Project (1977) *Canning Town to North Woolwich: the aims of industry*, 2nd edn, London and Oxford.

Carnoy, M. and Shearer, D. (1980) *Economic Democracy*, White Plains, New York, M. E. Sharpe.

Central Office of Information (1978) 'British industry today: textiles and clothing', *Central Office of Information Reference Pamphlet*, 150, London, HMSO.

Central Statistical Office (1973) *Input–Output Tables for the United Kingdom, 1968*, London, HMSO.

Central Statistical Office (1975) *National Income and Expenditure, 1964–1974*, London, HMSO.

Central Statistical Office (1976) *The Measurement of Changes in Production*, London, HMSO.

Central Statistical Office (1977) *Price Index Numbers for Current Cost Accounting*, London, HMSO.

Coalition to Save Jobs (1979) 'Saving jobs and communities: an explanation of ES.96, H.281 – the Notification and Assistance Act', Boston, Mass., mimeo.

Commission of the European Communities (1975a) *A Study of the Evolution of Concentration in the Food Industry for the United Kingdom* (2 vols), Luxembourg.

Commission of the European Communities (1975b) *A Study of the Evolution of Concentration in the United Kingdom Textile Industry*, Luxembourg.

Council for Science and Society (1981) *New Technology: Society, Employment and Skill*, London.

David, R. (1978) 'Sheffield cutlers under the Korean knife', *Financial Times*, 30 October.

David, R. (1981) 'Plessey plans £2.5 million plant on troubled Liverpool site', *Financial Times*, 14 September.

Department of Employment (1974) 'Women and work: a statistical survey', *Department of Employment Manpower Paper*, 9, London, HMSO.

Department of Employment (1975a) 'New estimates of employment on a continuous basis: employees in employment by industry 1959–73', *Department of Employment Gazette*, March, 193–202.

Department of Employment (1975b) 'New estimates of employment on a continuous basis: United Kingdom employees in employment by industry 1959–1974', *Department of Employment Gazette*, October, 1030–7.

Department of Employment (1981a) *Department of Employment Gazette*, April.

Department of Employment (1981b) *Department of Employment Gazette*, October.

Department of Industry (1977) *Report of the Footwear Industry Steering Group*, London, HMSO.

Dibben, M. (1981) 'How the habitat man is changing Hepworths' made-to-measure image', *Guardian*, 5 May.

Economist (1968) 17 February.

Economist (1980) 4 November.

Economists Advisory Group (undated) *British Footwear – The Future,*

Vol II: The Industry (A report prepared for the Department of Industry), London.

Edwards, R. (1979) *Contested Terrain: The Transformation of the Workplace in the Twentieth Century*, London, Heinemann.

Elger, T. (1979) 'Valorisation and deskilling: a critique of Braverman', *Capital and Class*, 7, Spring, 58–99.

Elliott, J. (1981) 'NEDO gives warning on productivity optimism', *Financial Times*, 6 August.

Etzioni, A. (1980) 'Re-industrialization: view from the source', *New York Times*, 29 June.

Farrant, D. L. (1977) 'The ironfoundry industry since 1952', *Foundry Trade Journal*, 18 August, 463–6.

Financial Analysis Group (1975) 'The paper and board manufacturing and converting industry', *Extract Information Services*, Wokingham.

Fisher, A. (1981) 'High hopes for re-opened newsprint mill', *Financial Times*, 22 July.

Footwear Industry Study Group (1976) *Production Efficiency and Technology, Phase 2: Cost Effectiveness of Investment in Machinery*, London, HMSO.

Fothergill, S. and Gudgin, G. (1978a) 'Long-term trends in the regional distribution of service activity in the UK', *Centre for Environmental Studies Working Note*, 481.

Fothergill, S. and Gudgin, G. (1978b) 'Regional employment statistics on a comparable basis, 1952–1975', *Centre for Environmental Studies Occasional Paper*, 5.

Fothergill, S. and Gudgin, G. (1979) 'Regional employment change: a sub-regional explanation', *Progress in Planning*, 12 (3), 155–219.

Foundry Industry Training Committee (1978) *Annual Report April 1977 to March 1978*, London.

Fyfe, J. (1978) 'The economic and employment aspects of technological change', *Technology Choice and the Future of Work* (Report of a symposium organized by the British Association for the Advancement of Science and Intermediate Technology), London.

Glyn, A. and Harrison, J. (1980) *The British Economic Disaster*, London, Pluto Press.

Gooding, K. (1977) 'Financial Times Survey: foundries' *Financial Times*, 28 April.

Gooding, K. and Garnett, N. (1981) 'BL to close Rover plant and end TR7 production', *Financial Times*, 13 May.

Hall, P. G. (1980) 'Planning with a human face', *The Times Higher Educational Supplement*, 13 June.

Hall, W. (1980a) 'UK newsprint industry struggles for survival', *Financial Times*, 19 May.

Hall, W. (1980b) 'UK papermakers suffer on three fronts', *Financial Times*, 22 July.

Harper, K. (1981) 'Ford asks for 40 per cent cut in workforce', *The Guardian*, 16 March.

Harrison, B. (1981) 'Rationalization, restructuring and industrial reorganization in older regions: the economic transformation of New England since World War II', mimeo, Joint Center for Urban Studies of MIT and Harvard University.

HMSO (1969) *Attainable Production Targets*, London.

HMSO (1975) *Strategy Alternatives for the British Motor-cycle Industry: A Report Prepared for the Secretary of State for Industry by the Boston Consulting Group Ltd*, London.

Institute of Workers' Control Motors Group (1978) *A Workers' Enquiry into the Motor Industry*, London, CSE Books.

Jackson, J. and Richardson, K. (1976) 'Rover builds a workers' palace for its new car', *Sunday Times*, 27 June.

Keeble, D. (1976) *Industrial Location and Planning in the United Kingdom*, London, Methuen.

Kershaw, R. (1970) 'Painful adjustment for wool textiles', *The Times*, 9 September.

Kershaw, R. (1971a) 'Wool fights back for its future', *The Times*, 29 March.

Kershaw, R. (1971b) 'A slimmer industry with more hope for the future', *The Times*, 25 May.

Kershaw, R. (1973) 'Wool textiles: paradox of a prop in prosperity', *The Times*, 18 July.

Lamfalussy, A. (1961) *Investment and Growth in Mature Economies: The Case of Belgium*, London, Macmillan.

Large, P. (1981) 'The age of robots is still a long time away', *The Guardian*, 11 February.

Leighton, M. (1978) 'The workers' triumph', *Sunday Times Magazine*, 4 June.

London Brick Company (1968) *Annual Report and Accounts*, London.

London Brick Company (1969) *Annual Report and Accounts*, London.

London Brick Company (1970) *Annual Report and Accounts*, London.

London Brick Company (1971) *Annual Report and Accounts*, London.

London Brick Company (1972) *Annual Report and Accounts*, London.

London Brick Company (1973) *Annual Report and Accounts*, London.

London CSE Group (1980) *The Alternative Economic Strategy. A Response by the Labour Movement to the Economic Crisis*, London, CSE Books.

Lonsdale, R. E. and Seyler, H. L. (1979) *Non-metropolitan Industrialization*, Washington D.C., Winston/Wiley.

Lorenz, C. (1975) 'Balancing the Anglo-German investment equation', *Financial Times*, 4 September.

Lorenz, C. (1981) 'Lack of innovation blamed for UK economic problems', *Financial Times*, 31 July.

Louis, H. and Currie, R. (1978) *The Story of Triumph Motorcycles* (2nd edn), Cambridge, P. Stephens.

McDowell, S. and Draper, P. (1978) 'Trade adjustment and the British jute industry: a case-study', *Fraser of Allander Institute Research Monograph*, 5 (UK) (in association with the Overseas Development Institute).

Manwaring, T. (1981) 'Labour productivity and the crisis at BSC: behind the rhetoric', *Capital and Class*, 14, Summer, 61–97.

Massey, D. (forthcoming) *Space and Class: Industrial Location, The Regional Problem and British Economic Decline*, London, Macmillan.

Massey, D. and Meegan, R. A. (1979a) 'The geography of industrial reorganisation: the spatial effects of the restructuring of the electrical engineering sector under the Industrial Reorganisation Corporation', *Progress in Planning*, 10 (3), 155–237.

Massey, D. and Meegan, R. A. (1979b) 'Labour productivity and regional employment change', *Area*, 11 (2), 137–45.

Metzgar, J. (1980) 'Plant shut down and workers response: the case of Johnstown, Pa.', *Socialist Review*, 53, 9–49.

Mitchell, B. (1978) 'Measuring value added from the Census of Production', *Statistical News*, 41, 41.4–41.9, London, HMSO.

Monopolies and Mergers Commission (1973) *Footwear Machinery: A Report On The Supply and Exports of Machinery for the Manufacture of Footwear*, London, HMSO.

Monopolies and Mergers Commission (1976) *Building Bricks: A Report on the Supply of Building Bricks*, London, HMSO.

Mooney, F. and Wheatcroft, A. (1977) 'Survey into the capacity of the brickmaking industry, 1975', *Statistical News*, 36, 36.18–36.23, London, HMSO.

Moore, B., Rhodes, J. and Tyler, P. (1977) 'The impact of regional policy in the 1970s', *Centre for Environmental Studies Review*, 1, 67–77.

Moreton, A. (1981) 'Trouble afoot for shoes', *Financial Times*, 16 November.

Moseley, M. J. and Darby, J. (1978) 'The determinants of female activity rates in rural areas: an analysis of Norfolk parishes', *Regional Studies*, 12 (3), 297–309.

Moseley, M. J. and Sant, M. (1977) *Industrial Development in East Anglia*, Norwich, Geo Abstracts Ltd.

National Board for Prices and Incomes (1970) *Report 150: Pay and Other Terms and Conditions of Employment in the Fletton Brick Industry and the Prices Charged by the London Brick Company*, London, HMSO.

National Economic Development Office (1969) *The Strategic Future of the Wool Textile Industry* (Report prepared by W. S. Atkins and Partners for the Marketing Study Steering Group of the Economic Development Committee for the Wool Textile Industry), London, HMSO.

National Economic Development Office (1971a) *Technology and the Garment Industry*, London, HMSO.

National Economic Development Office (1971b) *Work Study in the Clothing Industry*, London.

National Economic Development Office (1973) *Industrial Review to 1977*, London.

National Economic Development Office (1974a) *Industrial Review to 1977: Clothing*, London.

National Economic Development Office (1974b) *The Anatomy of Purchasing Clothing Machinery: A Study of the Attitudes of Clothing Manufacturers Towards the Purchase of Technologically Advanced Equipment*, London.

National Economic Development Office (1974c) *Low-Cost Work Aids for the Clothing and Garment Industries*, London.

National Economic Development Office (1974d) *Industrial Review to 1977: Iron and Steel Castings*, London.

National Economic Development Office (1975a) *Financial Tables for the Clothing Industry 1973/74*, London.

National Economic Development Office (1975b) *Unlocking Productivity Potential: The Experience of Seven Firms in the Clothing Industry*, London.

National Economic Development Office (1976) *NEDC Industrial Strategy: Clothing*, London.

National Economic Development Office (1978a) *NEDC Clothing EDC: Progress Report 1978*, London.

National Economic Development Office (1978b) *NEDC Paper and Board Sector Working Party Progress Report*, London.

National Economic Development Office (1978c) *NEDC Paper and Board Sector Working Party Progress Report Summary: The Paper and Board Industry*, London.

National Economic Development Office (1978d) *Increasing Your Sales in the UK Clothing Market: A Report on Case Studies Conducted for the Clothing EDC*, London.

National Economic Development Office (1978e) *Food and Drink Manufacturing: Biscuits*, London.

National Economic Development Office (1978f) *Food and Drink Manufacturing EDC: Productivity Growth in the UK Food and Drink Manufacturing Industry*, London.

National Economic Development Office (1979a) *NEDC Industrial Strategy: Wool Textile EDC Progress Report 1979*, London.

National Economic Development Office (1979b) *Small Craft Foundries – Their Present Role and Future Prospects* (Report by the Small Craft Foundry Working Party to the Foundries EDC), London.

National Economic Development Office (1980) *Wool Textile EDC Progress Report 1980*, London.

National Union of Tailors and Garment Workers (1978) 'Employment in the garment industry', Milton Keynes, mimeo.

New American Movement (1981) *Plant Closings Bulletin*, 11, Spring.

Odling-Smee, J. (1977) Introduction to S. McDowell and P. Draper 'Trade adjustment and the British jute industry: a case-study', *Fraser of Allander Institute Research Monograph* 5 (UK) (in association with the Overseas Development Institute).

O'Farrell, P. N. (1976) 'An analysis of industrial closures: Irish experience 1960–1973', *Regional Studies*, 10 (4). 433–48.

Office of Health Economics (1981) 'Sickness absence – a review', *Office of Health and Economics Briefing*, 16, London.

Organization for Economic Co-operation and Development (1975) *The Pulp and Paper Industry in the OECD Member Countries 1974–1975*, Paris.

Palloix, C. (1976) 'The labour process: from Fordism to neo-Fordism', in 'The labour process and class strategies', *CSE Pamphlet*, 1, London, Conference of Socialist Economists.

Policy Studies Institute (1981) *Microelectronics in Industry: Extent of Use*, London.

Poulantzas, N. (1975) *Classes in Contemporary Capitalism*, London, New Left Books.

Retail Business (1974) 202, December.

Rogers, N. M. (1979) 'The British motorcycle industry 1945–75'. *Centre for Urban and Regional Studies, University of Birmingham, Working Paper*, 67.

Rohatyn, F. (1980) 'The coming emergency and what can be done about it', *New York Review of Books*, 4 December, 20–6.

Rohatyn, F. (1981) 'Reconstructing America', *New York Review of Books*, 5 March, 16–20.

Rothschild, E. (1981) 'Reagan and the real America', *New York Review of Books*, 5 February.

Salter, W. E. G. (1969) *Productivity and Technical Change* (with addendum by W. B. Reddaway), Cambridge, Cambridge University Press.

Sayer, A. (1980) 'Some methodological problems in industrial location studies'. Paper presented to the Institute of British Geographers' Industrial Location and Economic Activity Groups, May.

Schott, K. (1981) *Industrial Innovation in the United Kingdom, Canada and the United States*, British North America Research Association, London.

Singh, A. (1977) 'UK industry and the world economy: a case of de-industrialization?', *Cambridge Journal of Economics*, 1, 113–36.

Sorrell, A. A. (1971) 'Some pitfalls in the use of net output statistics', *Statistical News*, 12 February, 12.5–12.8, London, HMSO.

Stanton, R. (1979) 'Foreign investment and host-country politics: the Irish case', in D. Seers, B. Schaffer and M.-L. Kiljunen (eds) *Underdeveloped Europe: Studies in Core-periphery Relations*, Brighton, Harvester.

Stock Exchange Official Yearbook (1973–4), London.

Taylor, G. (1979) 'The restructuring of capital in the Teeside chemical and steel industries', *Centre for Urban and Regional Studies, University of Birmingham*. Paper presented to the Regionalism Working Group of the Conference of Socialist Economists, University of Durham, 8 December.

Times, The (1969) 5 August.

Townsend, A. R. (1981) 'Geographical perspectives on major job losses in the UK 1977–80', *Area*, 13 (1).

Treasury (1976) 'Trends in UK manufacturing industry', *Economic Progress Report*, 71, February.

Treasury (1979) 'Productivity, wage costs and inflation', *Economic Progress Report*, 114, October.

Tyler, P. (1979) 'Manufacturing employment growth in the regions of the UK economy, 1950–1976', *Centre for Environmental Studies Working Note*, 522.

United Biscuits (1973) *Annual Report and Accounts*, Isleworth.

United Biscuits (1976) *Annual Report and Accounts*, Isleworth.

Varaiya, P. and Wiseman, M. (1978) 'The age of cities and the movement of manufacturing employment, 1947–1972' *Papers of the Regional Science Association*, 41, 127–40.

Varaiya, P. and Wiseman, M. (1980) 'Investment and employment in manufacturing in US cities, 1960–1976'. Paper presented to the Western Economic Association, San Diego, California, June.

Wainwright, H. and Elliott, D. (1982) *The Lucas Plan: A New Trade Union in the Making*, London, Allison and Busby.

Ward, D. (1978) 'A knife in the back', *The Guardian*, 24 July.

Wells, J. D. and Imber, J. C. (1977) 'The home and export performance of United Kingdom industries', *Economic Trends*, 286, August.

Wilkinson, M. (1980) 'Newsprint and the men from DG4', *Financial Times*, 2 July.

Williams, N. P. (1979) 'The profitability of UK industrial sectors', *Bank of England Quarterly Bulletin*, 19 (4) December, 394–401.

Wood, E. G. (1976) *British Industries: A Comparison of Performance*, Maidenhead, McGraw-Hill.

Woodcock, C. (1980) 'Computer Charlie makes a better tailor of Hepworths', *The Guardian*, 8 July.

Wragg, R. and Robertson, J. (1978) 'Post-war trends in employment, productivity, output, labour costs and prices by industry in the United Kingdom', *Department of Employment Research Paper*, 3, London.

Name index

Subject index